HANDBOOK OF
SOCIAL WORK PRACTICE

HANDBOOK OF
SOCIAL WORK PRACTICE

By

JOHN A. BROWN, D.S.W.

School of Social Work
San Jose State University
San Jose, California

CHARLES C THOMAS • PUBLISHER
Springfield • Illinois • U.S.A.

Published and Distributed Throughout the World by

CHARLES C THOMAS • PUBLISHER
2600 South First Street
Springfield, Illinois 62794-9265

© *1992 by* CHARLES C THOMAS • PUBLISHER

ISBN 0-398-05799-0

Library of Congress Catalog Card Number: 92-7203

Printed in the United States of America

SC-R-3

Library of Congress Cataloging-in-Publication Data

Brown, John A., 1931–
    Handbook of social work practice / by John A. Brown.
      p.   cm.
    Includes bibliographical references and index.
    ISBN 0-398-05799-0 (cloth)
     1. Social service.   2. Social service—United States.   I. Title.
HV40.B873   1992
361.3'2—dc20
                                    92-7203
                                     CIP

DEDICATION

A book of this magnitude owes its existence to many people who have influenced my life as a person and as a professional social worker. They include

Beverly, my wife, who encouraged this project from its inception and who has truly enriched my life with her love and devotion,

My mother and my sister, Lottie Jean, who have always been sources of support,

My past professors, Leon Lucas of Wayne State University, Detroit, Michigan who taught me the value of analytical thinking in practice and posthumously David McEntire at U.C. Berkeley who taught me the value of organizational theory and always was a source of encouragement,

Adele Aras of Catholic Social Services of Wayne County, Detroit, Michigan who was my field instructor, former supervisor, and now friend who taught me what social work practice was all about,

Timothy Ryan, former Executive Director and friend at Catholic Social Services of Wayne County who provided me with the opportunity to use the agency as a laboratory for practice, supervision, program coordination and administration,

Orpha Quadros, former Dean and colleague at the School of Social Work, San Jose State University, who always exemplifies by her behavior and compassion the finest example of the professional social worker

The many clients over the years who have provided me with the privilege of practicing with them. In many cases they taught me possibly more than they gained and to them I am truly grateful,

The students who have challenged my thinking even while they were eager learners and who are now my colleagues.

PREFACE

Social work practice is frequently described as a constellation of knowledge, value and skills. These are the components of practice used by all social workers in their professional practice with client systems. These components of practice are located in diverse sources which make their accessibility difficult and their integration problematic. The author, who has served as a caseworker, group worker, family worker, field instructor, supervisor, program coordinator and administrator, has been deeply aware of the need for a book which not only makes the components of practice easily accessible but also illustrates how they are integrated in practice. This book is the result of such thinking.

This book can be used by undergraduate and graduate social work students, practitioners, supervisors and those in the human services profession who feel a need for a ready source by which to refresh some of their thinking about the "nuts and bolts" of practice. Therefore, it can be used as a reference book, a primary text or a supplementary text. The knowledge, skills, values identified and the procedures discussed in planning and carrying out intervention through the beginning, middle and ending stages of contacts are integral aspects of sound social work practice which can be employed in any social work setting. These skills and procedures have remained constant throughout the history of the profession. While they may undergo refinement, their essential nature remains the same and new knowledge is incorporated into them. While no particular theoretical approach is stressed, the author adheres strongly to the problem-solving and psychosocial models of social work practice. However, the importance of a theoretical framework in guiding practice is stressed.

The book is divided into sections which focus on particular aspects of social work practice such as knowledge; skills and values; the beginning, middle and ending phases of contacts; practice with specific client populations such as ethnic minorities (transcultural practice), interracial families, Appalachian and low income families, vulnerable populations (women, gays and lesbians); prevention; and supervision and consultation.

Hopefully, this book fills a need in social work practice. It is one of the most comprehensive books on social work practice currently in existence. The revised curriculum at the School of Social Work, San Jose State University which stresses transcultural practice stimulated the author to think of ways of integrating materials on ethnic minorities, interracial families and vulnerable populations into the common base of social work practice.

CONTENTS

SECTION V THE PRACTICE OF SOCIAL WORK

SECTION VI TRANSCULTURAL SOCIAL WORK PRACTICE
WITH PEOPLE OF COLOR

SECTION VII SOCIAL WORK PRACTICE
WITH INTERRACIAL FAMILIES

HANDBOOK OF
SOCIAL WORK PRACTICE

SECTION I
THE NATURE OF
SOCIAL WORK PRACTICE

Chapter 1

SOCIAL WORK PRACTICE

Social work practice is commonly defined as a "constellation of knowledge, skills and values" employed by the social worker in assisting clients with problems in psychosocial functioning. Social work practice may also be conceptualized as those activities engaged in by social workers and clients as they engage in the change process. Gordon (1962, quoted in Brieland, 1977) views the basic idea of social work practice as being "the social worker in action." Actions engaged in by the social worker are sanctioned by society and relate to the basic purpose of the profession. Meyer (1976) conceptualizes social work as the institutionalized expression of society in meeting common human needs. Rein (1983) defines practice as "a special system of action unique to, and institutionally vested in a professional role," (p. 176). In Rein's view, practitioners are doers; they are professionals who apply skills and knowledge to the solution of a practical problem. In essence, social work practice may be defined as those actions engaged in by the social worker on the behalf of client systems. If the action is to be defined as social work practice, it must consist of knowledge, values and skills which are viewed as being unique to the practice of social work.

Knowledge consists of the information derived from empirical inquiry and used by the social worker in understanding the nature of and the reasons for problems faced by the client system. This knowledge is borrowed from other disciplines and also developed by the profession. Values are the principles subscribed to by the profession and the code of ethical behavior which influences the conduct of the social worker as he/she interacts with client systems.* Skills denote the capacity to perform with some degree of expertise specific functions in the application of specific techniques in assisting the client with his/her difficulties in psychosocial functioning. The professional activities implemented by the social worker are performed in a planned manner and they always

---

*While cumbersome, the author will use the term he/she in referring to the social worker.

5

relate to the purpose and functions of the social work profession in American society.

THE NATURE OF SOCIAL WORK PRACTICE

Social work is the profession assigned by society with the responsibility of providing social services in a wide range of organizations under public and private auspices. These services are consistent with societal objectives and are directed at addressing common human needs and problems in psychosocial functioning. Many writers have provided definitions of social work and its purposes. Boehm (1958) states

> Social work seeks to enhance the social functioning of individuals singly and in groups by activities focused upon their social relationships which constitute the interaction between man and his environment (p. 18).

Baer and Federico (1978) view social work as being concerned and involved with the interactions between people and the institutions of society. These interactions are viewed as adversely affecting the ability of people to accomplish their life tasks, to realize their values and to alleviate the distress they face (p. 61).

Generally definitions of social work contain common concepts. Such concepts are the improvement of social functioning, the enhancement of social relationship, and the mediation of stress in the interactions which occur between people and their environments. Those conditions, personality and social, which adversely impact on the psychosocial functioning of clients are the focus of social work practice. In assisting clients in improving their psychosocial functioning, the social worker may engage in activities with individuals, families, the small group, organizations and communities. His/her activities are directed at the eradication or amelioration of those conditions identified as contributing to stress and negatively influencing the capacities of clients to maximize their potentials and to achieve their aspirations. A preventive focus may also be included in these activities at the primary, secondary and tertiary levels.

Schwartz (1961) views every profession as having a particular function to perform in society. In his practice approach, referred to as the interactionist or mediating model, the role assigned to the social worker is that of a mediator or a "third force". As a "third force", the social worker enters into a stressful situation and attempts to mediate the stress(es) which characterizes the interactions of the interacting systems.

The mediating function is an appropriate activity for the social worker. In focusing on the interactions which occur between people and their environments, the social worker seeks to identify those conditions which contribute to systemic friction. Once this identification is accomplished, the social worker implements an intervention plan which is directed at mediating the existing problem so that a degree of harmony is restored between the interacting systems.

THE SOCIAL PURPOSE OF SOCIAL WORK

A purpose suggests the reason for the existence of some entity. Social work practice seeks to bring about social justice, the existence of a more just society in which the needs of people are met, and to remove obstacles to social functioning. These obstacles may include personality and/or societal conditions which prevent self-actualization. In essence the practice of social work is characterized by the following purposes which guide his/her activities with client systems: (1) enhancing the problem-solving and coping abilities of people, (2) locating and linking people to resources, (3) mobilizing the community to address unmet needs, (4) engaging in legislative advocacy to bring about desired laws and programs (5) humanizing organizations in their operations, particularly in identifying and addressing dysfunctional procedures and practices which impact adversely on client systems, (6) contributing to the development and formulation of social policy and (7) contributing to the knowledge base of practice through research and the dissemination of knowledge gained from research. The social worker's focus is always of a dual nature as he/she directs his/her attention at the interface of people and environments. This interface can be stress inducing and leads to a "lack-of-fit" between the interacting systems (individual, family, small groups, organizations, the community and the larger society). The intervention strategies may be directed at the micro-messo-macro levels of society based on his/her psychosocial assessment.

FUNCTIONS OF SOCIAL WORK PRACTICE

In American society, the profession of social work is assigned two broad functions. These functions are those of social change and social control. The purposes identified above are incorporated into these two functions. Through social change, the social worker seeks to bring about a more just society by modifying or eradicating those conditions which lead to social inequality. The social change function is basically of a structural nature. The social control function places social workers in the position of agents of social control as they attempt to aid society in dealing with its members who have been classified as exhibiting deviant behavior judged to be harmful to the well-being of society. The social worker also provides services of a tangible (financial aid, health care, housing) and intangible (interpersonal counseling) nature. These services are also referred to as environmental and psychological work. Several of these functionings may be performed simultaneously.

THE SOCIAL FUNCTIONING CONCEPT

The concept of social functioning is very important in social work practice. The objective of social work practice is frequently identified as improving the psychosocial functioning of people. Social functioning may be translated into role functioning. Social role is an interactional concept implying reciprocal behavior between individuals, individual and group, individual and family, and individual and the community. People in any given society are placed in specific role categories. Adequacy of social functioning is connected with how well people performed in particular role categories in a given society. Generally it is believed that people are self-actualizing, can problem solve effectively and cope with new conditions when these attributes have not been compromised by internal and/or external factors. The faulty interactions which occur between interacting systems and are stress inducing result from a basic lack of reciprocity between them. This lack of reciprocity may be viewed as being of a regressive instead of progressive nature. The social worker's task is to locate reasons for noxious interaction and to implement ways of releasing progressive capacities in people and their social environment so that social functioning is maximized and the individual is able to perform adequately in carrying out his/her social roles.

Bartlett (1970) defines social functioning as the "relation between the coping activities of people and the demand of the environment," (p. 116). She states that social functioning does not refer uniquely to social systems such as individuals and groups but to the transactions between people and their environment and the effects of these transactions. Perlman (1961) views social functioning as being essentially role functioning, the ability of people to carry out their life tasks in designated roles.

An important task of the social worker is to identify why individuals cannot carry out their specific roles in specific contexts. It is important for social worker to recognize the role stress which results for a person of one culture when he/she enters into another culture with different role expectations. Brown (1968) states

> Different social systems may call for different behavior on the part of the individual and may create confusion . . . in some areas of role performances. Therefore, as the individual goes from one social system to another, role problems, such as role strain, ambiguity, or discontinuity may become evident (p. 12).

A FRAMEWORK FOR SOCIAL WORK PRACTICE

The notion of interacting systems and those conditions which result in stressful transactions impacting adversely on psychosocial functioning provides a useful framework for the organization of social work practice. Role functioning is essentially ego functioning in action. A role may be viewed as a set of expectations applied to a position. It is an interactional concept borrowed from sociology. For every position in which an individual finds him/herself, there exists a counter-position which is referred to as a position sector. If a tenant is having problems, the counterposition is a landlord. Smelser and Smelser (1963) state that the unit of analysis of social systems are not persons as such but the selected interaction among persons such as roles and social organization. The position and position sector suggest that a particular type of interaction is occurring as the participants perform in designated roles. At various times the individual can occupy a variety of roles; he/she can be a sibling, a parent, a student or a worker. Interactions associated with these role performances can be of a growth or stress-producing nature. In assessment, the social worker seeks to identify those elements in the situation which are supportive and those of a noxious nature as the client interacts with social systems. Thus role analysis offers one way of organizing a practice approach which is compatible with a systems orientation.

Perlman's (1957) problem-solving approach also provides an organizing framework for practice. She develops her framework around problem solving efforts as the client and social worker engage in seeking solutions to the difficulty which brings the client to the agency. For Perlman, the client goes to a place to be helped by a profession utilizing a specific process which she refers to as social casework. In the problem-solving approach the following steps are evident: (1) problem identification, (2) assessment of contributing factors to the problem, (3) identification and assessment of possible alternative solutions, (4) selection and implementation of a solution, (5) follow-up and evaluation of solutions implemented for their effectiveness in goal achievement, (6) repeat problem-solving process if implemented solution(s) do not lead to goal achievement. In any organizing framework for social work practice, the activities implemented by the social worker and the roles assumed by him/her are directed at the enhancement of psychosocial functioning through the eradication or amelioration of those noxious transactions which are held to be responsible for faulty psychosocial functioning and the inability of the client system to adequately perform the various roles in which he/she is operating. As a result of the theoretical framework employed, the social worker comes to the change process with a particular view of the world, the way it should be, and interventive strategies and skills by which to implement an intervention strategy based on psychosocial assessment.

BASIC SYSTEMS IN SOCIAL WORK PRACTICE

The four basic systems of social work practice are (1) the client system, (2) the worker or change-agent system, (3) the action system and (4) the target system. A system is basically an aggregate of parts which are interdependent, interconnected and operate as a whole in performing its specific function. In social work practice, the individual is conceptualized as a biopsychosocial system that is influenced by and at the same time influences his/her social environment. The family is also a social system which is given specific functions to perform in American society. Small groups, communities and society in general can be conceptualized as social systems. In an ecological environment, all systems have specific functions to perform. These systems are referred to as ecosystems to reveal that they are parts of a larger environment. If some systems in the ecological environment fail to perform their intended functions, then other systems will be affected. A systemic view of stressful transactions which occur between interacting systems suggests that the individual or family does not need to be assigned the blame for problems faced or to be designated as target systems for change efforts. The shift is to systemic transactions. The client and his/her environment are viewed as being inextricably interrelated, each is affected by the performance of the other, and consequently failure in any part of the systems involved in the transactional process has consequences for the total system. When the social worker identifies the various systems which are involved in the client's situation, he/she is able to assess the contributions of various systems to the problem(s) faced by the client. On the basis of this knowledge, he/she is able to plan intervention. The client system is the system which seeks the services of the social worker. This system may be an individual, a family, a small group, or a community. It is facing some kind of difficulty in which it seeks the aid of the social worker in addressing. The worker or change agent system is composed of the social worker, the resources of his/her agency, and his/her capacity to involve other systems in the change effort. The primary role of the social worker is to lend direction to the change process and to assist in the resolution of the problem which brings the client system to the agency for help. The help provided will always be consistent with the function of the agency as reflected in its charter. The action system is developed and implemented by the social worker. It consists of other systems which need to be involved in the change effort. These systems will bring particular knowledge and expertise to the change process. The target system is the one which needs to be changed if the goals of the client system are to be achieved. The target system can also be the client system as in the case of a marital and/or family conflict.

SOCIETAL LEVELS OF PRACTICE

Depending on the needs of the case situation and the problem(s) to be addressed, social work intervention can be directed at various levels of society, singularly or in varying combinations. A focus on multilevels of society is necessary as clients' problems are of a multicausative nature. If social work practice is defined as focusing on people in transactions with their environment, then these transactions may include social systems at the micro, messo and macro levels of society. Micro practice focuses on individuals, families and small groups. In a micro approach, problems are viewed as relating more to the interpersonal problems of client systems as these systems interact in family, marital, peer-group or work relationships. Messo practice is directed toward the neighborhood level, and may focus on small groups, neighborhood institutions or local government. Intervention directed at a neighborhood school or local health institution may be viewed as a form of messo practice. Macro practice is directed at large scale complex social systems which include government, bureaucracies and policies. Macro practice includes work with community groups, governmental agencies and legislative bodies. In macro practice, intervention may be directed at social policy formulation and implementation at the Federal and state levels. Class action suits are an example of macro level intervention.

INTERVENING ROLES

In implementing the change process, the social worker will always find it necessary to activate specific roles. These roles will depend on an assessment of the problem, what needs to be done to institute corrective actions, and an identification of the necessary activities required in achieving identified goals. The social worker may find it necessary to assume different roles at different periods of time in the life of a case. Since role is an interactional concept, the roles employed by the social worker will always be directed at having some impact on the interacting systems, particularly those which are designated at the targets of change. Social workers have available a variety of roles which may be activated as indicated. At one point in the life of the intervention process, the social worker may act as a mediator, a social broker and at another point he/she may assume the role of an advocate, a role not originally considered at an earlier stage. The advocate role may be activated if the mediation role proves ineffective. Roles are never automatically assumed by a social worker in the absence of an assessment which suggests that a specific role in indicated if a specific objective is to be achieved.

The advocate role has become an important one in the role repetoire of the social worker. When the social worker assumes this role, he/she in effect becomes a partisan with the client, and has totally identified with the client's situation and the need for social action. The client may be viewed as being in a victimized status, and a degree of conflict may be indicated if desired change is to be achieved. An outcome of the advocate role is client empowerment. McGowan (1978) defines advocacy as "partisan intervention on behalf of an individual client or identified client group with one or more secondary institutions to secure or enhance a needed service, resource or entitlement" (p. 92).

As a social broker, the social worker locates and refers the client to those resources which can address his/her identified needs. The social worker in this role also identifies unmet community needs and planfully initiates a process of meeting these needs. The social broker roles carries with it the responsibility of monitoring and evaluating the quality of the services provided to insure that the client is not falling through the cracks. This role is a predominant one in case management. Frequently the social worker engages in out-reach efforts. In this role, he/she seeks to identify populations at risk and to bring services to them. This role contains preventive aspects at the primary and secondary levels of prevention and should be in the role repetoire of all social workers. The social worker frequently assumes the role of an enabler to the client system. As an enabler, he/she provides clients with needed information so that they can actively work on tasks directed toward goal achievement. Mediation is another important role for the social worker. As a mediator, the social worker seeks to mediate and resolve stressful transactions between interacting systems. He/she, as stated earlier, becomes a "third party" in attempting to mediate stress points and to restore systemic harmony. In the role of mediation, the social worker is essentially a neutral party as his/her effectiveness is dependent on the trust established with the involved systems. Conciliation is another role assumed by the social worker. In this role the social worker seeks to negotiate differences between systems while at the same time bargaining in the interests of the client. As a behavioral changer/therapist the social worker seeks to help clients to modify maladaptive behaviors or to develop understanding of psychological problems and their impact on the clients' situation. This role predominates in the area of interpersonal stresses. Within this role, the tasks of the social worker are to assist individuals, families, and members of small groups to modify behaviors which are stress inducing for the client and others in his/her environment. As an educator/teacher, the social worker provides clients with new information or knowledge which will assist them in coping more constructively with their situation. The social worker in carrying out this role acts as a teacher and models appropriate behaviors for the client to imitate. The intent of this role is that the client will make use of this knowledge and integrate it into his/her problem solving repetoire. As a consultant, the social worker acts as a third party in providing knowledge to the consultee which can be useful in helping him/her to deal more effectively with a particular problem or concern. As a systems manager, the social worker becomes a case manager in identifying client's needs, linking the client to needed services and following through to insure that services are performing intended functions in the interests of the client system.

While the systems manager also performs the functions of a social broker, this role has wider ramification for client systems. The systems manager attempts to avoid duplication in services and to prevent fragmentation. As a mobilizer of community efforts in addressing unmet needs in the community, the social worker acts as a community mobilizer and attempts to involve influential groups in recognizing the existing needs and to marshall community resources to address them. In the role of a community organizer, the social worker also acts as a community catalyst in initiating a change process at the community level. He/she organizes and influences community groups to act in their own best interests in developing social welfare resources and in making legitimate demands on the community to deliver an integrated service system. Two outcomes of this role are (1) the development of social welfare resources in a given community, and (2) some modification in the manner in which social welfare services are presently provided. As a researcher, the social worker collects and analyzes data which shed new light on existing problems, practice models, service delivery systems and social problems. Based on this analysis, the social worker suggests more effective ways of improving service delivery systems or addressing areas of concern. This information can be relayed to administrators, legislators and policy makers for further study and hopefully implementation. As a grant developer, the social worker develops proposals directed at addressing specific areas with innovative practice approaches. These proposals are submitted to funding bodies for financial support. The role of cultural broker is viewed as an emerging role for the future as the United States becomes a truly multiethnic society. As a cultural broker, the social worker will act as an educator and broker as he/she seeks to assist interacting systems to develop an improved understanding of the impact of culture on behavior and the importance of cultural sensitivity in intercultural contacts so that the stress which accompany these interactions may become minimized. It will be important for the social worker to educate participants in dominant group institutions about the impact of culture, race and class on behavior. This role also has preventive implications. Through educational groups, the social worker can educate clients and professionals about the importance of cultural awareness and cultural pluralism. The social worker also frequently acts as a case coordinator. This role is similar to that of the case manager. However, differences exist. In the role of a case coordinator, the social worker seeks to coordinate case activities and programs in the interest of client system. The role of case coordinator involves interorganization, intraorganization and interpersonal activities. Issues which present themselves in these areas require attention and amelioration if the client is to be the recipient of a variety of services based on his/her needs.

CONCLUSION

Social work practice is directed at the improvement of the quality of life for all people, the enhancement of psychosocial functioning, and the removal of obstacles to self-actualization. The focus of social work practice is directed to the interface of people in interactions with their social environment and the stress points which characterize these interactions, resulting in faulty psychosocial functioning. Intervention may be directed to various levels of society and may focus on the individual, the family, the small group, organizations, communities and society, in a singular fashion or in varying combinations. The social worker brings to his/her practice a theoretical framework and a variety of roles which are activated as he/she seeks to achieve specific goals relating to the client' situation. Basically, the social worker will work with four systems: client, change agent, action and target. In seeking to carry out the purpose of the profession, the social worker operates within the knowledge, skills and value base of the profession.

SELECTED BIBLIOGRAPHY

Baer, B. and Federico, R. (1978) Educating the baccalaureate social worker (Cambridge, MA: Ballinger Publishers).

Bartlett, H. (1970) The common base of social work practice (New York: Columbia University Press).

Boehm, W. (1957) The nature of social work, 3, 10–18.

Brieland, D. (1977). Historical overview, Special Issue on conceptual frameworks. SOCIAL WORK, 22, 341–346.

Brown, J. (1965). Role theory: Its contribution to social casework methodology. CATHOLIC CHARITIES REVIEW, 12, 11–19.

McGowan, B. (1978) The case advocacy function in child welfare practice. CHILD WELFARE, LVII, 275–284.

Meyers, C. (1976) Social work practice, 2nd. ed. (New York: Free Press).

Perlman, H. (1957) Social casework: A problem-solving process (Chicago: University of Chicago Press).

Perlman, H. (1961) Persona (Chicago: University of Chicago Press).

Rein, M. (1983) From policy to practice (Armonk, NY: M.E. Sharpe).

Schwartz, W. (1961) The social worker in the group. In SOCIAL WELFARE FORUM (New York: Columbia University Press).

Smelser, N. and Smelser, W. (1963). Introduction: Analyzing personality and social systems. In N. Smelser and W. Smelser (Eds.), Personality and social systems (New York: John Wiley and Sons).

Chapter 2

THE ORGANIZATIONAL SETTING OF SOCIAL WORK PRACTICE

Inasmuch as the majority of social work practice is performed in organizations such as child welfare, family services and mental health agencies, it is important that social workers possess knowledge of organizations and their specific functions. Social work is also practiced in organizations whose primary function is not that of providing social services. These agencies are referred to as host settings and include industry, corrections, education and health settings. While the primary reason for the organization's existence is not to provide social services, the importance of social work in assisting the agency to carry out its function is recognized and consequently social work becomes an important aspect of the delivery system of services provided by these agencies. The organizations in which social workers practice their profession have been legally chartered by society to perform specific functions. They may be under public or private auspices and some of them are also under religious auspices, such as Catholic, Protestant or Jewish agencies.

Social workers may not fully recognize the impact of organizations on the services they provide. Frequently, organizations contribute to client's dysfunctioning by their practice, procedures, policies and philosophies; they may also contribute to the social worker's distress and low morale by the demands placed on them and the lack of necessary resources by which to meet these demands. Organizations should legitimately be viewed as targets for change when it is recognized that they are contributing to the client and/or worker's distress. In order for social workers to effectively engage in practice directed at bringing about organizational change, they need to be knowledgeable about the structure and workings of organizations.

ORGANIZATIONAL THEORY

Organizational theory is basically a way of thinking about organizations and their behavior. While the body of knowledge about organizations has not yet achieved the stage of constituting a theory of organizations, according to Daft (1986) organizational theory provides approaches to organizational analysis. He identifies three high levels of development in organizational theory: (1) size and bureaucracy, (2) technology and structure, and (3) functional versus structural processes (p. 541). Organizational theory provides social workers with a knowledge base for understanding organizational structure and processes so that they are able to identify those areas which contribute to stress and impede goal achievement. If social workers are to become agents of organizational change, then it is imperative that they also become students of organizations. This knowledge is of extreme importance to the profession in the achievement of its mission. Organizations are pervasive in American society and, according to Rappaport (1977), "a great deal of behavior is under the control of the social structure of organizations" (p. 180). Consequently, the achievement of social change necessitates organizational change.

DEFINITION OF ORGANIZATION

An organization may be defined as a social system which has been deliberately established for the achievement of specific goals. As a social system, social welfare organizations take in inputs, put them through a conversion process and end up with specific products. In systemic terms, the client is the input, the method applied to him/her is the conversion process, and the product relates to the outcome of the client's contacts with the agency. In order for organizations to survive, they must achieve their goals and take on successor goals when previous goals have been achieved and the existence of the organization is threatened. Goal achievement is uniquely connected to organizational accountability and provides a means of demonstrating organizational effectiveness. This effectiveness demonstrates to funding bodies and the community at large the relevance of the organization to the society in which it exists and the importance of its continual support.

ORGANIZATIONAL STRUCTURE AND PROCESSES

All organizations have some type of structure. Structure is the organizational design which details the manner in which the organization will operate in carrying out its operations so that its mission will be achieved.

Structural aspects of an organization include (1) its board of directors or some governing body which is responsible for the overall operations of the organization, (2) an executive director who assumes the administrative responsibility for the organization, (3) middle management which is responsible for the daily or day to day operations of the organization, and (4) a service sector which provides the front line services of the organization to its clientele. The social worker should be aware of the differences between an advisory and governing board of directors. An advisory board has no administrative power. Its function is to advise, but this function itself can be a powerful influence on organizational practices. A governing board has the power to make decisions about programs, program changes and policies. It also has the authority to hire and fire the executive director.

Organizations also have divisions of labor, chains of communication, a hierarchy of authority and policies and procedures which govern the behavior of its employees. These rules and policies make it possible for every employee to know his/her particular function within the organization and how this function contributes to goal accomplishment. The work of divisions must be coordinated. Within an organization, policies and procedures may be written or unwritten. Unwritten policies and procedures are those which have been codified over time. They result from tradition, and usually few people know of their origin. When questioned about them, the usual response is that this is the way things have always been done.

Social welfare organizations to a high degree reflect the bureaucratic model of organizations by their emphasis on certain features such as clear-cut objectives, well-planned and executive activities, divisions of labor, coordination of efforts, centralized control, a formal system of authority, promotions based on merit and the collection of data from many sources. Blau (1968) conceptualizes social welfare organizations as people-changing institutions. While some theorists view bureaucracy as being the ultimate form of rational efficiency, others view it as being inefficient, cumbersome, unresponsive to change and conducive to the stifling of creativity. It is also felt that power in bureaucracies is in the control of a few powerful individuals.

Social welfare organizations utilize certain processes/methods for achieving their goals. Clients are provided specific services which are designed to achieve specific outcomes. Social casework, group work, family work and community work are some of the methods employed in the conversion process. The official goals of the organization are those outcomes which the organization strives to achieve. These outcomes relate to the agency's purpose, its reason(s) for existence, its operations, processes and the value system under which it operates. Goals are usually identified in the policy manual of the organization and in its annual report. While goals are manifest, the organization may also have latent goals, goals which it strives to achieve but are not articulated on paper. Usually the organizational chart will reveal the structure of an organization.

ORGANIZATIONAL MODELS

Organizational theorists have identified several models of organizations. Gouldner (1954) identifies the rational and natural models. The rational model represents a closed system of organizations. This type of organization has been referred to as one without men and women. Its structure is deliberately designed for achieving the highest level of efficiency and effectiveness. In such organizations, the emphasis is on rationality. Emotions are held to a minimum. This type of organization usually does not interact with its environment. It acts on the assumption that it knows what is best and attempts to keep the influence of external forces to a minimum. In contrast the natural model represents an open system of organization. Organizations which follow the natural model recognize the dependency of the organization on its relationships with large external systems. Its primary purpose is to survive and in order to survive it must adapt itself to environmental inputs. As an open system, organizations are conditioned to states of disequilibrium which result from the effects of other social units on it. These other units with which the organization interacts may include other complex organizations and the public. Thompson (1967) views organizations as being open-systems which while affected by uncertainty are at the same time subjected to the criterion of rationality.

Scott (1961) divides organizations into three models: classical, neoclassical and modern. The classical model, similar to the rational model, focuses on organizational structure and the achievement of goals in the most effective and efficient manner. The neoclassical model emphasizes participatory management and human relations as well as the impact of informal groups on organizational life. The modern school is systems oriented and views the organization as a social unit involved in an interdependent relationship with its external environment. The public school as a formal organization presents a good example of how organizations adapt to changes in the environment over a period of time. Its survival frequently depends on its adaptability. The public schools have evolved from a classical model to a neoclassical model and finally to a modern model as it has responded to the demands made on it by the clientele it serves, especially the minority groups. The concept community school illustrates the modern model of organization which has come to characterize the public schools.

PURSUING ORGANIZATIONAL CHANGE

Rappaport states that organizations and techniques for changing them are the key to the solution of social problems (p. 180). Finch (1976) states, "The effective worker will be skillful at modifying the organizational patterns to remove impediments to practice," (p. 373). Pruger (1973) identifies three roles assumed by the social worker within organizations: helper, organizer and bureaucrat. The change agent role is also a necessary one for the social worker in organizational life. When the social worker arrives at a decision based on organizational analysis that some aspect of the organization is dysfunctional, he/she then should assume the role of becoming a catalyst for organizational change. Daft (1986) states "Organizational change is the adoption of a new idea or behavior by an organization" (p. 365). Johns (1963) states,

> Organizational change can therefore be a modification in purposes or functions, in structure, in products or services, in methods of production, or ways of providing services or personnel. It can be a change in what a company or social agency is, in what it does, or where it operates. It can be a minor adaptation or a major adaptation (p. 21).

In attempting to implement a change process within an organization, it is important that the social worker engages in research to identify dysfunctional organizational behavior and the impact of this behavior on client systems or workers' morale. The social worker will also need to identify the type of change which is indicated. The need for change becomes evident when the social worker develops awareness that some aspect of the organization works against the interest of clients. In order to implement change within organizations, the social worker must be knowledgeable about their workings and possess technical and analytical skills.

The problem-solving approach is useful. Technical skills focus on problem identification and an analysis of those conditions external and internal to the organization which impede goal accomplishment. The organization should be viewed as an open-system as this perspective places the organizations within an ecological environment in interactions with other systems. Process skills focus on identifying, influencing and mobilizing various systems within the organization to become involved in the change process. Knowledge of organizations, their functions, processes, philosophy and the attitudes which they hold toward clients are extremely important in identifying dysfunctional organizational behavior which serve as a focus for change. Social workers must also be sensitive to the powerful people in the organization. As he/she attempts a change effort, these people may serve as support systems or adversaries to the change process. In general, organizational change may be viewed as those activities which are directed at moving the organization from one point to another point which will have more favorable impact on its operations.

Daft identifies a political model of organizations. The political model views the organization as being made up of groups that have separate interests, goals and values. Disagreement and conflict are normative aspects of this model. Disagreement and conflict make it difficult to acquire the needed power and influence which are necessary to make decisions. He identifies four areas in which politics play a role in most organizations: (1) structural change, (2) interdepartmental cooperation, (3) personnel change and (4) resource allocation. Daft suggests that the use of power should not be obvious and that structural change or reorganization strikes at the heart of power and authority relationships. Structural change leads to a reallocation of legitimate authority within the organization and a major reorganization can result in an explosion of political activity (p. 409). Daft also identifies the four types of changes that take place in organizations: (1) technological changes, (2) product/services, (3) administration, and (4) human resources. Technological changes refer to the organization's productive processes. Changes in this area lead to some modification of the transformation processes through which products go in the pursuit of organizational goals. Product/services changes refer to the product and service delivery system of the organization. Administrative change refers to the administrative domain of the organization and may include changes in structure, goals, policies, procedures, labor relations, change of command, control systems and data management.

Human resources change refer to modification in the attitudes, skills, beliefs, expectations or behaviors of employees. Human relations changes are viewed as being different from other types of change as its primary emphasis is on the skills and attitudes of workers and not the technological, products or administrative services. The social worker may focus on achieving change in one or several of these areas.

ORGANIZATIONAL ANALYSIS

Rosenthal (1978) identifies five steps which the change agent should follow in identifying the need for change and in implementing change strategies. The social worker should possess knowledge of the organization and its development over time. Knowledge of the organization, its adaptive capacity and the manner in which the organization responds to crisis will be useful to the social worker in assessing the rigidity and the flexibility of the organization in responding to change. In addition, knowledge of the organization's physical facilities, its personnel practices, operational procedures, values, technology and the social context in which the organization operates is also extremely important. This information makes it possible for the social worker to identify structural and attitudinal aspects of the organization into which intervention is indicated. The social worker should be aware of the personalities of the major players within the organization as he/she may need to cultivate their support. It is extremely important that the social worker be sensitive to his/her vulnerability as he/she engages in organizational change. The organization may resist change and establish and implement counterstrategies in addressing it. A counterstrategy may be directed at imposing sanctions on the social worker.

Sound efforts at bringing about organizational change are dependent on research which reveals the dysfunctional aspects of the organization. In securing this data, the social worker may engage in formal or informal research. Formal research requires the permission of the administration. The research efforts can follow a problem-solving approach. Crucial elements of this approach are (1) problem identification, (2) assessment of a need for change, (3) the engagement of managerial goals and support systems in the process, (4) the incremental implementation of the design plan for change and (5) the formulation of a plan to overcome resistance to the change effort (Daft, 1986). Such a plan would ideally include an alignment with the goals of the organization and the needs of its consumers, communicating this plan to others, and educating them about its objectives, and seeking to influence organizational personnel to support it. Influential organizational personnel should be made aware of the purpose of the change effort from its beginning.

ORGANIZATIONAL DEVELOPMENT

The accomplishment of organization change requires some knowledge of organizational development. Organizational development may be viewed as a means of contributing to the development of the organization so that it becomes more effective in goal achievement. Organizational development encompasses two major stages. One stage is an identification of the problem which impedes goal achievement and the other stage is the problem-solving one in which alternative courses of actions are identified and selected for implementation in bringing about desired change. The social worker needs to apply knowledge and techniques to this process. Brager (1967) identifies problem solving, education, persuasion, negotiation, bargaining and the use of pressures as representing strategies for institutional change. Sherman and Wenocur (1983) state that workers cannot singlehandedly bring about change in complex organizations. They state that the social worker's empowerment is dependent on the formation of mutual-aid groups and that a sustained mutual-aid group can provide a base of power (p. 377).

ADDRESSING THE RECALCITRANT NATURE OF ORGANIZATION TO CHANGE EFFORTS

Change in organizations disrupts existing equilibrium, and organizations may be willing or unwilling partners to the change process. The social worker must never rule out conflict in attempting to initiate change. Therefore, he/she should be prepared to engage in a variety of strategies. Conflict may be evident in the relationships which exist between client groups and the organization, or it may exist in intraorganizational groups when one group feels that change will deprive it of its power and status. Horizontal conflict may exist in administrative groups over the issue of control and power. Whenever possible, the social worker as a catalyst for organizational change should attempt to reconcile these varying interests in the interest of organizational health.

The social worker should not be fearful of conflict but recognize the purpose it serves in mobilizing people into action. His/her primary task is to bring about constructive actions on the part of organization participants while at the same time dispelling feelings of anger and suspicion which slow down progress. The social worker in addressing resistive forces to the process of change should employ intervention strategies which focus on consensus at one end of the change continuum to those of conflict and advocacy at the other end. The social worker always acts in changing organization on the assumption that administration is the responsibility of every individual in the agency. These individuals include social workers as line workers and clients who are the beneficiaries of the agency's services.

INSTITUTIONAL RACISM IN ORGANIZATIONS

Racism has been established as a dynamic in American life. Three types of racism have been identified: individual/psychological, cultural and institutional. Injustice and inequality of treatment are revealed when people are treated differently as a result of their culture or race. The social worker who seeks to achieve a just society must be prepared to combat racist practices wherever they present themselves. Individual/ psychological racism presents itself when members of the dominant group lay claim to superiority based solely on the happenstance of birth. Minorities are viewed as being inferior and to possess deficits which make it impossible for them to function in a similar manner as dominant group members. This type of racism presents itself when a white social worker thinks he/she is superior to a minority social worker, or a white family refuses to allow blacks to move into its neighborhood on the premise that the neighborhood will in some way suffer. Cultural racism provides the foundation on which racist practices (psychological and institutional) are built. Such statements as white man's burden or manifest destiny were used for slavery as well as colonialism. Sociological, biblical, psychological or practically any kind of knowledge can be used by dominant group members to rationalize and support a system or racism. Even though an individual may not have had any contacts with a minority person, based on the stereotypes which exist about them in American society, this individual will have formed a particular attitude toward minorities which will influence his/her perceptions of them.

Racist practices result essentially from the acceptance of cultural values and beliefs which are held about minorities. They are perpetuated through the institutions of the dominant society. Racist practices are of a systematic and invidious nature and reveal themselves in the latent functions of organizations. Swanson and Brown (1981) provide the following examples of racist practices located in social welfare organizations, (1) the repatriation of Mexican-Americans in the 1930s, (2) segregated social services agencies, (3) transracial and transcultural adoptions and (4) the manner in which the child welfare system has historically treated minority children. These are examples of institutional racism, perpetuated through social welfare organizations. As a result of racist practices in organizations, the quality of services provided to minorities are frequently less than adequate and sufficient resources are rarely allocated to address their needs. The social worker must be sensitive to racist practices and analyze the service delivery systems of organizations to determine if racist practices are being implemented.

PURSUING AND ACHIEVING ORGANIZATIONAL CHANGE

Merton (1957) states that each individual has available a choice of strategies in dealing with organizations. These strategies include the following: (1) conformity and acceptance of the organization's goals and procedures, (2) innovation that is subscribing to the goals but rejecting the procedures, (3) conforming ritualistically, that is, to reject the goals but to accept the procedures, (4) retreat, that is to reject both the goals and the procedures and (5) rebel, that is, reject both the goals and procedures and attempt to institute a new set of goals and procedures. Daft suggests that changing organizations can only be effective when the goals and needs are made explicit so that the organization can respond to them. He identifies several strategies for using power and influence in accomplishing change within the organization: (1) building coalitions, (2) expanding networks such as discussion of the situation with key employees who are likely to be sympathetic to the proposed change, (3) cooptation of key dissenters, (4) controlling decision premises, that is, choose or limit information to be provided to the higher ups, (5) enhance legitimacy and expertise, (This means that social workers can exert the greatest influence in areas in which they are recognized as having legitimacy and expertise) and (6) making preference(s) explicit but keeping the power and strategies implicit until support is secured.

Pawlak (1976) also identifies strategies for organizational change. He refers to this behavior as organizational tinkering and states that social workers can seek to bring about change through tinkering with organizational structure, modes of operation, rules, conventions, policies and programs. Change strategies suggested by Pawlak include (1) issuing a white or position paper, (2) making attempts at modification of board composition, (3) influencing grant reviewers, (4) leaking information, (5) resignation by protest and (6) bypassing legitimate channels of authority. The author questions some of these tactics, particularly the ethical aspects of them, since the social worker is placed in a position of duplicity, particularly in bypassing legitimate channels of authority, influencing grant reviews and leaking information. The author feels that the social worker should do everything in his/her power to bring about organizational change, but should not be expected to resort to subversive tactics or engage in behaviors which compromise his/her integrity. The author also questions resignation as a sign of protest since the organization may still continue its questionable policies and procedures. If the social worker remains within the organization, he/she may be able to pursue the change process and in time find a responsive audience. Social workers should have some loyalty to their employing organization and make known their dissatisfaction. All attempts in the author's view, to change organizations should be started within and then based on the response to these attempts become external if indicated. Daft's strategies, referred to earlier, appear more sound and systematic in nature in attempting to change some aspects of the organization's behavior.

In attempting to initiate a change process in an organization, the social should be sensitive to organizational responses. The organization may attempt to co-opt him/her through promotion, or attempting to place responsibility for the problem on him/her. The social worker may find him/herself under close scrutiny or receive a negative evaluation. It is important that the social worker follows a rational problem-solving approach in attempting to induce change and is able to articulate how the suggested changes will benefit the organization in goal achievement. Even though the social worker may question the policies and operations of the organization, he/she has an ethical responsibility to inform the administration of the need for change and why. The social worker should not assume that administration will automatically be resistive to change. In some instances, administrators may be aware of the need for change and can see the merits of the proposed outcomes. However, if the organization resists change and continues dysfunctional practices, then it must be viewed as a target for change and the social worker will need to develop an action system. The social worker must also recognize that once this action is implemented future interactions between him/her and administration may be characterized by stress and conflict. It is when such conditions appear that the social worker must seek support within and without the organization so that pressures for change can be brought to bear on it. Certainly in a closed or rational model of organization change may be more difficult to achieve than in an open-model.

LEVELS OF ORGANIZATIONAL CHANGE

The social worker can attempt organizational change at the micro or macro level. Scott states microanalysis focuses on the identification of problems which impact on individuals within the organization. These problems may focus on low workers' morale or working patterns that impede goal achievement. The problem of worker's burnout would accommodate a microanalysis. Macroanalysis focuses on a principle or characteristic of the organization that may also be having some negative impact. These characteristics or principles are held to be common to all organization and also include workers' morale in addition to processes and administrative behavior. Following an organizational analysis of the problem(s) faced by the organization and its impact on client systems or worker's morale, the social worker will then decide whether the problem requires intervention at the micro or macro level of the organization. Interactions with members of the board of directors, contacts with community groups, developing support groups within the organization, developing and implementing task committees, knowledge of the organization's relationship with funding bodies and other agencies in the community, writing proposals for demonstration projects, contacts with professional organizations—all of this knowledge and behaviors may be used by the social worker as he/she attempts to bring about organizational change.

CONCLUSION

If the social worker is to be successful in bringing about organizational change, he/she must be knowledgeable about organizational theory and dynamics. Organizational change is an extremely complex process. It is an area of extreme importance to social worker as it holds the key to structural change and the achievement of a just society. Organizations are also the primary means by which racist practices are implemented and perpetuated. The achievement of organizational change is so complex that an individual social worker cannot accomplish it alone. The social worker can and should serve as a catalytic agent in initiating and implementing a change process when he/she becomes aware of the need for such a change. The impetus for change should result from a recognition of a problem which impedes the capacity of the organization to achieve its stated goals. An analysis of this problem should reveal contributing factors which must be addressed if positive change is to occur.

SELECTED BIBLIOGRAPHY

Blau, P. (1968) Dynamics of bureaucracy (Chicago: University of Chicago Press).

Brager, G. (1967) Institutional change: Perimeters of the possible. SOCIAL WORK, 12, 56–59.

Daft, R. (1986) Organization theory and design (St. Paul, MN: West Publishing Co.).

Finch, W. (1976) Social workers versus bureaucracy. SOCIAL WORK, 21, 370–375.

Gouldner, A. (1966) Organizational analysis. In R. Merton, L. Bloom and L. Cottrell (Eds.) Sociology today (New York: Basic Books).

Johns, R. (1963) Confronting organizational change (New York: Association Press).

Merton, R. (1957) Bureaucratic structure and personality. In R.K. Merton (Ed.) Social theory and the social structure (Glencoe, IL: The Free Press).

Pawlak, E. (1976) Organizational tinkering. SOCIAL WORK, 3, 376–80.

Pruger, R. (1973) The good bureaucrat. SOCIAL WORK, 18, 26–32.

Rappaport, J. (1977) Community psychology: Values, research and action (New York: Holt, Rinehart and Winston).

Rosenthal, S. (1978) A clinical perspective of work organizations. PSYCHIATRIC OPINION, Fall, 19–23.

Scott, W. (1961) Organization theory; An overview and an approach. THE JOURNAL OF THE ACADEMY OF MANAGEMENT, April, 7–26.

Sherman, W. and Wenocur, S. (1983) Empowering public welfare workers through mutual support. SOCIAL WORK, 28, 375–379.

Swanson, A. and Brown, J. (1981) Supervision, racism and organizational environment. ADMINISTRATION IN SOCIAL WORK, 5, 59–68.

Thompson, J. (1967) Organizations in action (New York: McGraw-Hill).

Chapter 3

SOCIAL WORK METHODS

All professions contain methods which are essential for achieving their objectives. In social work, methods and/or processes refer to the steps or phases implemented by the social worker in the helping process. Contained within these steps or phases are specific activities. Gordon (1962) views the basic idea of practice as being the "social worker in action." The activities implemented by the social worker are directed toward the accomplishments of specific purposes which will lead to goal achievement. Methods have been defined as "an orderly and systematic mode of procedure." Others have referred to methods as the "how" of helping. Methods include all of the activities which are encompassed in the intervention plan and include (1) engagement of the client, (2) data collection, (3) assessment, (4) goal setting, (5) contract formulation and (6) intervention. The method is always implemented in a conscious and disciplined manner. The processes of social work have been referred to as constituting a series of actions with a progressive movement over time. These processes are divided into beginning, middle and ending phases. Procedures refer to tasks carried out by the social worker within the use of a method. For example, recording may be viewed as a procedure and a skill. Techniques are those behaviors/tools employed by the social worker in attempting to achieve certain outcomes which will facilitate the accomplishment of goals. Social work is also referred to as being a science and an art. Social work as art refers to the social worker's creativity, intuition, and use of him/herself as a professional. The social worker brings his/her use of self to the helping process in a unique manner. Social work as science refers to the utilization and application of knowledge derived from various disciplines in practice.

Bartlett (1961) identifies specific questions which the social worker should pose to him/herself as he/she engages in the helping process:

1. Purposes and goals: Why are you doing it?
2. Functions and services: What are you doing?

3. Methods and processes: How are you doing it?
4. Working relationships: With whom are you doing it?
5. Sanctions: under what authority are you doing it? Who gave you the right to do it?
6. Auspices and location: Where are you doing it?
7. Point of intervention: When are you doing it? (p. 28).

These are questions relevant to any profession which has been sanctioned by society. They form the crux of social work practice and are important in analyzing its nature. The use of social work methods must be supported by a sound knowledge base. In a general sense, the social worker should possess knowledge of people and situations. Situations include transactions with individuals, marital dyads, small groups, organizations, communities and the impact of environmental conditions on psychosocial functioning. The social worker also needs to possess interactional, interpersonal and analytical skills. Zastrow (1985) identifies a wide range of knowledge required by the social worker for effective practice. This knowledge base includes social work methods, socioeconomic and political theory, social work theories and practice approaches, knowledge of human growth and development, and the nature of social and environmental factors which impact negatively on client systems.

IMPORTANCE OF THEORETICAL PERSPECTIVE

A knowledge of one or several theoretical perspectives or practice models to guide practice is of inestimable importance if the social worker is to practice in a knowing and disciplined manner. A social work method cannot be employed in the absence of a theoretical framework to guide practice. This framework guides the social worker in the collection and assessment of data and the formulation of an intervention plan by which to achieve stated objectives. In the absence of a theoretical perspective, the social worker operates in a vacuum and will not be able to make sense of the data that he/she collects. Intervention approaches result from a choice made by the social worker in identifying contributing conditions to the problem and what needs to be done to correct the situation. This choice results from the theoretical framework employed. The theoretical framework invariably contains a particular view of the world, how it should be, what has gone wrong and the conditions which result in the problems faced by the client. As a result of this understanding the social worker is able to plan corrective actions into those conditions which are impacting adversely on the client system. In social work practice, theoretical perspective or practice approaches are behavior modification, the psychosocial approach, the problem-solving approach, ego-psychology, cognitive therapy, the ecological perspective and the life-model.

CATEGORIZING SOCIAL WORK METHODS

Social work methods may be categorized as direct and indirect. Direct methods imply face-to-face contacts with client systems and include the methods of social casework (clinical social work), social group work, family work and community organization. Indirect methods are those employed in the interest of the client system without involving a face-to-face contact. However, these methods are important if the client is to receive necessary services or if the service delivery system is to be improved. The client is the beneficiary of the indirect methods. Administration, consultation, supervision, social planning and research are indirect methods.

In applying a method, direct or indirect, the social worker follows an orderly, rational and systematic approach to developing an understanding of the client's situation, identifying the conditions contributing to it, and implementing an intervention strategy. It is difficult and literally impossible for social workers to intervene effectively into a situation if they do not know the reasons for their intervention. Cockerill et al. (1956) state, "The fundamental logic of action (treatment or remedy) based upon judgment (diagnosis) derived from social study (facts) rather than a capricious bias is the foundation of professional practice" (p. 9). While the processes of study (data collection), diagnosis (assessment) and treatment (intervention) are treated separately for discussion purposes, in actuality they are always implemented simultaneously.

The steps or stages in the methods approach include social study, diagnosis and treatment. In the social study or data collection stage, the social worker collects facts about the client and his/her situation. This step is necessary as it leads to an understanding of the person, his/her problem and his/her reactions to it. The engagement process may be viewed as a central aspect of social study. In the engagement of the client in the study process, the social worker initiates and facilitates forward movement in the change process through developing the helping relationship or therapeutic alliance. This crucial stage provides data for the social worker to develop inferences or hypotheses about the problem. As the social worker attempts to make sense of the data collected, he/she enters into the diagnostic or assessment stage. He/she thinks about the facts collected, identifies the problem(s), isolates the conditions which have led to it, and arrives at some determination of what needs to be done so that the stress felt by the client can be alleviated. In the assessment stage, the tasks to be accomplished as well as the roles and responsibilities of the participants in the change process are identified. In the intervention stage, the social worker and the client implement tasks and activities which have been identified as being necessary if goals are to be achieved. An evaluative stage is always on-going as the social worker and client evaluate the change process for its effectiveness or lack of effectiveness in goal achievement.

DIRECT METHODS

Social Casework. Perlman (1957) refers to social casework as "a process used by certain human welfare agencies to help individuals and families to cope more effectively with their problems in social functioning," (p. 4). The social worker engages in face to face contacts with client systems as he/she attempts to assist them in improving their psychosocial functioning. (Indirect methods can also be used as the social worker consults with psychiatrists, psychologist, supervisors or administrator about how best to handle certain facets of the client' situation.) The client' problem(s) may result from personality and/or environmental conditions, and these conditions are viewed as having a negative impact on the problem-solving abilities of the client. It is important for the social worker to remember that even though the individual may be the primary client, the influence of the family and/or significant others on his/her behavior is not overlooked. These people are always participants, even though they may be invisible, in the client's situation, and frequently the social worker must assist the client in addressing unresolved issues from earlier experiences. The social worker always seeks to help client systems to improve their psychosocial functioning and problem-solving capacities.

Clinical Social Work. This method has essentially replaced that of Social Casework. Clinical social work also focuses on individuals and families who are encountering interpersonal difficulties which adversely impact on their psychosocial functioning. Problems are viewed as the result of internal and/or external stresses. Brown (1980) defines Clinical Social Work as

> a form of social work therapy, psychosocial in nature which seeks to improve the social functioning and human conditions of individuals through lessening the internal stress acting on them as a result of psychological, social, cultural and physiological forces either singularly or in varying combinations (p. 260).

Social Group Work. This method seeks to help individuals through the small group to enhance their psychosocial functioning and coping abilities. The small group may be used to achieve individual and/or social change. It is viewed as providing the context and the environment for the achievement of individual and group goals. The small group is conceptualized as providing mutual-aid processes and curative factors which can be activated in facilitating group interaction and goal achievement. The small group can be used for a variety of purposes which include educational, therapeutic, recreational, orientation and support. Papell and Rothman (1966) identified three models of social group work: social goals, remedial and reciprocal. Recently they have incorporated features of these models into one which they refer to as the mainstream model of social group work.

Family Therapy. In family therapy the focus is on the family as the unit of attention in the change process. The identified patient is viewed as being symptomatic of a dysfunctional family. As the client has developed his/her problems in the context of the family, the family comes to be viewed as the environment which needs to be changed if the individual's behavior is to be improved. Family therapy also has preventive implications. If the family can resolve its issues, then other members may not be negatively affected by the family's interactional patterns. The family interactional patterns provide the line of inquiry into the individual's problems as well as the area for intervention. In this approach, the onus of the problem is shifted from the individual to the family. The social worker assumes the role of a participant-observer to the family processes and attempts to help the family to modify them by bringing these processes to the attention of family members. The social worker assumes a very active direct role in this approach as he/she captures and comments on the family processes as they are occurring in the here-and-now.

Marital Counseling. Inasmuch as social workers are involved to a considerable degree in marital counseling, no reason exists why marital counseling should not be viewed as a social work method. In marriage counseling, the focus is on the marital unit. The needs of the marital partners are viewed as resulting in marital friction and faulty psychosocial functioning. Parent-child conflicts often have their foundation in marital difficulties in which the child becomes the scapegoat for the marital stress. In marriage counseling, the social worker will direct his/her attention at the personality needs of the parents, the faulty communication patterns which exist between the spouses, and those interactional patterns which are dysfunctional and stress inducing.

Community Organization. In community organizing the social worker seeks to help community residents to organize to address pressing community needs. Community problems are identified as a result of a needs assessment or the recognition of an at-risk population whose social welfare needs are not being met. These needs may present themselves in the areas of social welfare, health, education, or recreation. The social worker helps community residents to become aware of pressing concerns and to organize and mobilize community groups in resolving those conditions which have negative consequences for community members. Roles assumed by the social worker in community organization are essentially those of an enabler and a facilitator. Community organization does not focus on individuals but on community groups. The residents serve as the primary change agents with assistance from the social worker. Rothman (1970) identifies three models of community organization. Locality development and social action may be viewed as direct social work methods. Social planning is an indirect method. These models provide different views of client systems, strategies and the role of the social worker in recognizing and addressing community needs.

Crisis Intervention. Crisis intervention is a time-limited approach to helping individuals, families, organizations and communities in crisis. As a methodology, it seeks to provide immediate assistance to individuals in stress brought on by crisis situation so that they can be restored to a previous or a higher level of precrisis functioning. A crisis is defined as an event which the client system cannot address with his/her usual coping skills and consequently he/she finds him/herself in a state of disequilibrium and high anxiety. If the individual is not given immediate assistance, then he/she may cope with the crisis through developing maladaptive coping habits. Since a crisis is viewed as being time-limited, it will ultimately resolve itself in one fashion or another. A strong assumption of crisis intervention is that the individual is healthy and merely requires some therapeutic assistance during this time. The focus is not on personalities but on events. The time frame for intervention is usually eight interviews or less. In crisis intervention, the social worker attempts to engage the cognitive abilities of the client in recognizing the crisis event. Assessment is extremely important as what constitutes a crisis for one individual may not constitute a crisis for others in similar conditions. Crisis intervention is an action-oriented approach which is aimed at crisis abatement. The help provided at this crucial time and the client's motivation to use this help prevent the development of dysfunctional behavioral patterns.

Planned Short-Term Treatment (PSTT). This approach is also a time-limited, task-oriented methodology in which assistance is given to an individual or family facing problems within a specific period of time. The time frame is usually twelve interviews or less. PSTT differs from crisis intervention is that it is not always a crisis which precipitates the need for intervention. It is also task-oriented and implies that clients may be functioning well in other areas of their lives but face a problem which is creating stress for them. This is also a cognitively oriented intervention. The client is provided with considerable guidance; tasks are identified which are crucial to the intervention and the client is expected to carry them out. The client is viewed as having ego strengths which can be called on and employed in this approach. Usually tasks are prioritized.

INDIRECT METHODS IN SOCIAL WORK PRACTICE

In the interests of client systems, the social worker often makes use of indirect methods. These indirect methods may be used for the following reasons: (1) to gain greater understanding of some aspects of the client's situation about which the social worker has questions, (2) to enlist the services of others in the change process, (3) to insure that quality services are being provided within the framework of agency's policy and procedures, or (4) to identify gaps in services which can be improved through specific actions. Even though the client may not be directly involved in the utilization of these services, they are used for his/her benefit and for the purpose of enhancing service delivery in a more effective manner.

Social Welfare Administration. Social welfare administration is viewed as the "process of transforming social policy into social services" (Trecker,

Glick and Kidneigh, 1952). Kramer (1966) refers to administration as "a process of working with people and individuals and in groups and relating them to each other in order to provide the best social welfare services to the community" (p. 50). Basically, social welfare administration concerns itself with the administration of agency services in an efficient and effective manner so that the goals of the agency can be achieved. Administration concerns itself with decision making, policy formulation and program development. Social policy directives result in programs carried out through agencies to meet societal objectives. The assignment of seeing that these programs are carried out in an intended manner is also a function of administration. Administration plays crucial roles in resource allocation and in the manner in which services will be provided to client systems. It may be viewed as the policy-making and decision-making structure of the organization. The social welfare administrator is assigned the responsibility for overseeing the operations of the agency and in insuring that necessary resources are available and tasks completed so that the mission of the organization is accomplished. Administration is basically a problem-solving process.

Supervision. Swanson and Brown (1981) identify supervision as a part of middle level management. The supervisor is delegated responsibility for the job performance of worker and carries out administrative, supportive functions. Administratively, he/she is charged with the responsibility of insuring that workers perform in according with their job descriptions, and is expected to evaluate these performances. He/she is also responsible for teaching the worker how to perform his/her job more adequately, and is expected to provide the worker with ego supports as the worker faces stress or other impediments which may adversely affect his/her job performance. The supervisor implements administrative directices and his/her primary responsibility is to insure that necessary functions are performed by workers so that the goals of the organization can be achieved in an effective and efficient manner. The social worker frequently turns to his/her supervisor for assistance and guidance in providing services or seeking answers to those areas of the organizations which are perplexing to him/her.

Consultation. Consultation is a problem-solving process frequently engaged in by the social worker. In consultation, the social worker seeks assisting from a third party in addressing an area of concern. The information provided by the consultant is advisory in nature. Psychiatric or organizational consultation are employed in seeking knowledge about dealing with certain aspects of the client or organization's problems. The social worker also provides consultation to others. The basic function of the consultant is to analyze the data presented and to make suggestions about the most effective way of addressing the problem presented. Based on the outcome of the consultative process, the social worker or consultee should be able to develop an appropriate plan of action in dealing with a specific problem.

Research. The social worker as a researcher seeks to apply methods of scientific inquiry to areas of concern for the profession. Research can focus on the improvement of practice or the prevention of social problems. Always the objective of social work research is the improvement of practice and to identify and seek solutions to social problems. Social workers constantly engage in research as they work with client systems and based on the outcome of their practice, they are able to evaluate its effectiveness. Inasmuch as social work is a practice-oriented profession, research findings should enhance the capacity of the profession to perform its functions in American society so that professional objectives are achieved. Research follows the scientific method which is similar to the problem-solving approach of social work practice. Research methods employed by social workers include case studies, surveys and statistical analysis.

Social Planning. Planning is a method within community organization; it is a process of identifying needs, evaluating the reasons for existing problems and developing and implementing programs directed at addressing social problems or community needs. In some communities, planning agencies exist. These agencies have the responsibility of identifying needs and allocating resources to meet them. The social planner is viewed as being an expert with substantive knowledge in a particular area. Client systems are viewed as the recipients of services and may or may not be involved in the planning process. The substantive knowledge held by the social planner in areas such as drug abuse, teenage pregnancies, delinquency or housing, is applied to the community concern and result in a particular program to address this concern. Social planning is viewed as being a very technical, analytical process.

Social Policy as Intervention. For the social worker, social policy is both a knowledge area and an intervention methodology. It is an intervention strategy because it can result in the development of specific programs to address human needs. Social policy statements reflect societal values which are translated into specific programs with specific societal objectives.

Head Start and Foster Grandparents provide good examples of social policy as intervention. Head Start is directed at providing children of low-income families with compensatory education at the preschool level as a means of preparing them so that they can be more successful educationally when they enter regular school. It is designed as a comprehensive program with a wide range of services. As an intervention program, Head Start encompasses both educational and War on Poverty objectives.

In American society, social welfare programs reflect a residual or institutional view of social welfare policy. These views are indicative of the values which are embodied in the specific program. The residual view of social policy carries a stigma and suggests personal failure in adequacy of psychosocial functioning. The institutional or developmental view contain no stigma. These are viewed as programs which are necessary for the benefit of the total society and basically all citizens benefit from such programs. Federal parks, highways and education represent the outcomes of social policies which reflect developmental or institutional values.

NEW AND EMERGING METHODS OF SOCIAL WORK PRACTICE

As the problems faced by society become increasingly complex, or old problems are magnified to the degree that they demand the attention of society, new and emerging methods come into existence to address them. Attention has been increasingly focused on the role of the environment in contributing to client's problems and the importance of sustaining certain categories of clients, such as the chronically mentally ill, in the community. These developing practice approaches make it possible for the social worker to embrace more strongly the duality of his/her practice focus—clients in interactions with their environment—and to direct his/her attention at the various levels of society, micro-messo-macro. These new and emerging methods are case management, case coordination, collaboration, case conference and the Generalist or Integrative Approach to practice.

Case Management. This practice model is receiving increasing attention in social work practice and can be used with a variety of client populations and problems including the aged, children and the chronically mentally ill. Case management is viewed as an appropriate model of intervention for delivering needed services to client populations with multiple needs. The social worker as a case manager assesses problems, identifies needs, links clients with resources and then coordinates, monitors and evaluates these services for their effectiveness. The objective of case management with the chronically mentally ill is to increase and maintain their community tenure through the utilization of a wide range of services which include self-care, social networks and community resources. In attempting to achieve this objective, the case manager seeks to prevent clients from falling through gaps in the system. He/she is also able to identify unmet community needs and to attempt to meet them through the mobilization of community groups. Moxley (1989) identifies the case manager as a designated person who organizes, coordinates and sustains a network of services directed at maximizing the functioning of clients with multiple needs. Inasmuch as the case management approach requires a focus on clients with multiple needs, the social worker is called on to assume the role of a systems manager. He/she may or may not act as the primary therapist. Educational requirements do not appear to be a factor in this model. Its functions can be carried out by paraprofessionals, BSWs and MSWs. The MSW may act independently while the paraprofessional and BSW require supervision. The case manager is expected to possess knowledge and skills in assessment, intervention, knowledge of the community and its resources, understanding of family dynamics and skills in crisis intervention, advocacy and community organizing.

Case Coordination. Case coordination is similar to case management. However, it has its differences. Case coordination is viewed as being a direct service which involves addressing issues in the interpersonal and organizational areas so that the client receives all of the services that he/she requires in a coordinated manner. Essentially the case coordinator seeks to coordinate programs and services in the interest of the client system. An objective of case coordination is to avoid duplication and fragmentation of services so that involved agencies do not work at cross purposes. Case coordination also prevents the client playing one agency against another agency since the case coordinator is informed of the services being provided by the involved agencies. According to Bertsche and Horejsi (1980) the case manager attends to the total spectrum of the client needs, and his/her focus is to determine if the client's needs are being met, and if so in what manner. Macht (1978) states, "In coordination, two or more people providing services to a client or program inform each other of their activities and attempt to synchronize their actions and develop ways of preventing unconstructive overlap, duplication, or counterproductive action as they work to provide separate but relative services" (p. 237).

Case Collaboration. Case collaboration is basically a joint effort between various systems to provide specific services to a client system. The involved systems identify the problem(s) and needs of the client system, and the services which they will provide. Case collaboration may be an outcome of a case conference. Case conference will be discussed below. An outcome of a case conference may be the identification and implementation of a service plan in which involved agencies are made aware of their roles in providing a range of needed services to the client system. Macht states that in collaboration two or more people work together to solve a common problem and share responsibility for the process or outcome (p. 407).

Case Conference. The purpose of a case conference is to bring together a group of agencies which are involved with a specific client. The purpose of a case conference is to discuss the client's situation, identify service needs, establish goals, and to plan services among the various agencies so that duplication is avoided and they do not work at cross-purposes. The client may or may not be involved in the case conference. However, he/she should always be informed of it and the reasons why. An objective of the case conference is to bring a sense of clarity to the change process and to insure that involved agencies are not giving the client conflicting messages. Due to the number of agencies involved, the social worker may assume responsibility for arranging the case conference. As an outcome of the case conference, the social worker may be assigned the role as the primary professional in coordinating the various services of the involved agencies. Case conference is an extremely important activity for the social worker. Through a case conference the mutual roles and responsibilities of involved agencies can be clarified and services provided become more comprehensive instead of fragmented in nature.

Information and Referral. If clients are to be assisted with problems in psychosocial functioning, they need access to information and referral services. Information and referral services must be viewed as an important aspect of the intake process where the social worker assesses client's problems and needs. Without such a service, the client may not know of the existence of those services in the community which are established to provide him/her with assistance in a time of need. Levinson (1988) provides a definition of Information and Referral Services provided by the United Way of America: "I & R is a service which informs, guides, directs and links people in need to appropriate human service which alleviates or eliminates that need (p. 7). She states that the goal of I & R "is to facilitate access to services and to overcome the many barriers that obstruct entry to needed resources" (p. 7). Through I & R services, the client is connected with appropriate resources. In addition unmet community needs can also be recognized as a result of I & R. The data collected about community needs can be useful in social planning, program development, advocating and in evaluating effectiveness of existing services and the need for new services (p. 7).

Generalist or Integrated Practice. The generalist approach is currently a popular one in social work practice. When the social worker follows a generalist perspective, he/she identifies the problem faced by the client, and based on problem definition and identification of those conditions contributing to it, he/she may employ a variety of intervention strategies in addressing it. A unique characteristic of the generalist practitioner is that he/she possesses sufficient skills and knowledge for using a variety of methods in addressing a specific problem while at the same time knowing his/her limitations. If he/she feels the situation is beyond his/her competencies, he/she will bring in specialists as indicated for assistance. Goldstein (1981) identifies several generalist typologies: the case manager, the generalist, the problem-focused generalist, the ideological generalist and the systems-oriented generalist. What is important or emphasized in generalist practice is that it is the problem faced by the client which determines the intervention. The client is not held captive to a method, i.e., a particular method is employed regardless of the problem faced by the client.

PROCEDURES WHICH CHARACTERIZE A METHOD ORIENTATION

In whatever practice approach employed by the social worker, he/she will follow the following procedures:

(1) Client engagement,
(2) Formulation of the helping relationship or therapeutic alliance,
(3) Problem identification and definition,
(4) Conduct the social study process in which facts are collected from a variety of sources: the client, collaterals, existing records, and psychological or psychiatric consultation,

(5) Apply a theoretical perspective to the facts, and formulate an assessment or psychosocial diagnosis based on the inferences drawn from the facts as to the nature of the client' situation and the reason(s) for it,

(6) Present the assessment to the client for his/her input and agreement. If the client does not agree with the assessment, then a process of negotiation is initiated. If the client agrees with the assessment, goals are identified and a contract is formulated,

(7) Design an intervention plan directed at goal achievement and identify mutual roles and responsibilities of the client, social worker, and others in this intervention strategy,

(8) Implement, monitor and evaluate the intervention strategy on a recurrent basis to evaluate its progress toward goal achievement,

(9) If progress is not shown toward goal achievement, obstacles are identified and different strategies are implemented to address these obstacles,

(10) Implement the revised plan and evaluate it for its effectiveness,

(11) Termination or ending when goals are achieved, or the client is referred to another agency, or a decision is made that future contacts will not result in substantive change in the client's situation.

CONCLUSION

In contacts with client systems, the social worker applies a specific method which will enable him/her to collect data, analyze it and to come to an understanding of the client's situation and the reasons for it. Based on this knowledge, he/she will implement an intervention strategy. The social worker follows a method or a process which implies an orderly procedure or a systematic approach in carrying out specific steps from the beginning to the ending of the process. Social work methods can be divided into direct and indirect categories. The problem-solving process which will be discussed later is applicable to all of the methods of social work practice.

SELECTED BIBLIOGRAPHY

Bartlett, H. (1961) Social work practice in the health field (New York: National Association of Social Workers).

Bertsche, A. and Horejsi, C. (1980) Coordination of client services. SOCIAL WORK, 25, 94–98.

Brieland, D. (1977) Historical overview: Conceptual framework issue. SOCIAL WORK, 22, 341–346.

Brown, J. (1980) Clinical social work with chicanos: Some unwarranted assumptions. CLINICAL SOCIAL WORK JOURNAL, 4, 256–265.

Cockerill, E. et al. (1956) A conceptual framework for social casework (Pittsburg, PA: University of Pittsburg Press).

Goldstein, H. (1981) Generalist social work practice. In N. Gilbert and H. Specht (Eds.). Handbook of social services (Englewood Cliffs, NJ: Prentice-Hall, Inc.).

Kramer, R. (1966) community organization and administration: Integration or separate but equal? JOURNAL OF EDUCATION FOR SOCIAL WORK, 2, 48–56.

Levinson, R. (1988) Information and referral networks: Doorways to human services (New York: Springer Publishing Co.).

Macht, L.B. (1978) Community psychiatry. In M. Nicholi, Jr. (Ed.). The harvard guide to modern psychiatry (Cambridge, MA: Harvard University Press).

Moxley, D. (1989) The practice of case management (Newbury, CA: Sage Publications).

Papell, C. and Rothman, B. (1966) Social group work models: Possession and heritage. JOURNAL OF EDUCATION FOR SOCIAL WORK, 2, 66–77.

Perlman, H. (1957) Social casework: A problem-solving process. (Chicago: University of Chicago Press).

Rothman, J. (1970) Three models of community organization practice. In F. Cox et al. (Eds.). Strategies of community organization (Itasca, IL: F.E. Peacock Publishers).

Swanson, Al and Brown, J. (1981) Racism, supervision and organizational environment. ADMINISTRATION IN SOCIAL WORK, 5, 59–68.

Trecker, H., Glick, F. and Kidneigh, J. (1952) Education for social work administration (New York: National Association of Social Workers).

SECTION II
VALUES AND ETHICS
IN SOCIAL WORK PRACTICE

Chapter 4

VALUES AND ETHICS IN SOCIAL WORK PRACTICE

T he profession of social work has an identifiable value base which guides the social worker in his/her practice with clients. This value base must be evident if the activities engaged in by the social worker are to be designated as social work practice. Pincus and Minahan (1973) define values as "beliefs, preferences and assumptions about what is desirable and good for man," (p. 38). Trecker (1975) states social work is based on certain assumptions and convictions about people. These convictions are translated into the values which underlie all actions taken by a social worker (p. 30). Vigilante (1974) states that values are the "fulcrum of practice" (p. 12). Noble and King (1981) state that values and ethics compose an important unifying bond in the social work profession and give meaning and identity to it.

A value system makes it possible for the social worker to determine what constitutes desirable and undesirable behaviors in his/her interactions with clients. In essence the social worker incorporates a value system and always demonstrates it in practice. The values of the profession are inextricably connected to the values of the society in which the profession of social work is practiced.

SOCIAL WORK VALUES

The following values have been identified as being basic to social work practice:

(1) The individual is the primary concern of society,
(2) A state of interdependence exists between the individual and society,
(3) Individuals and society have a mutual responsibility for the welfare of each other,
(4) Human needs exist which are common to each person, yet each person has a uniqueness which makes him/her different from each other,

47

(5) A necessary attribute of a democratic society is to make it possible for each person to achieve his/her full potential and to actively participate in the society in which he/she holds membership, and

(6) It is the responsibility of society to provide for the common human needs of its members through the removal of obstacles to self-realization (NASW, 1958).

VALUES IN AMERICAN SOCIETY

Social work values flow from the value system of the society in which social work is practiced. Bayles (1981) states, "A liberal society and its citizens are devoted to the values of governance by law, freedom, protection from injury, equality of opportunity, privacy and welfare" (p. ix). When these values become distorted, are not played out in the process of human affairs and when people are treated differently in spite of these values because of unique characteristics which they possess, the social worker must intervene to ameliorate or eradicate those conditions which contribute to an injust society. Intervention may be indicated at various levels directed at bringing about individual and/or societal change. A primary function of the profession is to contribute to social change which suggests organizational and societal intervention. Inasmuch as these democratic values hold particular significance for social worker, they will be discussed in limited detail:

(1) *Governance by Law:* It is through laws that people come to know what is expected of each other. Laws are communicated to citizens and find expression not only in government, but in the institutions of society and the behaviors which govern interpersonal contacts. When laws are being violated or administered in an unjust manner, it is the differential application of laws that social workers frequently locate points for intervention.

(2) *Protection from Injury:* People must be protected from injuries which are self-inflicted or inflicted by others. Bayles feel that this value is essential for social life is not possible without protection from injuries inflicted by others.

(3) *Equality of Opportunity:* All people should have the same opportunity to participate equally in society and to reap its benefits. This value in effect states that people should not be victimized or discriminated against as a result of sex, race, ethnicity or religion. In this aspect it is extremely important that the social worker be sensitive to the existence of institutional racism. In American life, institutional racism

has been the primary mechanism for the denial of equality of opportunity.

(4) *Welfare:* All people have a right to expect society to provide the resources required to fulfill common human needs so that individuals can attain a minimal standard of living. To receive social, health, educational and mental health services must be viewed as a right and not a privilege.

These are but a few of the democratic values which have become incorporated into social work values and serve as guides to the social worker in contributing to his/her practice efforts toward the achievement of a more just society.

ARTICULATION OF SOCIAL WORK VALUES IN INTERPERSONAL CONTACTS WITH CLIENTS

Biestek (1957) identifies several behaviors on the part of the social work in interpersonal contacts with client systems which have also come to be viewed as social work values:

(1) *Individualization:* Individualization focuses on the uniqueness of clients and their right to be treated as individuals. This is an important value as it emphasizes that people are unique and even though they may present a similar problem they have come to their difficulties by different routes. Therefore, the social worker cannot place clients in specific categories.

(2) *Purposeful expression of feelings:* This value supports the need and the right of clients to be able to express positive and negative feelings without fear of retaliation. It is crucial if the client is to be honest in his/her contact with the worker; the client needs to be able to express his/her feelings about his/her condition and his/her attitude toward the social worker.

(3) *Controlled emotional involvement:* The social worker as a professional is expected to reveal sensitivity and empathy toward the client's situation and to respond in a purposeful manner to it. The social worker may disclose personal information about him/herself as indicated in facilitating the helping relationship. Self-disclosure has been shown to be of particular importance in social work practice with minorities. However, the social worker is always expected to act within professional boundaries and this value is directed at preventing the social worker from becoming overly involved with the client to the degree that he/she loses his/her professional objectivity.

(4) *Acceptance:* In the expression of this value, the social worker accepts the client with all of his/her strengths and weaknesses, positive and negative attributes. In this acceptance, the client always remains an individual endowed with dignity and self-worth. An important aspect of this value is that the social worker sometimes must accept the client while at the same time reject his/her behaviors. For some social worker, especially in cases of child abuse and sexual molestation, this is a difficult value to implement in some of their cases. This difficulty may result from their own life experiences and the painful memories associated with these experiences. Nevertheless all clients have a right to professional services and to be treated in a humane manner. If the feelings of the social worker prevents the development of a healthy helping relationship, then he/she must work to resolve these feelings, or recognize his/her limitations in working with such clients. If the social worker selects not to engage in therapy directed at working through these feelings, then he/she should seek employments in a setting where the likelihood of engaging such clients is limited.

(5) *Self-determination:* This value is the recognition of the right of the client to be fully involved in those decisions which affect his/her life. This value is sometimes difficult for social workers to fully understand as they view it as being an absolute. Self-determination has its limitations. It is limited by the law, i.e., people cannot do harm to themselves or others; it is limited by the agency' function; the client cannot make demands on the agency which are not within its purposes and boundaries, and self-determination is limited by the mental capacity of the client.

(6) *Nonjudgmental attitude:* This value results from the belief that social workers should not judge clients' behaviors by imposing a moral value on it. The social worker in effect does not attempt to judge the client's behavior. No moral standard is attached to it. While the standards and values of society are not imposed on the client, the client needs to know the manner in which his/her behavior conflicts with the norms of society and the consequences of this behavior. This is especially important in practice with the involuntary client who comes to the attention of the social worker because he/she has violated in some manner the norms of society.

(7) *Confidentiality.* This is an extremely important value for the social worker, however, a degree of confusion also surrounds it. By maintaining confidentiality, the social worker seeks to treat in a confidential manner the information provided by the client. Sometimes social workers do not understand the limitations of this value. They act on the

assumption that what the client reveals is between them and the client. As a representative of an organization, whatever the client reveals to the social worker must legitimately be shared with others in the organization, particularly the worker's supervisor and administration. The behavior of the worker may have consequences for the organization, and this is why administration has a right to know what is happening in a given case. It is always expected that the client will give consent to the use of the information in either psychiatric or psychological consultation, and in its release to other agencies which may request it.

Clients should be made aware of the limits of confidentiality. This knowledge is of particular importance in cases involving child or adult abuse, or in situations in which harm may result to another person. The client should be informed that the information provided by him/her will be shared with the social worker's supervisor and that confidentiality will be insured to the maximum degree possible. A safeguard for the social worker is to warn the client that since he/she cannot promise absolute confidentiality that the client may want to reconsider if he/she wants to reveal this information to the worker. Honesty is an important aspect of building and maintaining the helping relationship. The social worker should be as honest with the client as possible. Dishonesty in contacts with clients reflects negatively on the helping relationship and the integrity of the social worker.

THE RIGHTS OF CLIENTS

Social work clients are not always informed of their rights. Clients have the following rights which must always be respected by the social worker:

(1) Clients have a right to treatment and to participate responsibly in it,
(2) Clients have a right to be treated with courtesy and dignity,
(3) Clients have a right to voice their opinions without fear of retaliation,
(4) Clients have a right to confidentiality within the limits of the law and agency's constraints,
(5) Clients have a right to know the conditions under which treatment is to be provided and what will be expected of them,
(6) Clients have a right to expect that workers will be honest with them and not engage in dishonest activities,
(7) Clients have a right to know the process involved in filing a complaint against the worker or in filing an appeal against an agency's decision, and

(8) Clients have a right to refuse treatment, and if they are involuntary clients to be informed of the consequences of their decisions.

In contacts with clients, social workers are expected to translate values into behaviors. The social worker must always follow a code of ethics and conduct him/herself in a professional manner. Bayles suggests that ethics describe the standard of conduct expected of practitioners and the manner in which they are to utilize their skills and knowledge. Further, Bayles states that ethics represent ideal behaviors to be exhibited by the professional concerning what is correct in professional conduct. They serve as guides to decisions when the professional is conflicted about what to do.

From an ethical standpoint, the social worker is expected to be a competent individual, professionally trained and educated to provide services to client systems. He/she is expected to be a person of integrity and not to take advantage of vulnerable clients who are suffering from psychosocial stresses which make them susceptible to unprofessional behaviors on the part of the social worker. The welfare of the client is the top priority.

In contacts with other professionals, the social worker is always expected to exhibit professional conduct. He/she should provide his/her employing agency with the highest quality of services and respond with promptness and efficiency in providing these services to clients. In all aspects of his/her performance, the social worker is held accountable to his/her employing agency, the client system, the social work profession and the society which sanctions the profession.

A primary reason for a code of ethics is to provide social workers with guidance as to what is appropriate and inappropriate behavior. Violations of ethical standards can lead to organizational and professional sanctions. Regarding the Code of Ethics of the National Association of Social Workers, Berliner (1989) states,

> The ethical code has many important functions. It imparts knowledge of the professional standards of behavior to the laity and to clients, helps socialize aspirants to the profession, clarifies the demarcation between social work and other professions, helps define the social worker-client relationship, supports client's rights and interests and provides the basis for evaluating whether a violation of ethical conduct has occurred. The Code's avowed purposes, then, address the promotion of ethical behavior and control of ethical infraction by prescribing parameters of professional conduct (p. 69).

VALUE DILEMMAS OF THE SOCIAL WORKER

The social worker will face situation(s) in which the values of the profession may contrast with his/her value system, the values of the client, the values of the organization, and the society in which he/she holds membership. These value dilemmas present themselves in his/her personal and professional life. From the author's perspective, if the social worker views certain situations as being legitimate or accept racist practices in his/her personal life, then it is difficult to see how these values will not intrude into his/her professional life. The values of the profession must be constant in personal and professional life.

Some social worker will be employed in religious agencies in which certain religious values are advocated. In a Catholic social service agency, it would be unethical to provide or assist the client with information on abortion. In seeking employment, the social worker should be made aware of the agency's philosophy and asks him/herself if he/she can work in such a setting in which professional values must be placed in a subordinate position to the values of the agency. Some have suggested that correctional settings conflict with social work values and social workers should not work in these settings. The social worker may find him/herself in many situations in which the values of the profession will be tested. Such value dilemmas always should be resolved in such a manner that the client is not harmed and the values and ethics of the profession are being upheld. When acting as a professional social worker, it is expected that the professional values supercede personal and organizational values. Such incidents may place the social worker in conflict situations, but for the common good and in the pursuit of a just society they must be addressed.

CONCLUSION

Values and ethics are important aspects of social work practice. As Noble and King, quoted earlier, state values and ethics compose an important and unifying bond in social work practice and give meaning and identity to the profession. In order for the social worker to engage in social work practice, he/she must exhibit those values and ethical behaviors which underlie and support professional social work practice.

It is necessary that the social worker possesses full awareness of his/her personal value system and to never attempt to impose it on client systems.

As Corey, Corey and Callahan (1979) state, "Counselors and therapists should be aware of their own needs, areas of unfinished business, personal conflicts and vulnerabilities—and how these may intrude of their works with their clients" (p. 26). In addition, the social worker should also be sensitive to those behaviors exhibited by societal institutions which are at odds with the value base of the profession. If these behaviors are evaluated as being detrimental to the welfare of clients, then the social worker must initiate a change process even in the face of stiff opposition. While it is recognized that the social worker will encounter value dilemmas in practice, hopefully these are always resolved in the interests of the values of the profession which he/she represents. As stated earlier, social work values constitute one of the essential elements of social work practice. If they are absent or subverted, then the social worker is not truly engaging in the practice of social work.

SELECTED BIBLIOGRAPHY

Bayles, M. (1981) Professional ethics (Belmont, CA: Wadsworth Publishing Co.).

Berliner, A. (1989) Misconduct in social work practice. SOCIAL WORK, 34, 69–72.

Biestek, F. (1957) The casework relationship (Chicago: Loyola University Press).

Corey, G., Corey, M. and Callahan, P. (1979) Professional and ethical issues in counseling and psychotherapy (Monterey, CA: Brooks/Cole Publishing Co.).

Noble, D. and King, J. (1981) Values: Passing on the torch without burning the runner. SOCIAL CASEWORK, 62, 579–584.

Pincus, A. and Minahan, A. (1973) Social work practice: Model and process (Itasca, IL: F.E. Peacock Publishers).

Trecker, H. (1975) Social group work: Principles and practices, 2nd. printing (New York: Association Press).

Vigilante, J. (1974) Between values and science: Education for the profession during a moral crisis, or is proof truth? JOURNAL OF EDUCATION FOR SOCIAL WORK, 10, 107–115.

SECTION III
THE KNOWLEDGE BASE OF
SOCIAL WORK PRACTICE

Chapter 5

KNOWLEDGE BASE OF
SOCIAL WORK PRACTICE

Theory without practice is futile; practice without theory is ignorance.

Norman Brod

Social work practice to be applied in a discipline manner and to be effective must be supported by a sound knowledge base which sheds light on people and their environments and the nature of the reciprocal transactions which exist between them. In attempting to develop an understanding of the nature of the client's problem, the reason(s) for its existence and to arrive at a plan of intervention, the social worker will need to apply a theoretical framework to practice. The activities of social workers must always be guided by knowledge. Allen-Meares and Lane (1978) state "social work practice requires grounding in theory and an understanding of the profession's mission" (p. 515). Spiro (1979) states knowledge required for practice in any profession can be viewed as having two substantive components: (1) an understanding of the relevant system, and (2) specification of possible interventions and their outcomes (p. 79). Skills alone are insufficient for practice. Hepworth and Larsen (1986) state that practice skills alone do not assure competence but must be accompanied by a knowledge base. Shulman (1979) states a practice theory should (1) describe what is known about human behavior and social organization, (2) lead to the establishment of specific goals or outcomes based on this knowledge and (3) enable the social worker to describe those activities which will result in desired change and goal achievement. Specht (1988) interestingly states that theories about practice are intellectually limiting and sometimes hazardous to professional development (pp. 274–275). While he presents the view that theories are not a necessary requirement for practice, he emphasizes that social work practice consists of "the skillful application of knowledge about human development, interpersonal interactions, intervention models, methods and policy and programs." The author takes the position that a grounding in a theoretical orientation, one or several, is a necessary prerequisite for effective social work practice. The essence of a professional in action is his/her application of knowledge, skills and values which can be explained to others. The social worker will find him/herself severely limited in practice if he/she acts without a theoretical foundation.

KNOWLEDGE IN SOCIAL WORK PRACTICE

Specht states knowledge may be viewed as "those words, concepts and theories that professionals use to communicate their ideas to one another" (p. 8). Knowledge may also be viewed as the information or facts employed by the social worker in developing and understanding of the client's situation and the reasons for it. As a profession, social work has made its own contributions to the knowledge base of practice. Dempsey (1981) states,

> The knowledge base of social work practice is eclectic. In the early days it borrowed heavily from psychiatric, but sociology gained prominence in the 1950s and many recent social work publications may be called "applied sociology" in reflection of the rather homogeneous social science base in them (p. 12).

In general, it may be stated that social work practice is informed by the following knowledge:

(1) A knowledge of human development and the social environment,
(2) A knowledge of social welfare programs
(3) A knowledge of social policy, and
(4) A knowledge of social work practice which includes its methods, skills and the value base which underlies practice.

Social work practice is of a dualistic nature, focusing on individuals in interactions with their environments. The social worker must see clients as social systems involved in reciprocal relationships with other social systems in an ecological environment. Inasmuch as these relationships may be stressful, the social worker needs to identify those conditions which contribute to the client's stress. These conditions become the focus of social work intervention. It is the theoretical approach employed by the social worker which will influence his/her understanding of the problem, its nature, and the type of intervention which will be employed.

THEORETICAL ORIENTATIONS/
CONCEPTUAL PRACTICE MODELS

A theoretical orientation or a conceptual model to practice provides the social worker with a frame of reference for making sense out of the client's situation. Through a theoretical orientation, the social worker is able to explain the why and how of his/her intervention. The activities, techniques, roles and intervention activated by the social worker are a direct result of his/her theoretical orientation. Fawcett (1984) suggests that the utility of a conceptual model comes from the organization it provides in thinking, observing, interpreting and making sense of what is seen. The social worker's theoretical assumptions about the nature of the person-environment engagement will influence his/her line of inquiry, i.e., based on his/her conceptual framework the social worker will emphasize certain aspects of the client's situation and draw inferences from them as to the reason(s) for the client's difficulties. In initial contacts with client systems, the social worker will have a view of the nature of society, the way it should be, and apply his/her theoretical framework in determining what has gone wrong and what actions are indicated to correct the situation.

Social workers can make use of a variety of theoretical orientations to practice. Theoretical orientations and conceptual frameworks to practice can be located in a number of social work texts (Roberts and Nee, 1970; Strean, 1971; Roberts and Northen, 1976, and Tolson and Reid, 1981). These texts have identified theoretical orientations used by social workers in their practice with individuals, the small group and families. Some of these theories will be discussed in limited detail. It should be emphasized that theoretical approaches discussed in this chapter have utility for practice with individuals, the small groups and families, and are applied essentially in the direct methods of social work practice.

The Psychosocial Approach. This approach is primarily identified with Florence Hollis (Woods and Hollis, 1990). Turner (1978) views this approach as a form of therapy in which the bio-psycho-social knowledge of human behavior, skills in relating and competence in mobilizing resources are used to help clients to alter their personality, behavior or situation so that they can live more satisfying lives. This approach incorporates knowledge from Freudian psychology, ego psychology, role theory, and systems and communication theories. Its essential focus is directed toward the person-situation configuration and an identification of the external and/or internal forces contributing to the client's problem in psychosocial functioning. The social worker who employs this practice approach should possess knowledge of the psychosexual stages of development, the structure and levels of the personality, transference and countertransference phenomena and ego functions and defenses. An important concept within this approach is "average expected environment." People require certain psychological and social experiences if they are to illustrate competence in living. The absence of these experiences or a distortion of them can result in faulty psychosocial functioning. In this approach, emphasis is placed on the personality, inner drives, and the environment, external pressures and the role each of them play in the problems faced by the client. Problems are viewed by Woods and Hollis as resulting from (1) infantile needs and demands which are made on the adult world, (2) life events and stresses and (3) faulty ego and/or superego functioning. The objectives of this practice approach are to enhance the psychosocial functioning and coping abilities of individuals who are facing stress in living. The social worker seeks to identify the reasons for this stress which is viewed as hampering the ego and its functioning. Social study, diagnosis and treatment are the sequential steps employed by the social worker in developing (1) an understanding of the problem, (2) its contributing factors and (3) in planning and implementing an intervention strategy. Hollis has developed treatment procedures which the social worker can employ in assisting the client in addressing his/her problem. Some of these treatment procedures are of a sustaining or reflective nature directed at ego support or insight development. Treatment in the psychosocial approach is highly individualized and attention is usually focused on micro-level practice. This approach also emphasizes the impact of the environment on psychosocial functioning and the importance of environmental work in identifying and connecting clients to environmental resources.

Case Management. While this practice approach has received considerable attention, it is not much different from the environmental work which earlier characterized social casework. A basic assumption of case management is that a category of people such as the chronically mentally ill has a multitude of problems and needs which require attention if they are to maintain self-sufficiency or attain an improved level of functioning so that their community tenure can be maintained and strengthened. Case management is appropriate to any population with multiple needs such as children and the elderly. Professional assistance is required in linking these clients with agencies in the community which can address their identified needs. Without this specialized assistance, these clients will not receive necessary services, may further deteriorate and their community tenure may be decreased. Moxley (1989) defines case management as "a client-level strategy for promoting the coordina- of human services, opportunities or benefits" (p. 11). In following this conceptual framework to practice, the social worker identifies with the client system the nature of his/her needs and then plans and implements a service delivery system. He/she seeks to integrate, coordinate, monitor and evaluate these services for their effectiveness. Basically the sequential steps employed in the case management model are (1) assessing the client's needs, (2) developing a service plan, (3) linking the client to needed services, (4) coordinating these services, (5) monitoring these services to insure that client is receiving services and (6) evaluating these services for their effectiveness. Two models of case management present themselves. One model calls for the social worker to act as the primary therapist and a systems manager. The other model places the social worker entirely in the role of a systems manager and therapeutic needs are addressed by others who are involved in this vast service network which is organized by the social worker. Whatever the model employed, pure (systems manager) or mixed (systems manager and primary therapist), the social worker as a case manager will collect data, analyze it, identify the client's needs and develop and implement a service plan directed at addressing the needs of the client. With the chronically mentally ill, the objectives of case management are to help the client to develop self-sufficiency so that his/her community tenure can be stabilized and maintained. In achieving these objectives, the social worker and client systems make use of social networks and societal resources.

Case management requires that the social worker makes use of a variety of skills. Some of these skills are problem-solving, advocacy, crisis intervention, and dealing with the mass media. Written and communication skills are of extreme importance. The roles assumed by the social worker as a case manager are also varied and may include those of broker, mediator, educator and coordinator of services. As a practice model, case management seeks to make maximum use of the environment. Its focus is on the integration and coordination of services in a sustained manner. It may be described as a client-centered, goal-directed approach which seeks to provide individuals with multiple needs with a variety of services.

The Problem-Solving Approach. Perlman (1957) is the social work theorist who is most identified with this approach. She views the social casework process as one which employs an orderly systematic approach. This systematic approach is identified as being basic to any effective thinking and implementation of intervention. The problem-solving approach has relevance for all of the social work methods. Northen (1969) refers to the group as a problem-solving medium. Community organization and family work can also make use of this theoretical orientation. A problem is identified as a situation confronting the client which has overtaxed his/her ego functioning to the degree that the client feels overwhelmed and seeks professional assistance. An assumption of this approach is that it is natural for people to engage in problem-solving as they engage in this process throughout their lives. However, sometimes life events of either a personal and/or environmental nature impair their problem-solving capacities and they are unable to address it with their usual problem-solving skills. The objective of this approach is the enhancement of the social functioning of the client through a problem-solving process. Theoretical supports for this model include Freudian psychology, ego psychology, role theory and communication theory. The focus of intervention is to engage the healthy parts of the ego in a process of problem-solving. This approach emphasizes the partialization of goals. Partialization of goals emerges from the belief that minor successes strengthen and motivate the client to address larger problems.

The problem-solving approach is viewed as a process as it is orderly and systematic in nature, and denotes a recurrent patterns of activities over time which seek to achieve specific objectives through sequential steps (Perlman). Steps in the problem-solving process are:

(1) Problem formulation and definition,
(2) Identification of contributing factors to the situation faced by the client,
(3) Identification of possible solutions to the problem,
(4) Selection and implementation of a solution(s),
(5) Evaluation of implemented solution for its effectiveness,
(6) If progress toward goal attainment is effective, continue the process and if goals are not being achieved, repeat process,
(7) Goal attainment and termination.

Behavioral Modification. This theoretical approach to social work practice derives basically from social learning theory and rests on the assumption that behavior is learned and maintained by contingencies in the environment. Inasmuch as it is learned, it can also be unlearned through the application of specific techniques. Behavior is viewed as being a function of a stimulus (B = F(S), or the result of an A (antecedent event) which activates B (behavior) which leads to C (consequences). Within this approach, the social worker seeks to secure a precise picture of the deviant or maladaptive behaviors which have been evaluated as being problematic by significant people in the client's environment. The social worker attempts to establish a baseline of the behavior, i.e., how often it occurs. Effectiveness of intervention can be evaluated by a decrease in the behavior over time ultimately to its extinction. Two important tasks for the behaviorist social worker are (1) to identify and specify the area in which behavioral change needs to occur, and (2) to identify the contingencies in the environment which maintain the behavior. The objective of this approach is to modify or eradicate these environmental contingencies so that they no longer maintain the client's behaviors. When these contingencies are modified, the client will learn new behaviors or the instances of the problematic behaviors are decreased. Since the eradication or extinguishing of each set of maladaptive behaviors requires a specific change regimen, the social worker directs his/her attention at eradicating one set of maladaptive behaviors at a time. Behavioral modification techniques can also be employed by parents when they have been trained in their use.

In behavioral modification, the focus of the change effort is not the individual, but his/her behaviors. Techniques employed in this approach are those of modeling, token economy, behavioral rehearsal, and assertive training. Knowledge of the past is not important and the importance of the helping relationship in this approach is not viewed as being as important in other theoretical frameworks. Attention is directed toward modification of current environmental conditions which are assessed as playing an important role in the maintenance of the behavior. Sequential steps employed by the behaviorist social worker in this approach are:

(1) An initial analysis of the problem to identify the required services,
(2) An identification of the behavior(s) to be increased or decreased in frequency or to be modified in some form,
(3) An identification of the environmental conditions that maintain or play a role in its occurence,
(4) An identification of what needs to be changed in order to alter the behavior,
(5) Development and establishment of the treatment regimen,

(6) Implementation of the program,
(7) Monitoring of the program,
(8) Evaluation of the program for feedback and measurement of its effectiveness, and
(9) Termination.

Cognitive Therapy. This approach is increasingly receiving attention in social work practice. As a therapeutic approach, it focuses on changing people's thinking patterns so that their behavior can become more rational in nature. A basic assumption in this approach is that distorted thinking leads to the presence of anxiety and dysfunctional behaviors. The distorted thinking is viewed as being a result of the beliefs held by people. These beliefs and cognitive judgments held about people, events, traits or abilities lead to anxiety and problems in psychosocial functioning. Human emotions are viewed as being essentially a direct result of what people think, tell and believe about themselves and their social situations. The ABCs of emotions are (1) an outside event or situation happens, (2) this event or situation acts on the belief systems which people have about themselves, and (3) these belief systems lead people to feel badly about them. Usually these beliefs are colored by the incorporation of "shoulds" and when these "shoulds" are not met, the individual feels bad or guilty. The beliefs which lead to distorted thinking are viewed as being distorted and resulting from earlier experiences of the client. When people's thoughts and beliefs are rational, the emotions which they feel are functional; when people's thoughts or beliefs are irrational, they develop dysfunctional emotions which in turn lead to anxiety and bad feelings about themselves. These feelings or emotions can lead to dysfunctional behavior. In cognitive theory, the tasks of the social worker are to discover the evaluations of these events by the client, i.e., what are the client's feelings toward them. The outcome of this assessment may reveal that these events are benign, positive, stressful or irrelevant.

The objective of the social worker in this approach is to help the clients in changing their irrational ideas and beliefs. If this is accomplished, then the dysfunctional behavior may disappear as the client will come to view situations and events differently. This change is accomplished through cognitive problem solving. Several assumptions underlie cognitive theory. One assumption is that most dysfunctional behaviors result from the misconceptions which people hold about themselves and their environment. A second assumption is that these belief systems are outside of the conscious awareness and people lack awareness of what beliefs and misconceptions they are using to bring about the dysfunctional state. Lantz (1978) identifies six treatment procedures that the social worker with a cognitive orientation can use in helping clients to change their patterns of thinking: (1) use of the therapeutic relationship, (2) clarification and communication, (3) explanation, (4) imagery, (5) experiential learning and (6) therapeutic bond. Self-talk is also a technique employed in the cognitive approach. In self-talk the client engages in a dialogue with him/herself in an attempt to correct his/her distorted thinking or misconceptions about events and people.

The Interactionist Approach. This practice approach is most identified with Schwartz (1961) and Shulman (1979). In this practice approach, the social worker as a means of identifying systemic conflict and the reason(s) for it focuses on the interactions which occur between interacting systems within the context of the society-individual encounter (individuals involved with such agencies as child welfare, family services, corrections). If these interactions are stressful, a lack of mutuality is evident and systems are unable to perform their intended functions. When such situations present themselves, the social worker enters into these encounters as a "third force" with the stated objective of restoring a degree of harmony between the interacting systems. Anderson (1984) refers to this as a generic practice approach and states, "This approach offers a useful conceptual framework for integrating human behavior and the social environment, and practice content and skills in generic social work practice" (p. 323). An essential role within this approach for the social worker is that of mediation. He/she mediates systemic conflict so that involved systems can carry out their intended functions. For various reasons obstacles can present themselves which prevent systems from carrying out their purposes of addressing specific human needs. Whatever the reasons for systemic stress or failure, the social worker must seek to establish a degree of equilibrium between the involved systems. The social worker does not act as a partisan to either system; he/she must maintain a stance of neutrality if he/she is to be effective.

This approach does not utilize a formal assessment process. The work to be identified and performed results from a tuning-in process in which the social worker listens to each party to gain his/her description of the problem. Based on this tuning-in process, he/she is able to locate those areas which are stress-inducing for the involved systems. Essentially the sequential steps employed in this approach are (1) preparatory empathy in which the social worker seeks to place him/herself in the situation of the client to develop sensitivity to how the client may feel about his/her situation, (2) tuning-in, (3) contracting, (4) work and (5) endings and transitions (Shulman). Shulman has identified a number of skills which can be used in this practice approach in contacts with individuals, small groups, the family and organizations. In all he has identified twenty-eight basic helping skills.

General Systems Theory (GST). General systems theory is not basically an intervention approach. Rather it is a framework for collecting and organizing large amounts of data which can be analyzed for identifying points of intervention. A system is conceptualized as a set of interdependent parts with specific functions to perform so that a system can operate in a coordinated manner in performing its intended function. The inter-relationships of these various parts create a whole which is greater than the sum of its parts. The sum of the parts refers to the transactions and relationships which occur between the various parts of the system. Because of this wholeness, a change in any part of the system will affect the total system (systemic reverberation). A social system may be closed or open. In a closed system, a resistance to change is evident. The system may become dysfunctional as energy it incorporates is not used in exchange with its environment, i.e., it is not responsive to environmental input. Such a system may become dysfunctional and eventually self-destruct. In contrast an open system is responsive to feedback from its environment and adapts itself to necessary change in the interest of insuring its survival.

In following a general systems perspective in practice, the task of the social worker is to institute actions which are directed at restoring a state of dynamic equilibrium between the interacting systems. The objective is to restore a state of harmony or homeostasis. Some systemic terms which are of value to the social worker in understanding the characteristics of systems are input, throughput (conversion process), entropy, negative entropy, equilibrium, roles and equifinality (Janchill, 1969). Equi-finality is an important characteristic. It suggests that when a system is in a state of disequilibrium, equilibrium can be restored by directing intervention at various points within the system. This perspective transfers the onus of responsibility for systemic stress from the individual to the interactions which occur between the involved systems, leading to stress or dysfunctional behavior. General systems theory provides a description of the world, empirical reality, with some predictive value. Using the information gained from his/her analysis of the data collected, the social worker is able to make sense of it as it relates to the client system and to identify where intervention should be directed. Inasmuch as the problem is viewed as being a systemic problem, the social worker has a multiplicity of choices for intervention. A problem-solving approach is a useful one to employ with a general systems orientation to practice as it contains intervention techniques. The social worker needs to possess awareness of the fact that general systems theory is not an intervention. Basically it is a way of identifying stress points between interacting systems and identifying points for intervention. Intervention seeks to restore a state of dynamic equilibrium to the involved systems in the problems faced by the client. Systems thinking has represented a dramatic change for social work practice and the manner in which the social workers view problems and their causation. It shifts the focus for problems from the individual to the transactions which occur between him/her and other involved social systems. It has made more practical the dual focus of social work practice, people in interactions with their environments.

The Ecological Metaphor. Ecology as a science seeks to understand the manner in which organisms adapt themselves to their environment and achieve a mutual fit. The mutual fit is characterized by the organism and the environment making positive contributions to the growth of each in such a manner that the ecological environment is healthy, strong and growth producing. The ecological metaphor has been applied to social work practice. As applied in social work practice, ecological social work would focus on understanding the reciprocity which exist between people and social systems in an ecological environment. A lack of fit in the transactions of people with their environments suggest that noxious conditions are at work which are interferring with the ecological balance. The tasks of the social worker is to address these noxious conditions which are stress inducing and debilitating to the degree that the psychosocial functioning of the client is impaired. In this perspective, the focus of attention is shift from so-called pathological states to problems in living or to the transactions which exist among the various ecosystems which are in interaction and make up the ecological environment. Germain and Gitterman (1980) state that the ecological perspective holds the view that human needs and problems result from the transactions which occur between people and social systems. They refer to their model which is ecologically-based as the life model to social work practice. The goals of the life model are to strengthen the adaptive capacity of people and to bring about positive responses from their environments. Stress for the client system is viewed as resulting from (1) life transitions, (2) environmental pressures and (3) interpersonal processes. The social worker assumes a variety of roles in this approach. An important one is that of social broker. Other roles are those of mediator, advocate, enabler to the client system and educator.

Time-Limited Interventions. Time limited approaches make maximum use of definite time periods in assisting clients to address their difficulties. Time-limited interventions include crisis intervention and planned short-term treatment. They may also be referred to as brief therapies. While these intervention approaches share similarities, differences exist relative to the amount of time allocated for intervention. However, they are basically action-oriented, goal-directed approaches. Common characteristics shared by them are (1) time is used as a crucial element in the intervention process, (2) the ending of intervention is clearly stated in the beginning stage, (3) the focus is on specific problem areas instead of mental states, (4) the client is actively engaged in the change process, (5) they are action-oriented. The social worker assumes a very active, directive role, and (6) they focus more on the here and now instead of the past. The cognitive processes of the clients are actively engaged in the planning and implementation of the change strategy. Clients are viewed as being relatively healthy individuals who have encountered a situation or condition which creates stress for them and impairs their usual effectiveness in psychosocial functioning. These approaches act on the assumption that intensive help within a short period of time can be helpful in preventing the development of maladaptive patterns or restoring the client to a higher or precrisis level of functioning.

Crisis Intervention. A crisis is perceived as a stressful event with which an individual cannot address effectively with his/her usual coping mechanisms. The individual finds him/herself in a state of crisis characterized by excessive anxiety. Inasmuch as a crisis is perceived as being time limited, the individual, if he/she does not receive immediate help, may develop maladaptive coping patterns as the crisis moves toward some resolution. The client in a crisis state is not viewed as being mentally ill or incompetent. Rather, he/she is viewed as being overwhelmed by the event (crisis) facing him/her to the degree that his/her usual coping skills are ineffective.

Within a crisis intervention framework, the social worker must quickly engage the cognitive capacities of the client in recognizing the event responsible for his/her condition and his/her reaction to it. Assessment is extremely important. Similar events do not constitute a crisis for all people and the social worker must determine why this event has placed the client in a state of crisis. It is also important that the social worker learns how the client has problem-solved in the past so that the client gains awareness of his/her capacity for problem solving as this has been effectively demonstrated in the past. Eight interviews or less are felt to be sufficient time for the achievement of crisis abatement. The goal of crisis intervention is not to change personalities, but to address the event that has brought on the crisis state. The expected outcome is to restore the client to a precrisis or higher level of functioning. Crisis abatement does not mean that the client no longer has problems. It means that he/she can again function with less anxiety being evident. As a result of the crisis work, the client may become involved in more intensive therapeutic work as he/she recognizes issues which require some resolution.

Crises are usually of two types: developmental or situational. The social worker acts as an enabler, a facilitator, a resource locator, and as a support system. Effective crisis intervention requires that the social worker assumes an active role with the client as he/she engages the client is developing a sense of hope that the situation can be addressed and that help is available to him/her in finding solutions to his/her situation.

Crisis theory is predicated on several assumptions. The client in crisis is perceived as being a well-functioning individual prior to the onset of the crisis; the client is receptive to help and suggestions made to the client during this period will be acted on; the client is able to incorporate these suggestions into his/her behavioral repertoire. The help provided by the social worker is fairly specific and aimed at achieving a fairly quick and satisfactory resolution to the crisis. The process or method involved in crisis intervention constitutes basically four phases: (1) assessment, in which the social worker seeks to idneity the hazardous event which has placed the client in a state of crisis, (2) planning, the social worker and the client identify what needs to be done if the crisis is to be resolve, (3) intervention, the social worker and the client implement activities which are directed at strengthening the client's ego functioning so that he/she can more effectively address the crisis and (4) termination. The helping process is accelerated; assessment is rapidly completed and intervention is quickly implemented. The client actively engages him/herself in this process and make use of community and social networks as he/she seeks to resolve his/her situation.

Planned Short-Term Treatment (PSST). In planned short-term treatment more time (usually 12 interviews or less) is allocated for achieving the goals of intervention. A crisis does not need to be the reason for agency's contact. The focus of planned short term treatment is on a specific stressful situation which is confronting the client system. The clients are viewed as being motivated and fairly well functioning people who can make use of a cognitive, task-focused, action-oriented approach in working on their problem. From the initial contact, the client is informed of the duration of intervention, and an identification is made of the areas to be addressed and the goals to be achieved. The problem to be addressed is very specific and deep-seated problems if they exist in the client's personality are not addressed. The specific incident to be addressed borders on being a crisis situation which threatens an otherwise functional situation.

The focus is on the here and now as the social worker attempts to assist the client in developing and implementing actions that will improve the situation. Some of the techniques employed in this approach are suggestions, advice, logical discussion, education, and support. The assessment is extremely important. Through assessment, an identification is made of those areas on which work is required as well as what areas are most susceptible to change.

Planned short-term treatment follows the principles of effectiveness (goal achievement) and efficiency (what can be accomplished in the shortest period of time) in social work practice. The social worker attempts to identify the triggering event which brings the client to the agency (life transition, dissatisfaction in the role which one is carrying or the threat of a divorce) and to focus on it. Phases in this process are (1) problem exploration, (2) assessment, (3) identification of problem to be addressed, (4) implementation of change strategy, and (5) termination. In the initial contact phase, the social worker and the client engage in a deliberate process of identifying the problem to be addressed, establishing goals, establishing the time frame of the intervention, identifying roles and responsibilities of the participants, formulating a contract and developing the change strategy. Work is then implemented towards goal achievement. Depending on the progress, the time frame can be shortened, or upon renegotiation it can be extended. Effective planned short-term treatment will be characterized by (1) the alleviation of a specific condition in the client's psychosocial environment which is stress inducing, or (2) the strengthening of the client's ego functioning, especially in the area of cognition. As a result of the intervention process, the client may learn something about him/herself that will enable him/her to function more effectively in the future.

The Task-Centered Approach. Epstein (1980) defines the task-centered approach as "a structured and time-limited model in which goals are to reduce the client's acknowledged problem by developing and accomplishing a series of problem-resolution tasks, a set of guiding value assumptions, giving prime value to the client's expressed wants and an underlying theoretical and empirical base" (p. 397). In the task-centered model, the client identifies his/her problems and what he/she wants to be changed. The client also assumes the role of the primary change agent in the task-centered model. Usually three problems are identified and prioritized. The primary philosophical assumption of this model is that effective intervention can be accomplished within a limited time frame. In this aspect, it has similarities to other time limited therapies such as crisis intervention and planned short-term treatment. Its essential difference is its task focus. A task is conceptualized as a unit of work to be accomplished in achieving a goal. The client is viewed as an essentially healthy individual who is competent and motivated to work actively in the change process. He/she is encouraged to accomplish tasks which are directed toward goal accomplishment by the time constraints and the activities in which he/she engages in. These activities are directed at bringing about problem reduction. The social worker has the task of assisting the client in this effort by providing resources and in removing obstacles to task accomplishment.

This is a problem-solving model with theoretical underpinnings from the psychosocial model of social work practice. Its major focus is on specific problems identified by the client with which he/she wants assistance. The problems selected for intervention are not of a global nature, but are specific and manageable. Following an identification of the specific problem(s) which the client wants to change, an agreement is reached by the client and the social worker on the problem which becomes the focus of intervention. Tasks are then identified which will be necessary in goal achievement and they are carried out by the social worker and the client. Again, as is true of all the time-limited approaches, problems are not viewed as resulting from pathological states. Difficulties are conceptualized as problems in living with which the client requires some assistance. The problems are viewed as representing temporary breakdowns in psychosocial functioning. The historical origin of the problem receives scant attention. Rather, the intervention is directed at addressing current obstacles to effective psychosocial functioning. The emphasis is on the here and now as the client and social worker engage in tasks which are goal-directed. Techniques involved in this model are similar to those located in the psychosocial approach: advice giving, support, role playing, encouragement, modeling and logical discussion. Homework assignments are an important part of the intervention strategy. Epstein identifies the following as steps in the task-centered approach: (1) Starting up (initial contact with the client system), (2) identifying and clarifying the client's target problem (as stated previously, usually three problems are prioritized), (3) contract formulation, (4) engaging in the problem-solving work which includes identification of those activities which are directed at problem reduction and goal attainment, and (5) termination (pp. 4–6).

Ego Psychology. Ego psychology constitutes a theory of personality development over time as the individual goes through the psychosocial stages of development. As a practice model, ego psychology provides a model for developing an understanding of those conditions which impact adversely on psychosocial functioning and hamper the ego capacities in performing its functions in a healthy growth-inducing manner. As stated previously, ego psychology is one of the theoretical underpinnings of the psychosocial model, the problem-solving approach and the task centered model of social work practice. In this conceptual framework, the ego does not develop from the Id as characterized in Freudian psychology, but develops autonomously free of conflict and is present at birth. Difficulties for the individual emerge when social demands are placed on him/her. These demands at each stage of psychosocial development constitute a crisis. The manner in which these crises are resolved will have a positive or negative impact on ego functioning. The ego is the psychic structure which mediates between internal demands and external reality. Its overall function is to mediate between these two forces and to maintain a state of dynamic equilibrium within the personality as it is constantly being threatened by inner and external forces. Psychosocial functioning has been referred to as essentially being ego or role functioning.

Ego functions are those of perception, reality testing, integration, judgment, synthesis, execution, object relations, handling of impulses (regulation and control of ID drives. When the social worker is engaging clients, he/she is also evaluating the strengths of the client's ego as revealed through his/her psychosocial functioning. An identification is made of those areas of ego functioning which are strong and those which required strengthening. The ego may become overtaxed by external pressures and/or inner stresses to the degree that behavior becomes dysfunctional or anxiety levels become extremely high. In defending itself from a situation perceived as threatening, the individual may resort to ego defenses. It is important that the social worker recognizes that ego defenses serve an important purpose for the individual; they should be respected and no attempts should be made to penetrate them until the social worker is able to replace them with attributes of a more positive nature. To arbitrarily remove a defense mechanism is to place the client in a vulnerable state. Rarely, are all of the individual's ego functions severely impaired. If they are, then the individual may well be in a psychotic state. Invariably the social worker seeks to identify the strengths within the client and to build on them in helping the client to cope with his/her life stresses. Some concepts in ego psychology are ego-alien (dystonic), ego syntonic, ego functions, ego defenses, lending one's ego to the client, ego supportive casework and working with the ego's adaptive capacity. The ego is adaptive and its movements are of a forward nature as it attempts to adapt to and master its environment. Sometime, this trait is referred to as ego competence. Stress can overwhelmed the ego to the degree that its functions take on a regressive nature and the individual is ill-equipped to deal with life demands. The social worker in assessing the problem faced by the client essentially focuses on the client and those systems in which he/she is involved (the dual focus of social work practice). The objective of this dual focus is to develop an understanding of those factors, personality and/or environmental, which are stressful to the ego and impairing its functions. The outcome of an ego-psychological approach is the enhancement of the psychosocial functioning of the client.

As a developmental theory of the personality, ego psychology emphasizes the impact of sociocultural factors on personality development. The social worker needs to be able to make a distinction between ego psychology and Freudian theory. While ego psychology is Freudian base, important differences exist. As stated earlier in Freudian psychology, the ego develops from the id and begins to present itself in the anal stage of psychosexual development. The personality of the individual is also felt to be securely established during the oedipal stage and adolescence ends the stages of psychosexual development. In the psychosocial stages of personality development, the individual is confronted with a crisis at each stage of development, and the manner in which this crisis is handled will affect the next stage. There are eight stages of psychosocial development, starting with infancy and ending at old age. In ego psychology the social worker needs to understand the structure of the personality (id, ego and super-ego), its levels (unconscious, conscious and preconscious), ego functions and ego defenses if he/she is to develop an understanding of the client's strengths, vulnerabilities and to plan intervention.

In this framework as stated earlier, the ego is perceived as being an autonomous structure with which the individual is born. The ability to walk, talk and to see are necessary for the mastery of one's environment and these functions develop automatically. Thus, it may be stated that individuals are born with the innate ability to adjust to and to master their environment. While these are basically conflict free areas, problems develop for the individual when environmental demands are imposed on him/her. Physical injuries, environmental constraints, unmet childhood needs and childhood traumas are some of the forces which may act adversely on the ego and impede its functioning. In addition, in this theoretical perspective, it is not always necessary for the individual to resolve early trauma in order to improve his/her psychosocial functioning due to the progressive nature of the ego. As the individual gains some understanding of him/herself in the therapeutic relationship, he/she may be able to synthesize earlier experiences in a growth-producing manner so that they no longer have a debilitating impact on his/her psychosocial functioning. For example, a good termination can help a client who fears separation because of earlier, traumatic separation experiences to see that all separations are not bad, and they are in effect a part of life.

Role Theory. If psychosocial functioning can be translated into role functioning, then social workers need to possess knowledge of role theory. This social psychological perspective is useful in evaluating the effectiveness of psychosocial functioning in the specific roles which the client is occupying at a given time. An important task of the social work is to identify those conditions, social, psychological, physiological or cultural, which prevent the individual from successfully performing life roles in an appropriate manner. It is through the socialization process that individuals gain knowledge of what constitutes appropriate behaviors in specific life roles. Cherscher (1979) states, "Social roles is the coordinating link between character and social structure and an understanding of the discrepancies that occur in role transactions can guide the practitioner in establishing the appropriate goals of treatment" (p. 93). Cherscher also suggests that in evaluating the discrepancies that occur in a role relationship, the social worker will discover clues as to the nature of that relationship. Social role is a dynamic, not a static concept. Perceptions of appropriate role behavior may undergo change as societal values change. As a transactional concept and the unit of analysis for the workings of social systems, an analysis of the role behaviors exhibited by the participants and the reasons for this behavior will be useful to the social worker in identifying reasons for systemic stress. Brown (1968) suggests that ego psychology should be used in tandem with role theory. Ego psychology provides an understanding of the strengths and weaknesses of the individual in specific areas of psychosocial functioning and role theory helps the social worker to identify environmental demands made on the person and his/her difficulties in carrying out these expectations. He states,

> Role theory helps social caseworkers in understanding the social dynamics and determinants of behavior. It helps to reveal the situation to which the individual is not adjusting at a given time and poses some reasons why (p. 13).

A role is a set of behaviors associated with a particular status. It calls for a position (wife) and a position-sector (husband) which implies interactions between the system participants as they perform in their respective roles. Personality, environmental influences and culture can affect the manner in which people perform in designated roles. In utilizing role theory in practice, the social worker seeks to help client systems to perform appropriately in given roles, or to modify role behavior so that conflict is minimized. Role theory has practice implications for individual and societal change. For example, if the role behaviors of participants within an organization (position) are viewed as being detrimental to the client or worker system (position-sector), then the social worker must identify for the reasons for the existing behaviors and attempt to modify them. Role incongruency is an important concept. Many reasons can exist for role incongruency, lack of environmental resources, cultural dissonance, physical injuries (the sick role) and personality factors. By its focus on the external validation of behavior, the social worker is able to employ role theory in identifying the reasons for role conflict or failure; he/she will then be able to identify points for intervention in achieving greater role compatability between systems participants. Role theory makes it possible for the social worker to evaluate role performances of individuals in specific social contexts and to identify the reasons for faulty role performances.

THE MINOR THEORIES IN SOCIAL WORK PRACTICE

The author believes that the theoretical frameworks discussed above are the major ones used by social workers in their practice. Ideally all frameworks for social work practice should enable the social worker to focus on the transactions which occur between people and their environments. This approach has been called the dual focus of social work practice. However, social workers also employ a number of theoretical perspectives which are not entirely suited to a dual focus. The book, *Social Work Treatment* (Turner, 1986), contains 23 theoretical approaches. All of these theoretical approaches are not widely used by social workers. Some of them may be classified as minor theoretical frameworks in social work practice. They are given this classification not due to a lack of complexity in their philosophical assumptions or their suitability to practice in specific problem areas, but because they are more individually focused and confine their intervention to interpersonal and individual conflicts. Examples of these minor approaches are Transactional Analysis, Existentialism, Gestalt Therapy and the Client-Centered Approach. Two of these theories, the Client-Centered Approach and Gestalt Therapy will be discussed as they have received considerable attention in social work practice.

Client-Centered Therapy was developed by C. Rogers (1951). It is an interpersonal approach which is directed at assisting the client in the process of self-actualization. It is important that the social worker views the problem through the eyes of the client. The effectiveness of the counseling approach is dependent on the client being the center of the helping relationship. The objective of this approach is to assist the client in becoming a fully functioning individual through the acceptance and unconditioned regard which he/she finds in the relationship. Problems are viewed as being a result of the distorted views which people have developed from their contacts with significant others. As a result of these experiences, the client has developed distortions in his/her view and disorganization in his/her thinking. Through the client-centered approach, the social worker helps the client to eliminate some of his/her distortions and denial which are operating in his/her situation.

Essentially, client-centered therapy is also a form of existentialism as the client is expected to fully integrate him/herself into an integrated human being. The social worker in this process exhibits a high regard for the client and a faith in his/her potential to use his/her powers in addressing his/her problems. He/she intuitively knows the answers to what he/she must do. The social worker in a skillful manner validates the client's thinking. The relationship is one characterized by permissiveness, acceptance, empathy, genuineness, active listening and reflection. In reflecting on the client's statements, the social worker enables the client to come to a realization of what powers he/she has and how he/she can move forward. The client presents the potentialities for development and the social worker acts as a guide in this process.

In this approach, the focus is on the individual in the here and now. Little attention, if any, is given to the past. Attention is directed toward the immediate situation confronting the client. The process itself is viewed as being a growth experience, and is not viewed as being a preparation for change as it is change itself. A formal assessment is not required in client-centered therapy. The emphasis is on the client and his/her growth capacity. The dynamics of the relationship will enable the client to grow. It is important that the social worker does not take responsibility for the client and informs the client from the beginning of contacts that he/she does not possess answers to his/her situation. It is the client who is expected to find the answers to his/her problems. The social worker encourages expressions of feelings from the client, accepts, recognizes and clarifies negative and positive feelings. The social worker does not praise or criticize the client, but communicates his/her total acceptance of the client through the attributes expressed in the relationship. As the client develops awareness of his/her situation and views alternative courses of action, he/she is able to assume control of his/her situation and to act accordingly. When the client reaches the stage of recognizing his/her powers to act and to take responsibility for his/her decisions, then the relationship can come to an end. Spontaneity and genuiness characterize the interactions between the client and the therapist.

In this approach the social worker must perceive as accurately and sensitively as possible the client's view of the situation as it is being experienced by him/her. When this transformation occurs, the social worker informs the client of the extent that he/she is seeing things through the client's frame of reference. In becoming joined with the client, the social worker creates a client-centered relationship and a safe environment in which the client can reveal him/herself and in doing so gain a more clear picture of him/herself as a person. The client through reflection and discussion is helped to integrate distortions so that a whole person can emerge. Client-centered therapy is basically a form of nondirective therapy within a humanistic framework. It is Roger's belief that the objective of therapy is to assist clients in their growth process. This growth enables them to address present and future problems.

Gestalt Therapy may also be viewed as a person-centered approach within the humanistic, existential framework. A major assumption of Gestalt therapy is that people have left over business from their life experiences which prevents their total integration as individuals. Emphasis in this approach is placed on the client developing conscious awareness of these concerns so that they can be integrated into his/her personality. This is basically a process-oriented approach to individual growth. In following a Gestalt framework, the social worker would direct attention on the manner in which the client is pursuing or not pursuing this process leading toward self-actualization and completeness. The client in developing awareness of these gaps or unfinished business is able to integrate them so that they no longer are anxiety producing. This process of awareness is facilitated by assisting the client to see the incongruencies in his/her behaviors, physical and verbal. The transformative process is accomplished through the medium of the relationship. The relationship is not viewed as being completely mutual as its purpose is directed solely toward the client. The client works with the social worker in this transformative process. The work is accomplished in the here and now and references to the past are held to a minimum. The task for the client is to see what is happening, to do something about it, to develop the capacity to cope and to learn from these encounters how to live a more satisfying life.

The therapeutic environment provides the client with a secure environment in which he/she can experiment with his/her feelings and learn ways of addressing them that are of a productive nature. Confrontations can occur within this relationship. The social worker needs to confront the client when indicated and to challenge him/her to face and come to grips with unfinished business. The social worker is very sensitive and alert to the client's behavior as it is presented in the session, and brings the incongruencies revealed to the conscious awareness of the client. As Perls states: "A frightened person does not smile." Some of the techniques employed in Gestalt therapy are (1) the empty chair, (2) confrontation,

(3) sharing hunches, (4) role playing and (5) homework assignments. These techniques are employed in helping the client to develop a greater sense of self-awareness so that he/she can grow and assume self-responsibility for his/her actions. Perls (1961) states the objective of therapy is "to make the patient not dependent upon others but to make the patient discover from the very first moment that he can do many things, much more than he thinks he can do" (p. 29).

MODELS OF SOCIAL GROUP WORK, FAMILY THERAPY AND COMMUNITY ORGANIZATION

Social group work, family work and community organization are methods of social work practice which also have different theoretical frameworks and conceptual models. Knowledge of these methods are necessary if the social work is to engage in social change or to present a dual focus to practice.

Social Group Work. The three models of social group work, social goals, interactionist and remedial, identified by Papell and Rothman are best viewed as constituting a continuum of group work practice. Depending on the problem area to be addressed, the social worker may employ either one of them. In actuality, all of these models may be used concurrently in practice but the use of one of them may predominate at a given moment. In reaction to the seemingly separateness of these three models, the mainstream model of social group work practice has been proposed. This model emphasizes the similarities instead of the differences which characterize the social goals, interactionist and remedial models of group work practice. The mainstream model presents an integrated model of social group work practice.

The models in social group work have theoretical underpinnings. A psychosocial perspective, a problem-solving approach, behavioral modification, and the task-centered model are practice approaches which can be used in social work with groups. The social worker needs to possess specific knowledge and skills. He/she should be knowledgeable about group dynamics, the developmental phases of the group, the curative and mutual-aid dynamics which present themselves in the life of the group, the use of program, the goals of the group and be sensitive to process and content as they are presented in the life of the group. The small group has been defined as consisting of two or more people who come together for the achievement of a specific purpose. The social worker in group work practice usually works with the formed group, a group deliberately planned and structured to achieve a specific purpose.

A group may be developed around a problem, a value, a concern or an issue. It is important that members share something in common which can serve as a bond. In social group work practice, planning is very important. The social worker needs to identify the purpose of the group, the function(s) it will serve, what type of group will be developed, its membership composition, if the group will be a closed or an open one, and if its membership will be of a homogeneous or heterogeneous nature. Major differences exist in the formed group, the natural group and the family. The family shares many characteristics of a group. However, membership is imposed by birth, and family members may leave the family but always remains a part of it. The natural group comes into existence on its own such as the gang, the work group or a neighborhood group. While it will share many characteristics of the formed group, its existence is of an on-going nature. The class room also shares group characteristics. However, the difference is that students will come to the classroom, assigned to a specific role, and expect to partake of the knowledge which will be provided by the teacher. Groups organized by social workers are characterized by movement over time, guided interaction, spontaneity of expressions and feelings, and a growing recognition among the members of their mutual dependence on each other. In effect, depending on the theoretical framework employed, the small group in social group work practice may be viewed as a social system, a place for interpersonal learning, a problem-solving medium or a mutual aid system.

The social worker can employ the small group for a variety of purposes: diagnostic, educational, information giving, orientation, socialization social change, psychological growth, the building of self-esteem and support. Groups can focus on subject matter (family life education), problems (marital stress, interpersonal communications) and governance (committees and boards). Ad-hoc committees are viewed as task-centered groups which are given a particular task to perform. Once this task has been completed, they go out of existence unless they are requested to continue by the individual or committee with such authority. Within the small group, the social worker assumes a variety of roles: information giver, resource locator, therapist, educator, facilitator and enabler. Vinter (1974) in the remedial model of social group work identifies three ways of exerting influence on the group: (1) extra-group (external to the group, (2) indirect (manipulation of group processes by the social worker), and (3) direct (dealing directly with group members).

Whatever the reasons for developing the group, its purposes will always be directed at meeting individual and group objectives. Its focus of intervention may be directed at the micro-messo-macro level as its members attempt to achieve individual and/or social change. The basic elements of social group work practice are (1) group members, (2) group processes, (3) the developmental phases of the group over time, (4) the group worker and (5) the use of program for the achievement of group purposes. While the author recognizes the emergence of the mainstream model of social group work, he finds considerable utility in the identification of these three models even though they may blend. Rarely will they present themselves in a pure form. The social goals model is necessary for macro level intervention. It focuses on the development of social consciousness and social responsibility. Implicit in this model is the interdependence of the group member and society. A social goals group would be directed at holding society accountable for the meeting of the needs of its members in a democratic society. Therefore, its activities of a social action nature can be directed at structural change or social policy development. As members work together for the achievement of common and valued goals, they gain a sense of empowerment. Society in response to the legitimate claims of its citizens assumes its responsibility for the welfare of its members. Certainly a social goals model must be able to accomodate conflict. The reciprocal or interactionist model is a useful one for achieving organizational change at the neighborhood level. While it does not focus on restructuring society or the achievement of social change, it does attempt to mediate differences between people and the organizations they call on for human services. It directs its focus on the stress which characterizes the transactions between interacting systems (the school and the family as an example) and seeks to mediate these differences so that each can carry out its intended functions. A primary objective of this model is the full integration of the group member into the institutional life of his/her community. This model is an adaptive one as it seeks to bring about a well-ordered, functioning society. The remedial model is basically micro-level intervention. Its focus is basically of a therapeutic nature as it seeks to extinguish maladaptive behaviors through the use of group interaction. The small group becomes the environment and the context for the achievement of individual change and the amelioration of interpersonal conflicts.

Each of these social group work models have a theoretical foundation. The theoretical underpinnings of the social goals model are of an electic nature. It may be supported by theories of powerlessness, social conflict, government, ethnicity and social policy. In this model the social worker may assume the role of an advocate, an enabler, a facilitator and information provider as he/she seeks to organize people and to develop a sense of social consciousness and responsibility. This awareness is viewed as influencing and motivating group members to take actions in their own interests and the well-being of society. Theoretical supports for the remedial model are social learning theory, ego psychology, group dynamics. Its theoretical foundation may be any of the theories of personality development and interpersonal dynamics. In this model, the social worker acts primarily as an agent of change. Theoretical underpinnings of the interactionist model are basically systems theory and knowledge about mutual-aid processes. The social worker in this model assumes the role of mediation.

Community Organization. Community organization is best conceptualized as being a problem-solving process at the community level. Unique to community organization practice is that the citizens or community residents act as the change agents. They are assisted by the social worker in an identification of their needs. The identification of needs results from a need-assessment which reveals that a condition exists in the community which has negative consequences for its residents. An individual is never the focus of community organization intervention. It is always the community or a group of people who share a common need and finds itself in need of assistance in addressing this needs. Sometimes, it is the community organizer who must sensitize community residents to the existence of this need. Other times, this awareness can come from the community itself. The task of the social worker is to assist in the development and implementation of groups for the purposes of improving the life of the community. As a community organizer, the social worker may assume such roles as enabler, facilitator, information provider, resource locator, advocate and educator. He/she seeks to unite and mobilize the community in problem-solving work. A primary objective of the community organization process is the development of indigenous leadership, the empowerment of citizens and the enhancement of community life.

Community work is essentially group work in the community. In the process of sensitizing people to their needs and rights, the social worker acts as an educator. Community needs may present themselves in the areas of housing, health, social welfare, neighborhood maintenance or recreation. Specific populations such as the elderly, children or minorities, may serve as the focal point of community organization activities. An important organizing task centers around influencing, developing and mobilizing community groups for action. The planning task involves (1) identification of needs, (2) history of the problem and what has been done about it in the past, (3) an assessment of those conditions which contribute to the problem and need to be changed, (4) formulating an intervention strategy, (5) implementing this strategy and (6) evaluating it for its effectiveness. Activities engaged in by the community organizer in the interest of the community group may include those of mediation, negotiation, fund raising, mobilizing action systems, legislative advocacy and confrontation.

The community organizer makes use of two types of skills: analytical and interactional. Analytical skills are those of problem formulation, assessment, planning and implementing change strategies and termination. Interactional skills focus on establishing relationships, facilitating a change process, motivating and influencing people to take actions in their own interests, sustaining motivation and developing indigenous leadership. The analytical skill of evaluation should reveal that the needed changes have occurred in the community and that community life has improved. Always the desired outcome of community organization is the total integration of citizens into the institutional life of the community and the provision of social welfare services to address human needs.

As stated earlier, Rothman (1970) identifies three models of community organization practice: locality development, social planning and social action. Rarely are these models pure in their execution. It is best to view them as existing on a continuum. For example, the social worker may initiate a change process at the neighborhood level using the model of locality development. If this approach should prove ineffective, then either the social planning or social action model may be implemented. Locality development seeks to bring about a community building process directed at addressing community needs. Its hallmarks are democratic participation, consensus building and community actions relative to how community problems may be addressed. This model has a cooperative dimension, and while conflict may be present, it is usually resolved in terms of citizen participation. The participants are viewed as having a vital interest in the welfare of the community. The community organizer brings together citizens, rich and poor, the powerful and the powerless, in order to inform them of community needs and to engage them in a process of community problem solving. Representative participation is extremely important in this model and the participants should represent a broad spectrum of the community with different skills and knowledge.

In contrast to the locality development model which is basically process-oriented, the social planning model of community organization practice represents a rational, technical, analytical approach to community problem solving and in the addressing of community needs. However, the citizens within this model are viewed more as recipients of services rather than as active participants in the process of community problem solving. Social planners are usually professionals who are employed in city planning offices or welfare councils of large voluntary fund raising organizations such as United Way. They are viewed as possessing substantive knowledge in social problem areas. Through research and systems analysis, social planners identify community needs and propose ways of addressing community problems. Their decisions influence resource allocation, program development, the location of services, and their coordination. The decisions of social planner may result in conflict situation as the proposed recipients of them may not feel that these are priority services. When decisions are imposed on citizens without their active participation by social planners, this is referred to as the "top-down" model of community organization practice to reflect the fact that citizens may not have been active participants in the process. When citizens are actively involved in the decision-making process and actions are initiated as a result of their concerns, this is referred to as the "bottoms-up" model to reflect the fact that citizens are articulating their needs and the community is responding to them.

The social action model of community organization practice is designed to address social conflict in which citizens are placed in a disadvantaged status and are viewed as being powerless and victimized. In this model, an important role of the community organizer is that of an advocate to a population which is being exploited and disenfranchised. Change strategies are directed at changing institutional policies and practices or to alter existing power structures through a redistribution of power. The social worker clearly aligns him/herself with the disadvantaged group in seeking to bringing about community changes. Social action techniques such as boycotting, picketing, demonstrating, and media attention are used to illustrate what the community seeks to accomplish and to identify the forces which seek to maintain it in a state of disenfranchisement. The objectives of these techniques are to influence public opinion so that pressures can be exerted at achieving institutional change. As a result of these strategies, other organizations or citizens which share similar goals may become involved in the community change process. The social worker may also assume the role of a negotiator as he/she attempts to negotiate the demands of the community with the power structure which holds the key to institutional change. Welfare Rights organizations, tenants associations and some civil rights organizations have used this model in pursuing their goals.

In essence in community organization practice, the social worker seeks to improve the community in a tangible manner in such areas as health, social welfare services and community improvement so that community residents can receive the services they need in order to live a more rewarding and satisfying life. The community organization process is basically an orderly, sequencing of events which take place over time and are directed toward the achievement of specific goals. Community work may be characterized by beginning, middle and ending phases or sequential steps such as problem identification, data collection, analysis and interpretation of data, developing and implementing a change strategy, evaluation of change strategy for goal achievement and termination. The organization of community residents for institutional change is viewed as being the primary means to improving community life. Key concepts within community organization are social development, allocation and mobilization of resources, integration and administration of services, policy formulation, decision-making, planned change and constituents.

Family Therapy. Family therapy has emerged as a major intervention strategy for social workers and within this field are located a variety of theoretical approaches. The family as a system is the focus of intervention. As a social system, the family is viewed as exhibiting dysfunctional interactional and transactional patterns which hold negative consequences for its members and the family as a unit. The social worker in family therapy becomes a participant-observer to the family processes and attempts to help the family to address them in a more functional manner as members develop awareness of these processes and their consequences. As the family develops awareness of its dysfunctional patterns, its members may seek to modify them so that future transactions become more positive and the family is able to function more effectively. A primary philosophical assumption of family therapy is that a dysfunctional individual is a symptom of a dysfunctional family. The family has contributed to and maintained the behavior(s) exhibited by its members. Therefore, attention should be directed at altering the environment which is held to be responsible for the existing conditions. The task of the social worker is to weaken the pathogenic forces within the family. The goal of family therapy is always to improve the psychosocial environment of the family so that dysfunctional familial patterns are weakened. Intervention is focused on the total family so that all family members will benefit.

Goldenberg and Goldenberg (1985) have classified the theoretical orientations to family therapy as falling into four categories: (1) psychodynamic, (2) behavioral, (3) experiential and humanistic, and (4) the family as a system. Systems-oriented family therapists are Satir (1967), Minuchin (1974) and Bowen (1978). The behaviors assumed by family therapists have been identified as those of conductors and reactors. As a conductor, the family therapist is active and directive as he/she attempts to regulate family processes. Family members are assisted to become more aware of their interactional, transactional and communication patterns through the attempts of the family therapist to bring these processes to their awareness. He/she gives direction to the family in identifying and focusing on problematic areas. In accomplishing this task, he/she acts as orchestrator of the family processes. The objective of this orchestration is to promote interactions between the family members as the family therapist assumes a focal point in the family/communication processes.

While other family therapists may also act within a systems framework, they assume the role of reactors to the family processes. They analyze the system processes and react to what they see occurring. Included in this group of family therapists are Haley (1976), Jackson (1965) and Zuk (1967). The reactors can be divided into two groups: analysts and systems purists. The analysts may employ a psychoanalytic orientation in identifying and explaining family interactions. To a great degree, their focus is on the internal processes of the family members which influence the interactional and transactional behaviors of family members. It is the psychological needs of the family members which motivate their behavior. In contrast the systems purists focus on the family as a social system or organization and view it as being a network of influence, power alliance, governed by rules and roles which contribute to the family's interactional patterns. It is also of value to the social worker to evaluate the family as an open or closed system. As an open system, the family is receptive to feedback from its environment and can make adjustment to it so that it can function more effectively in addressing internal and external influences on its members. As an open system, it is a dynamic entity which takes in energy, transform it, and receives feedback from its environment so that it can make the necessary adjustments in maintaining its equilibrium. As a closed system (This classification has frequently been given to the multiproblem family.), the family does not respond to new inputs; it continues to take in energy but does not transform it in a positive manner and its systems become overloaded to the degree that its survival is threatened and its functioning as a family seriously impaired. It may be stated with a high degree of accuracy that the primary function of the social worker in family therapy is to help the family in becoming an open system.

Tolson and Reid (1981) have edited a book on family models employed in social work practice. In this section, the author will briefly discuss a few of the major family therapy models. The reader should recognize that while each theorist is focusing on the family as a system or organization, each is giving attention to different aspects of the family such as structure, communication and intergenerational influences on behavior or unresolved issues from the family of origin. Family therapy basically requires a here-and-now focus as the social worker seeks to capture the family's interactional and transactional patterns as they are occurring. He/she becomes an active participant-observer to the family processes and captures and comments on its interactional and transactional patterns within the interviewing sessions. The emphasis is not on the individual (a linear approach to problem causation) but on the family processes and their impact on family members (a circular approach to causation). The effects of these transactions on one or several family members will reverberate throughout the total system affecting other family members.

Structural Family Therapy. In this approach to family practice, the family is conceptualize as an organization or a social system with specific structural elements, processes and boundaries. Its transactional or interactional patterns are viewed as having developed over time and they govern how the family addresses and resolves its conflicts. Structural elements and processes are those of communication patterns, rules, roles, decision-making mechanisms, family alignments and a power structure or hierarchy of power. The family has three subsystems: spousal which include the marital and parental dimensions of family life, parent-child which include the socialization and parenting functions, and sibling. The marital or parental system is viewed as the executive system within the family. Other subsystems may include grandparents, relatives and friends depending on their involvement and role in the family. In this model, the social worker directs his/her intervention toward the goal of bringing about modification in some aspects of the family structure. As behaviors exhibited by family members are altered, each family member experiences a change which can result in modification of the behaviors of family members. Structural change is indicated as the existing family operational patterns are viewed as being a result of the rigid patterns which exist in the family and have been reinforced over time to the degree that family members act in habitual ways. While the social worker will need to work with all subsystems in varying degrees, a primary objective is always to strengthen the executive system of the family. The dysfunctional family patterns are identified and specific techniques are directed at altering them so that the family may learn more effective ways of functioning as a unit (Minuchin and Fishman, 1981).

When the social worker enters into the family system, in effect, he/she becomes a part of it and a therapeutic system is formed. The social worker identifies dysfunctional transactional patterns and then attempts to upset the family's existing way of functioning. In this process, attention is directed toward helping the family to develop more effective coping mechanisms. As the social worker brings the transactional patterns to the awareness of family members and challenge them, a process of growth can be induced into the family's environment. The new experiences and their positive impact on the family lead to a questioning of the rigid, structural patterns which have characterized the family for generations. Frequently, the executive unit will state this is the manner in which parental figures in the past have addressed family conflicts. The restructuring focus has the primary objective of bringing into existence new patterns which will better serve the needs of the family as it progresses toward becoming more of an open system.

Communication Theory. A system must have communication patterns by which messages are conveyed to its members. In this theoretical orientation to family therapy, the social worker focuses on the communication system within the family and the emotions which influence them.

The objective is to identify the manner in which family's communications contribute to a dysfunctional family environment. Satir suggests that the capacity to communicate is related to self-esteem. An individual with a positive self-esteem is able to communicate/relate in an open manner and to send clear communications. In contrast, individuals with low self-esteems give out ambiguous messages and rarely assume any responsibility for their actions. A basic assumption of the communication approach to family therapy is that family stresses are a result of faulty communication patterns and the covert messages/feelings which are behind the messages transmitted.

As a participant-observer to the family processes, the social worker acts as an orchestrator in identifying these messages, their contents, to whom they are conveyed and the feelings which surround them. He/she then brings these messages/transactions to the attention of family members so that they may derive insights from them. Sculpting is one of the techniques in this family therapy model in which members may present a drawing or illustration of their views of the family members. The awareness gained from sculpting is useful in family members gaining some perceptions of how they are viewed by other family members. The here and now focus of this orientation necessitates that the social worker observes and captures these transactions as they occur. The communication system within the family serves as a point of inquiry into the messages being conveyed as well as the focal point of intervention. The social worker must act as a model of clear communication, and thus it is important that he/she is able to communicate in a clear, unambiguous manner if he/she is to serve as a model of communication. Communication may be defined as those verbal and nonverbal processes which occur between family members as they interact.

In family sessions, communication among the family members provides clues as to the nature of the problems facing the family. As these patterns are brought to the awareness of family members, communication styles may be modified, and the feelings behind the messages identified as family members recognize the impact of the messages on family members and the manner in which these messages, covert and overt, are conveyed. The alteration of communication patterns thus becomes the primary objective of this approach. The concern is with process (how the family members respond to messages) instead of content (the subject matter before the family). The focus is also on effect (outcome) instead of cause (reasons for the messages) and the emphasis is present instead of past oriented. As a role model for effective communication, the social worker assumes a very active stance in identifying dysfunctional communication patterns. Even though he/she attempts to support the family in its efforts to change and to alleviate its problems, he/she can also be confrontive as he/she will need to overcome resistance to open communication.

Bowen's Family Theory: Bowen's theoretical orientation to family therapy has an intergenerational focus and addresses unresolved issues from the family of origin. It is concerned with family patterns that emerge over generations as parents transmit varying levels of their own immaturities to their children who in turn carry them over to the next generation. Bowen conceptualizes the family as existing in time and space. Family histories are constantly repeated through powerful intergenerational transmission and projective processes. The genogram or family mapping provides a diagnostic tool for the identification of persistent family patterns and the events which have happened to the family over the years in one generation after another. The genogram presents a pictorial picture of what has happened to the family for several successive generations. Within Bowen's intergenerational framework of family therapy, the primary objective of the social worker would be to strengthen a sense of identity in the client while at the same time helping him/her to differentiate from the dysfunctional aspects of his/her family of origin. The social worker also needs to be aware that the total family does not have to be present in sessions. Work can be done with the individual but it is always in the context of the influence of family of origin materials on his/her particular problem.

The social worker in this theoretical approach to family therapy would assume the role of a coach; he/she would provide suggestions and guidance to the client in finding answers to his/her distress. The client takes on the primary responsibility for the work to be accomplished in arriving at discoveries about him/herself and his/her family and its impact on his/her behavior. A philosophical assumption of this model is that the individual problems of family members result from "the excessive garbage" which has been carried over from the family of origin. As a result of this "excessive garbage," family members develop immaturities and a lack of differentiation which lead to enmeshment. In his/her role as a couch, the social worker focuses attention on family patterns over generations so that the client develops some understanding of them and gains awareness of the options available to him/her in addressing them.

The emotional responses which maintain certain attitudes need to be replaced with rational responses. Analysis of the family proceeds on the levels of (1) the interacting family processes, and (2) the relationships which exist between them. Bowen's model contains many useful concepts which are of value in identifying and analyzing family behavioral patterns over time. Some of these concepts are (1) differentiation of self (how people distinguish between emotional and intellectual factors), (2) triangulation (when people involved in a dyadic relationship attempt to bring in a third person to stabilize the system), (3) nuclear family emotional system (the emotional functioning of the family in a single generation) and (4) the family projective process (the process by which undifferentiated parents triangulate and create dysfunctional behavioral patterns in their children). Within this approach, social work activities may be directed at assisting family members to achieve a higher degree of differentiation so that they are able to disengage from the "undifferentiated ego mass" which contribute to their present stress. This task is accomplished by working with family members, encouraging them to discuss their situation with their family of origin, reworking emotional-cut-offs, helping clients to develop an intellectual instead of an emotional response to problems and in the modification of triangular processes.

FAMILY THERAPY IN REVIEW

Many other approaches to family therapy are not discussed in this section. These approaches include (1) developmental, (2) behavioral, (3) psychodynamics of family life and (4) crisis intervention and brief short-term family therapy. These approaches for the most part are discussed in the Tolson and Reid book or any book on family therapy (Erickson and Hogan, 1972). The reader should bear in mind that all theoretical approaches to family therapy provide a particular view of the family and its functioning, particularly the role it plays in the development of problems among its members. The structure and processes which distinguish the family serve both as a focal point of inquiry into family problems and intervention. From an ecological perspective, consistent with the dual focus of social work practice, the social worker needs to be always cognizant of the fact that the family is also a subsystem within a larger social system with which it interacts while at the same time being influenced by it. These larger social systems include the community, the church, social welfare, law enforcement and health agencies. The ethnic family to be discussed in a later chapter is also influenced by its cultural system. These systemic transactions also must be evaluated for their positive or negative effects on the family's psychosocial functioning. As the genogram reveals a pictorial view of the family and the experiences which it has had over time and throughout generations, the ecogram is also a useful diagnostic tool in revealing the nature of the interactions which transpire between the family and its ecosystems. The ecogram makes it possible for the social worker to identify the sources of support which are available to the family as well as those systems which create stress for it. This knowledge provides points for intervention into the ecological environment. A general principle of family practice for social worker is that intervention efforts should be of a dualistic nature, the family in interaction with its environment, and should be directed at opening up the family boundaries so that the family becomes an open system receptive to looking at its internal structure while at the same time being receptive to inputs from its external environment. The environment may well serve as a target for change if its processes are viewed as being dysfunctional and detrimental to the well-being of the family.

GENERALIST–SPECIALIST APPROACH
IN SOCIAL WORK PRACTICE

The generalist-specialist debate to social work practice has received considerable attention. The specialist is viewed as a methods oriented social worker and the generalist is viewed as a problem-specialist who makes use of a variety of methods depending on the problem presented by the client system. The generalist approach is sometimes referred to as the unitary or integrated approach to practice. It is the author's conviction that all professions require generalist and specialist practitioners, and therefore this debate takes on a specious quality, centered around vested interests. Social work practice by its dual focus must take into consideration the transactions which occur between people and their environments and direct its intervention at those conditions which prevent self-actualization and the meeting of common human needs. Intervention may focus on the individual, the environment, or the individual and the environment. As stated previously social group work and community organization practice contain models which make micro-messo and macro levels intervention possible. Elsewhere the author has stated a conviction that all of these models may be required depending on the problems faced by client system and the levels of society to which intervention must be addressed. This practice approach has been referred to as the multimodel perspective (Arevalo and Brown, 1979; Brown and Arevalo, 1988).

A generalist approach to practice suggests the employment of a flexible use of methods and skills by the social worker across client systems (individuals, families, small groups, organizations and communities). Practitioners identified as generalists possess basic or foundation knowledge of the various social work methods and are able to employ them as indicated. The impetus for a generalist approach results from a view that the client's situation usually involves a number of social systems and areas to which intervention must be directed. This practice approach shifts the attention of the problem from the client and transfers it to the transactions which take place between interacting systems and are stress-inducing. It is viewed as having applicability to the totality of conditions impacting on the client system. Klenk and Ryan (1974) state that the philosophy behind the generalist approach is that the social worker does whatever activities are necessary in intervening into situations that are affecting client systems. The concern of the generalist social worker is the client in need, and not specific tasks or techniques, or professional pregogatives (p. 4).

Generalist practitioners begin with a holistic approach to the client's situation; he/she identifies those conditions impacting on the client and plans and implements an intervention strategy. He/she starts with the problem and is more problem- than method-focused. In contrast the specialist with a methods orientation is viewed as starting with the person. Pincus and Minahan view the social work process as being one in which certain steps are followed regardless of the problem or systems involved. Steps in this process are problem identification, data collection, data analysis, intervention, evaluation and termination. In effect the generalist approach is perceived as providing a broader base to practice than the specialist orientation. Basically its theoretical underpinning is located in systems theory.

Social work academicians present a penchant for challenging and immediately discarding the old when they introduce different practice approaches. The downgrading of different practice approaches leads to a strain between academicians and practitioners as new models of practice do not always easily translate into practice or fit the realities of the problems faced by the social worker. A need exists for academicians and practitioners to work more closely in developing and field testing new approaches to practice. Additionally, the question always exists if schools of social work are to prepare students for the realities of practice or to produce the model of practice which they feel is most suited to the social purpose of the profession. For example, some social work academicians may question if the social control function is a legitimate one for the profession. However, the reality is that some social work positions exist because of this social control function. This function finds expression particularly in child welfare and correction settings. In order for the social worker to function effectively in these settings, he/she must possess specific skills, knowledge and values, particularly in the purposeful use of authority. A specialist orientation is well-suited for these areas of social work practice.

In the author's view, the generalist approach has much to offer but should not be viewed as being the preferred way to perform social work practice. Its limitations must be acknowledged. The generalist should know his/her limitations and level of competency and turn to the specialist when indicated. While generalist practitioners have a repetoire of roles and follow problem-solving steps in addressing problems, it is unrealistic to expect the generalist to provide intensive therapy to people with severe psychological impairments. The social worker who specializes in a method, a field of practice, or a problem area will need to possess in-depth knowledge of these areas in addition to the foundation knowledge of the generalist. The generalist can be compared to the family practitioner in medicine. The family practitioner can treat a variety of illnesses; however, he/she recognizes when a condition exists which exceeds his/her level of competency, and he/she seeks consultation or refers the patient to a specialist. The same procedures should be followed by the generalist. While a place certainly exists in the profession for generalist practice, a place also exists for the specialist. Unnecessary division is created when one practice approach is presented as the preferred one, or of being more relevant to the mission of the profession. Given the functions of the profession in American society and the complexity of the problems it must addressed, generalist and specialist practice are required in carrying out the functions of the profession.

APPLICATION OF KNOWLEDGE TO PRACTICE

In essence, social work practice is distinguished by a knowledge base, a value system, a social purpose, professional sanctions and skills. As stated earlier, the knowledge base of social work practice is informed by knowledge of human behavior and the social environment, the wholeness of the individual, and the reciprocal influences of people in their transactions with social systems which comprise their ecological environment. This knowledge base includes a strong understanding of a psychology of giving and taking, the manner in which people communicate, group processes, the social services, the structure of society, the community in which people live, and social work methods. The social work method constitutes a systematic observation and assessment of client systems in interactions with their environments followed by a plan of action. Skills are an important part of the methods employed by the social worker in facilitating a change process. Technical expertise on the part of the social worker is illustrated in his/her ability to apply knowledge in an effective manner in implementing appropriate activities in the execution of his/her performance as he/she works to accomplish the purpose of the profession. Three methods of facilitating change exist: (1) within the individual in relations to his/her personality and social environment, (2) within the social environment and its impact upon the individual's psychosocial functioning and (3) within the individual and the environment as they interact and engage in stressful systemic transactions.

Always, the social worker must be guided by a theoretical orientation or practice model as he/she seeks to develop understanding of the nature of the client's problems, in isolating contributing factors to them, and in planning and implementing an intervention strategy. A conceptual model leads to a disciplined practice approach and enables the social worker to collect the required data so that inferences can be drawn from this data which eventually lead to a change strategy. Values influence practice and the outcome of any intervention with client systems regardless of the theoretical orientation employed. Self-awareness assists the social worker in keeping his/her value system in check so that it does not influence the view held of the client or the manner in which services are provided.

Regardless of the conceptual model employed, the social worker's activities must be directly related to the mission of the profession in American society. If the social worker is not guided by a practice theory, then he/she engages in a kind of serependitious practice and will not be able to articulate the reasons for his/her activities. A theoretical orientation should possess a predictive value as to the outcome of intervention. This outcome is influenced by specific contingencies in the client's environment and the manner in which they are addressed. Intervention at some point must proceed on the basis of a formal assessment even though any contact with client systems may be viewed as having intervention implications. It is the theoretical framework employed that will direct the social worker's attention to specific areas of the client-situation configuration and will make it possible for the social worker to ask relevant and necessary questions in securing the data for assessment which will lead to planned intervention.

CONCLUSION

This chapter emphasizes the importance of knowledge in social work practice. This knowledge base includes a theoretical perspective as a guide to practice. The purpose of knowledge is to inform the social worker so that he/she can bring a disciplined approach to his/her practice; it also enables the social worker to make some sense of the client's situation. In the application of knowledge in practice, the social worker demonstrates specific skills, assumes certain roles, performs specific functions and engages in specific activities as he/she attempts to assist the client in achieving stated and agreed on goals. The activities of the social worker are always consistent with the value base of the profession. It is only when the social worker demonstrates knowledge, skills and values which characterize the practice of social work can it be said that he/she is engaging in social work practice, a practice orientation which is distinguish from other professions by its unique focus on people in interactions with their environments.

SELECTED BIBLIOGRAPHY

Allen-Meares and Lane, B. (1987) Grounding social work practice in theory. SOCIAL CASEWORK, 68, 515–521.

Anderson, J. (1984) Toward generic practice: The interactionist approach. SOCIAL CASEWORK, 65, 323–329.

Arevalo, R. and Brown, J. (1979) An emerging perspective on school social work. SCHOOL SOCIAL WORK QUARTERLY, 1, 197–207.

Bowen, M. (1978) Family therapy in clinical practice (New York: Aronson).

Brown, J. (1968) Role theory: Its contribution to social casework methodology. CATHOLIC CHARITIES REVIEW, 12, 11–19.

Brown, J. and Arevalo, R. (1986) Group work with chicano youth in the school setting. In P. Glasser and N. Mayadas (Eds.), Group workers at work: Theory and practice in the 80s (Motowa, NJ: Rowman and Littlefield Publishers).

Cherscher, M. (1979) Social role discrepancies as clues to practice. SOCIAL WORK, 24, 89–94.

Dempsey, J. (1981) The family and public policy: The issues of the 1980s. (Baltimore, MD: Paul H. Brooke Publishing Co.).

Epstein, L. (1980) Helping people: The task-centered approach (St. Louis, MO: C.V. Mosby).

Erickson, G. and Hogan, T. (1982) (Eds.) Family therapy: An introduction to theory and technique (Monterey, CA: Brooks/Cole Publishing Co.).

Fawcett, J. (1984) Analysis and evaluation of conceptual models of nursing. 3rd. printing (Philadelphia, PA: F.A. Davis Co.).

Germain, C. and Gitterman, A. (1980). The life model and social work practice (New York: Columbia University Press).

Goldenberg, I. and Goldenberg, H. (1985). Family therapy: An overview. 2nd. edition (Monterey, CA: Brooks/Cole).

Goldstein, H. (1981) Generalist social work practice. In N. Gilbert and H. Specht (Eds.). Handbook of the social services (Englewood Cliffs, NJ: Prentice-Hall).

Haley, J. (1959) The family of the schizophrenic: A model system. JOURNAL OF NERVOUS AND MENTAL DISEASES, 129, 357–374.

Hepworth, D. and Larsen, J. (1986) Direct social work practice: Theory and skills. 2nd. edition (Chicago: Dorsey Press).

Jackson, D. (1965) Family rules: Marital quid pro quod. ARCHIVES OF GENERAL PSYCHIATRY, 12, 589–594.

Janchill, M. (1969) System concepts in casework theory and practice. SOCIAL CASEWORK, 50, 74–82.

Klenk, R. and Ryan, R. (1974) The practice of social work. 2nd. edition. (Belmont, CA: Wadsworth Publishing Co.).

Lantz, J. (1970) Cognitive theory and social casework. SOCIAL WORK, 23, 361–366.

Minuchin, S. (1974) Families and family therapy. (Cambridge, MA: Harvard University Press).

Minuchin, S. and Fishman, C. (1981) Family therapy techniques. (Cambridge, MA: Harvard University Press).

Moxley, D. (1989) The practice of case management (Newbury Park, CA: Sage Publications).

Northen, H. (1969) Social work with groups (New York: Columbia University Press).

Papell, C. and Rothman, B. (1966) Social group work models: Possession and heritage. JOURNAL OF EDUCATION FOR SOCIAL WORK, 2, 66–77.

Perlman, H. (1957) Social casework: A problem-solving process (Chicago: University of Chicago Press).

Perls, F. (1969) Gestalt therapy verbatim (Moab, UT: Real People Press).

Pincus, A. and Minahan, A. (1973) Social work practice: Model and method (Itasca, IL: F.E. Peacock Publishers).

Robert, R. and Nee, R. (1976) Theories of social casework (Chicago: University of Chicago Press).

Roberts, R. and Northen, H. (1976) Theories of social group work (New York: Columbia University Press).

Rothman, J. (1970) Three models of community organization practice. In F. Cox et al. (Eds.) Strategies of community organization (Itasca, IL: F.E. Peacock Publishers).

Satir, V. (1983) Conjoint family therapy (Palo Alto, CA: Science and Behavioral Books).

Schulman, L. (1984) The skills of helping individuals and groups (Itasca, IL: F.E. Peacock Publishers).

Schwartz, W. (1961) The social worker in the group. New perspectives on services to groups (New York: National Association of Social Workers).

Specht, H. (1988) New directions for social work practice (Englewood Cliffs, NJ: Prentice-Hall).

Spiro, S. (1979) The knowledge base of community organization practice. In F. Cox et al. (Eds.) Strategies of community organization (Itasca, IL: F.E. Peacock Publishers).

Strean, H. (1971) Theories of social casework in action (Metuchen, NJ: Scarcecrow Press).

Tolsen, E. and Reid, W. (1981) Models of family treatment (New York: Columbia University Press).

Turner, F. (1978) Psychosocial therapy (New York: Free Press).

Turner, F. (1986) (Ed.) Social work treatment: Interlocking theoretical approaches (New York: Free Press).

Vinter, R. (1974) The essential components of social group work practice. In P. Glasser et al. (Eds.). Individual change through the small group (New York: Free Press).

Woods, M. and Hollis, F. (1990). Casework: A psychosocial therapy 4th. edition (New York: McGraw-Hill).

Zuk, G. (1967) Family therapy. ARCHIVES OF GENERAL PSYCHIATRY, 16, 71–79.

SECTION IV
THE SKILLS OF SOCIAL WORK

The social worker applies a variety of skills in practice with client systems. Skills may be defined as expertise, technical competence or the capacity to apply knowledge in the execution of tasks which are crucial to the achievement of desired goals. Skills serve a facilitative function. They move the work forward in a dynamic manner. Without the effective use of skills, the social worker would face insurmountable obstacles in facilitating the change process toward goal achievement. Therefore, skills must be viewed as being a necessary and inherent part of sound social work practice.

This chapter focuses on the skills used in social work practice. They include the following; (1) interviewing, (2) development of the helping relationship or therapeutic alliance, (3) data collection, (4) diagnostic formulation or assessment, (5) goal establishment, (6) contract formulation, (7) implementing the intervention strategy, (8) evaluation of the change strategy, (9) termination and (10) recording. These skills are used across varying client systems (individuals, families, marital dyads, the small group and the community). Sometimes they are referred to as generic skills as they are used in all social work practice settings even though they may be applied differently.

Chapter 6

INTERVIEWING

Interviewing has been referred to as being both a science and an art. It is a science because it has a knowledge base and it is an art in that the social worker uses him/herself in a creative way in the interviewing process. Edinberg, Zinberg and Kelman (1975) state the interview is the foundation of any therapeutic intervention. This is especially true for social work practice. While the helping relationship or therapeutic alliance (Chapter VII) is the medium through which change is accomplished, it is through the interviewing process that movement is facilitated toward goal achievement. An interview can be described as a professional conversation or a communication process. It is characterized by a specific purpose and focus. The purpose is the reason for the interview; the focus is directed toward content (subject matter) and process (the manner in which the content is addressed) by the client and the social worker. The effectiveness of any interview is influenced by (1) the degree of the social worker's self-awareness, (2) the social worker's understanding of the dynamics inherent in the psychology of giving and taking, (3) the capacity of the social worker to develop a helping relationship, (4) the capacity of the social worker to respect the client and to actively engage him/her in the communication process, (5) the capacity of the social worker to skillfully phrase and present questions to the client, (6) the purpose of the interview, (7) the atmosphere and setting in which the interview is conducted, (8) the degree of privacy, and the social worker's awareness of the dynamics which occur in the interviewing process such as transference, countertransference. The interviewing process is also affected by racial and/or ethnic factors.

Effective interviewing is necessary for the engagement and maintenance of the client in the change process, for the collection of data and the achievement of goals. The dynamic aspects of the interview are revealed in the communication process which takes place between the social worker and the client as each responds to the questions and comments of the other. While the social worker always approaches the interview with a specific purpose in mind and some preparation, he/she must always show flexibility in modifying the contents in order to address the urgent problems of the client as they present themselves. Unless urgent pressing situations are addressed, the client may find it extremely difficult to discuss other areas. An axiom of the interviewing process is that materials can always be addressed in subsequent contacts. When the client has agreed to become a client of the agency, later contacts with him/her should be referred to as sessions instead of interviews. Sessions imply the establishment of the therapeutic alliance and cooperative efforts between client and social worker in problem solving. An interview suggests that the worker is carrying primary responsibility for the activities conducted within it. He/she is the interviewer (position) and the client is the interviewee (position-sector).

DEFINITION AND PURPOSE OF INTERVIEW

As stated previously, an interview is defined as being a professional conversation or a communication process which is characterized by purpose and is goal-oriented. Stewart and Cash (1985) define the interview "as a process of dyadic relational communication with a predetermined and serious purpose designed to interchange behavior and involving the asking and answering of questions" (p. 7). Interviews may be divided into beginning, middle and ending phases. The interactive nature of interviews is revealed in the behaviors of the participants as each participant is affected by other participants in the interviewing process.

Purpose is a key characteristic of the social work interview. The purpose will influence the manner in which the social worker conducts the interview. An identification of purpose is helpful to the social worker in preparing for the interview particularly in the manner in which it will be directed and the nature of the information to be gained from it.

The purposes of the interview have been identified: (1) data collection, (2) establishing and maintaining the therapeutic alliance, (3) providing the client with information, (4) identifying and addressing obstacles to the helping process, (5) identifying and implementing activities directed at goal achievement and (6) in general to facilitate the helping process. As a goal-directed activity, the interview has the following characteristics: (1) structure, (2) objectivity, (3) time-constraints and (4) outcomes. The achievement of the purpose of the interview should result in one or several of the following outcomes:

(1) The social worker develops a greater understanding of the client and his/her situation, i.e., how the client feels about it, what the client wants from the agency, knowledge of the client's motivation and capacity to use the services of the agency.

(2) The social worker and the client identify the nature of the client's problem, the areas to be addressed in alleviating it, the goals to be achieved, and the mutual roles and responsibilities of the client and the social worker in this process.

(3) The social worker and client reach agreement on intervention and intervention is then implemented. If obstacles are presented to goal achievement, the social worker and client discuss how they can be addressed.

(4) The social worker and the client following the implementation of the change process will monitor and evaluate the implemented activities for their effectiveness. (Monitoring and evaluation are on-going processes throughout the life of the professional contacts between the social worker and the client.)

(5) The social worker and the client engage in the termination process.

Following a series of interviewing sessions with the client system, it is helpful for the social worker to review his/her recording in order to analyze his/her interviewing style for its effectiveness.

Benjamin (1969) states an important task of the interviewer is to become aware of what is involved in the interviewing process. The interview serves as a means of data collection which makes it possible to develop an understanding of the client and his/her situation and to identify and isolate those conditions which appear to be contributing to the client's problem. The interview serves the therapeutic function of establishing and maintaining the therapeutic alliance through the skillful manner in which the social worker uses him/herself and the dynamic interactions which characterize the behaviors between the client and the social worker. It is important that the purpose of the interview is clear to the social worker and the client, and the social worker always applies a theoretical orientation to the process of interviewing. His/her theoretical orientation will influence his/her behavior and the nature of the questions to be asked in seeking and securing relevant information. In essence it is through the interview that the social worker will gain the necessary information to develop an understanding of the client and his/her situation so that an intervention plan can be developed and implemented.

PREPARATION FOR THE INTERVIEW

Whether the client is a drop-in, is being seen for the first time by appointment, or is being seen on an on-going basis, the social worker should begin every interview with a specific purpose. He/she will bring to the interview a fund of knowledge obtained through his/her education or practice experience about people and their situations, a role repetoire, specific skills and a value system. Information from the Intake form, previous records, correspondence from other agencies, or contacts from collaterals can provide useful information in the preparation for the interview. However, the social worker should guard against contamination of his/her thinking by being influenced by the contents of past contacts with previous professionals as he/she reads or receives past information on the client.

In preparation for the interview, the social worker may well engage in the following procedures:

(1) The social worker should reflect over the nature of the client's request for services, identify the areas in which the problem presents itself, and reflect over the client's reactions to seeking help. (Preparation is also important in alleviating the anxiety of the social worker relative to how he/she will perform.)

(2) After the reason for contact is identified, the social worker should then identify the nature of the questions to be asked so that desired information is secured about the client and his/her situation.

(3) The social worker should plan to focus the interview so that desired information can be obtained. This means that to whatever degree possible the social worker will maintain a focus and seek to prevent the client from rambling, becoming unfocused or going off into tangents.

(4) The social worker should be prepared to approach all interviews with some flexibility so that attention can be focused on the urgent matters facing the client at the time of the interview. This urgency will usually be related to the fact that the client is feeling overwhelmed in some area which needs to be addressed. Unless it is addressed, the client will not be able to work on those areas previously identified as a focus of the interview. If the social worker should feel at the end of the interview that the planned purpose was not achieved, he/she identify why.

(5) The social worker is aware that clients communicate in a verbal and a nonverbal manner. Therefore, he/she must be prepared to observe

these means of communication, particularly the nonverbal and to identify the topics which appear to activate nonverbal behavior.

(6) The social worker should identify the merit in determining if general or specific questions will be asked. This determination is based on the nature of the information to be collected. General questions are useful in preventing undue anxiety. Many times important information is contained in the client's general responses to the questions posed if the social worker is actively listening. Specific questions may be anxiety provoking in that they call for a specific instead of a general response. The nature of the question may be anxiety provoking and the client may feel trapped with no escape route except silence, the expression of anger or in showing resistance. In addition the client may not yet be ready to face or to deal with the emotions aroused by such questions. The willingness of the client to deal with such questions of an anxiety provoking nature appears related to the strength of the helping relationship and the trust and confidence which the client feels toward the social worker.

(7) Sometimes the social worker may spontaneously ask questions of clients. This spontaneity is genuine and related to the feelings which surround the interview. However, the social worker should always be prepared to respond to clients when they ask the reasons for such questions and how they relate to their situation. Therefore, social workers should not ask questions for the sake of curiosity.

(8) The social worker should determine if he/she will take notes during the interview, and if so, how it will be explained to the client. The same applies for tape-recording or video-taping. In these areas, It is important to secure the client's permission before such activities are implemented.

(9) The social worker should always be prepared to summarize the contents of the interview, the work which has been accomplished, and to engage the client in this process by seeking his/her feedback.

(10) If sessions are of a continuing nature, the social worker should always engage the client in the process of planning the next step. This activity reveals the continuity which characterizes the helping process and identifies future work.

The preparation process can only be carried out in a sound manner if the social worker possesses the following knowledge:

(1) Knowledge of the agency's purpose and function,

(2) Possesses a clear understanding of his/her role as a helping person and his/her limitations,

(3) knowledge of how people react to seeking help and the ambivalence which characterizes such requests,

(4) Knowledge of the principle of beginning where the client is and proceeding at his/her pace,

(5) Knowledge of the time-limits of the interview,

(6) Knowledge of the fee schedule if one is used by the agency and the feelings that his/her services are worthwhile. (Social workers can be uncomfortable in discussing fees with clients.)

(7) Knowledge of the importance of showing respect to the client and of conducting the interview in privacy, preventing interruptions. The client should be the center of attention as he/she tells his/her story.

(8) Knowledge of the limits of confidentiality. The social worker is required by law to report acts of child abuse and neglect. He/she cannot allow the client to harm him/herself or others and must take action when such information is presented to him/her. In addition as a representative of an organization, the social worker may be called on to share information revealed by the client with his/her supervisor or others in the administrative hierarchy. The social worker cannot forget that as a representative of the agency his/her actions are binding on the agency. Therefore, the agency has not only a right but a responsibility to know what is happening in his/her cases. However, the client should be informed that confidentiality will be protected to the maximum degree that is possible.

RESPONSIBILITIES OF THE SOCIAL WORKER IN THE INTERVIEWING PROCESS

The social worker has a responsibility to structure the interview so that time is used to the maximal effectiveness. The social worker is given the responsibility of interpreting to the client the policies and procedures of the agency and to correct any misconceptions which the client may hold about them. The social worker ethically can never exceed the agency's functions and boundaries relative to the client's request or demands and should not promise to do something that he/she has questions about or that he/she cannot deliver on. In such situations, the social worker should delay in responding to the client's request until he/she has checked with superiors. The social worker should attempt to avoid the use of professional jargon and to communicate with the client in a nontechnical manner. If the social worker does not understand the messages being conveyed by the client, he/she should seek clarification from the client and not feel uneasy when the client is put into the position of being a teacher.

Another responsibility of the social worker in the interviewing process is to keep the discussion relevant to the client's problem. While he/she recognizes the value of ventilation, he/she also recognizes that ventilation for the sake of ventilation is rarely therapeutic over a period of time and distracts from the real work which needs to be addressed. When the focus of the interview is lost and its contents become rambling in nature, the social worker must skillfully seek to refocus it. It is important that the social worker be able to recognize resistance and possesses the skills to address it. The social worker has the responsibility of facilitating the interview through purposeful questioning and meaningful interactions with the client system.

STRUCTURAL ASPECTS OR
DIVISIONS OF THE INTERVIEW

Interviews can be divided into beginning, middle and ending phases. Benjamin refers to these phases as (1) initiation and statement of the matter, (2) development and exploration and (3) closing. These structural aspects are part of each interview as well as the entire helping process. Each of these phases relates to the accomplishment of specific activities and objectives. The beginning phase of the interview relates to the purpose of the meeting, the reason for the contact, the work to be done, and a review of what has gone before if the interview is one of series of interviews (sessions). In the beginning phase, the client may bring the social worker up to date on his/her situation, or the social worker may provide the client with some new or additional information. The beginning phase of the interview sets the stage for the work of the interview which is referred to as the middle or work phase. The middle phase finds the client and the social worker actively engaged in the problem-solving process. They devote their energies and attention to the client's situation, and give consideration to what the client and social worker have done and must do to address it so that the goals of the case can be achieved. In this work phase, one or several solutions are proposed in further facilitating the work to be done. Time is devoted to a discussion of the progress made and in strengthening the client's resolve that his/her situation can improve. Obstacles are identified and ways of addressing them discussed. Discussion may also be devoted to how the work to be performed relates to the client's goals. In the beginning and middle phase of the interview, the social worker may find it necessary to address resistance and a lack of perceived or real effort on the part of the client to carry out his/her roles and responsibilities in the change process. The ending phase of the interview finds the social worker and the client engaged in the process of summarizing the work which has characterized the interview. Past work may be recognized and on-going work identified. In this phase, the communication process between the social worker and the client is marked by honesty, clarity, a mutual respect and a commitment to future work directed at problem resolution.

The social worker should always be sensitive to the on-going dynamic nature of the interviews. Interviews exist over a continuum of time. The social worker does not have to respond to client's comments at the moment they are made, but may select to comment on them at a later period of time when the client may be more receptive. The social worker must also guard against spontaneous insight and a desire to communicate this insight to the client without a full understanding of the possible impact which this information may have on the client. It is always necessary for the social worker to remember that the problem always belongs to the client, and it is the client, not the social worker who must solve it. The social worker is at best an instrument for the client to use as the client seeks to improve his/her situation.

In the beginning, middle and ending phase of each interview, the client always remains the center of attention. The central task of the social worker is to facilitate movement through skillfully asking questions, providing information, and engaging the client in the change process. Through the application of knowledge, the employment of skills and the demonstration of social work values, the social worker assists the client in exploring and understanding his/her situation, in identifying reasons for its existence and in performing necessary actions for goal achievement.

TYPES OF INTERVIEWS

Kadushin (1972) identifies three general purposes of the majority of social work interviews; (1) informational (securing data for the social study), (2) diagnostic (making an assessment) and (3) therapeutic purposes (effecting change). Mahoney (1958) identifies several types of interviews which are located in social group work: (1) marginal, fringe or drop-in, (2) intake, (3) casual, (4) formal and (5) interviews in the home.

The marginal or fringe interview, sometimes referred to as the doorknob interview, takes place following the formal group meeting when a group member remains behind to discuss something with the group worker. This interview takes place on the fringe of the group following the ending of the group session. The casual interview is an unplanned one and usually occurs in the community when a group member meets the group worker, possibly at the supermarket or a theater. The intake interview relates to the screening and selection of members for the group. The formal interview takes place by appointment. It occurs when the group member of social group worker arranges an office appointment to discuss a particular area of concern relating to the group member's situation. Interviews in the home occur when the group worker wants to discuss a topic usually relating to a child with his/her parents or to see the group member in his/her natural surroundings. Mahoney also identifies some interviewing principles for the social group worker: (1) acceptance of the client with his/her needs, (2) self-determination, (3) encouragement of client participation, (4) control use of authority and (5) the social group worker' purposeful use of self.

In family therapy, the composition of the interview may vary depending on the purpose. Family members may be viewed individual, conjointly or as a total family. An individual interview is usually arranged when the social worker seeks to obtain historical information which may be related to a family's secret, or seeks to clarify reasons for the client's behavior in the family session. In the individual interview, the social worker may prestructure the contents of the next family session by setting the groundwork for the discussion of specific topics which the client has previously illustrated a reluctance to address. A joint or conjoint interview consists of either the marital dyad, a parent-child combination or siblings. The purpose of such an interview is to explore in greater detail some facet(s) of the family situation which involves the dyad individuals being interviewed. It is important that the information gained in these interviews be related to the total family situation as it reveals insight into family dynamics and patterns of behavior. Family interviews consist of seeing all family members in the session. A reason for such an interview is that the social worker wants to observe or identify the communication and interactional patterns which characterize family behavior and lead to its dysfunctional environment. In family interviews, the social worker observes family content and its processes and the manner in which family members deal with the forces being evident. In this interview, the social worker operates in the here and now, is a participant-observer and assumes an active role in identifying and commenting on family processes as they are occurring. He/she is comfortable with confrontation and the display of hostility and aggressive behavior from family members as they challenge his/her interpretation(s) of what is happening in the family. Interview composition is closely related to the purpose of the interview. If the social worker feels the marital dyad does not share mutuality relative to their problems or the same motivation in addressing it, he/she may arrange for an individual interview. If the social worker has been seeing the couple on an individual basis, then he/she may arrange for a joint interview to clarify specific issues. If individuals are threatened by what goes on in an individual interview, then joint interviewing may be indicated to allay their fears and anxieties about the content of individual sessions. Individual interviews are indicated if the focus is on the securing of historical information or the exploration of individual or family secrets which are viewed as being taboo areas. In the joint and family sessions, historical information is minimized. However, historical information helps the social worker to recognize family dynamics and to understand the reasons for them.

Individual, conjoint and family sessions may be used in family therapy as long as the social worker is aware of their purposes. It is the author's belief that all interviews are family focused to some degree. Even though other members of the family are not physically present, they are present psychologically and their contributions to the client's problems clearly present themselves. A family therapy interview consists of the physical presence of all family members; a family-focused interview may consist of an individual, but the invisible family is also present and a picture of its impact on the individual's psychosocial functioning is revealed as he/she tells his/her story.

Home visits are an important aspect of social work practice. Observing clients in their natural environment reveals clues to family dynamics which may not be presented in office interviews. Possibly, this occurs because the family is being seen in its natural environment and some of its defensive behavior may be weakened as family members respond in a spontaneous manner. Interviews in the home can be used for social study, diagnostic and intervention purposes. In the home, the social worker as a participant-observer enters into the family system in a way that is not possible in the office. In the office, behaviors are described; in the home, behaviors are acted out. When the family is on its own ground, natural patterns of behavior are revealed more readily as they do not go through a filtering process. In this sense, office interviews may sometimes be viewed as an inhibiting force in the expression of natural behavior as family members seek to be on guard. Home interviews are conducive to a weakening of the inhibitions which may characterize the behavior of family members in the office. In the home, family members may forget for a moment the presence of the social worker and lower their defenses. When this happens, communication patterns, family alignments, power struggles, roles assigned, feelings expressed and control mechanisms become more clearly evident, and the social worker is able to address them as a part of the family system while these behaviors are occurring.

In recapitulation, it may be stated that the social worker depending on the purpose of the interview will determine its composition: individual, conjoint or family. Sometimes the client systems will express a particular preference for the composition of an interview. The social worker should value this request. However, he/she needs to inform the client that at a later time the composition of the interviews may be modified. Conjoint and family interviews are more geared to a focus on interactional and transactional patterns as revealed in the client's behavior, particularly communication modes. The individual interview appears more appropriate for the collection of historical data, the establishment of the therapeutic alliance, and for focusing in an in-depth manner on intrapsychic problems. If it is evident that individuals in the family constellation find conjoint or family interviews to be threatening, then these feelings should be more fully explored in individual sessions. Individuals should not be forced to participate in conjoint or family interviews if they express feelings of discomfort. While the social worker may wonder about this reluctance, their requests should be honored. Individual contacts with them will reveal reasons for the reluctance which hopefully can eventually be weakened. In contacts with clients, the social worker should not be wedded to one type of interview but should present flexibility in interview composition. The composition of the interview must always be related to purpose. It is imperative that the social worker be able to convey this purpose to the client system.

TIME: AN INTERVIEWING CONSTRAINT

Time is an interviewing constraint and the use of time is also directly related to purpose. Usually social work interviews are expected to last for fifty-five minutes. Group work and family interviews are expected to last for ninety minutes. Attributing an expected time limit to an interview is an artificial constraint. The social worker should not be guided by time as he/she will attempt to extend the interview to meet this expectation. Rather, he/she should be guided by purpose. It is not necessary to use up all of the time allocated for an interview if the purpose is achieved before this time expires. In the author's view, whenever the purpose of the interview has been achieved, then it is appropriate to end it. If the purpose has not been achieved in the allocated time and unless compelling reasons exist for extending the session, the materials should be carried over to the next session. This gives a sense of continuity to the work to be done. A brief interview can be as effective as an extended one if the purpose is clearly delineated and adhered to.

SKILLS IN THE COMMUNICATION PROCESS

Earlier, the interview has been defined as a professional conversation or a communication process. The social worker gives direction to the facilitation of the interview through the use of such skills as (1) active and focused listening, (2) purposeful use of self, (3) full involvement of the client in the communication process, (4) clarification of unclear communication, (5) the installation of hope which contributes to the client's full involvement and (6) the creation of a climate of of privacy and respect in which the client feels comfortable and nonthreatened. Berger (1977) emphasizes the importance of the therapist being tuned in to the verbal and nonverbal communications of the client. Berger identifies five qualities which relate to effective communication: speaking, listening, understanding, interrupting and interacting. Others (Schulman, 1984; Middleman and Wood, 1990) have identified interpersonal skills which are not only important to the development of the helping relationship but which can also be employed in facilitating the interviewing process. Some of these skills are active listening, clarifying, restating, summarizing, questioning, supporting, reflecting feelings, empathizing, giving suggestions (advice), providing feedback and reaching for unverbalized messages.

While it is a difficult task to identify and discuss the many skills employed by the social worker in his/her contacts with clients, some skills and the purposes to which they relate will be discussed:

Exploration: The social worker explores specific areas in order to gain more clarity and a greater understanding of different facets of the client's situation. Exploration also leads to the presentation of more detailed social study data and reflective thinking on the part of the client.

Encouragement: The social worker encourages the client to talk, to bring up taboo areas which the client presents a hesitancy to discuss. In encouraging the client to talk, the social worker shows acceptance of the client and presents the view that the client will not be judged.

Articulating the client's feelings: When the client struggles to put a statement into words and cannot readily do it, the social worker may articulate what he/she thinks the client is attempting to express and seeks feedback on the accuracy of his/her interpretation. This skill is particularly useful when the client is struggling to express contents of a negative or taboo nature.

Universalization of the client's situation: Universalization is frequently used in conjunction with encouragement. In encouraging the client to talk or reveal feelings, the social worker may universalize his/her situation through informing the client that he/she has heard many things and is sure that he/she has heard previously what the client is finding difficult to express. In universalization, the social worker puts the client's situation into the context of human experiences with the objective of helping the client to see that others have faced similar experiences and have conquered them. This skill aims at stalling a sense of hope into the client's situation and the dispelling of feelings of unworthiness and low self-esteem.

Clarification: The social worker seeks clarity from the client relative to a statement that he/she has made. The client may have made different statements in earlier sessions, or his/her statement may be of an ambiguous nature. The social worker through clarification seeks to make clear exactly what the client is stating. (Clarification is also a therapeutic technique in the psychosocial model of social casework in which the social worker attempts to clarify distortions in the client's behavior and the reason for it. For example if the client following an argument with his wife becomes angry with the social worker for no reason, the social worker clarifies for the client the reason for his displaced anger).

Confrontation: The social worker uses confrontive techniques in confronting the client relative to behavior illustrated or statements made. Confrontation is employed to face the client with some aspect(s) of his/her behavior.

For example, the social worker may confront the client about his/her inability to live up to the terms of the contract. The strength of the therapeutic alliance is an important factor in determining the use of confrontation.

Summarization: The social worker summarizes the work of the session, a previous session, or the work over time to illustrate the progress of lack of progress made by the client. Summarization is also employed to elicit feedback from the client as to the accuracy of the summarization.

Advice: The social worker presents the client with specific information or advice about a planned action and assists the client is seeing the consequences as well as the need for such actions.

Information giving: The social worker gives the client information about resources or clarifies an area that has in the past been confusing to the client, usually as a result of a lack of knowledge.

Appropriate use of silence: Following a question, the social worker tolerates the silence which follows until the client responds. The success of this skill often rests on who (the client or the social worker) can tolerate silence for the greater period of time.

Refocusing: When the interview is of a rambling nature and work is being evaded, the social worker refocuses it by returning it to the topic which previously was under discussion or to other areas which need to be addressed. Even while refocusing the interview, the social worker seeks to develop understanding of the reasons for the client going off into tangents, shifting from one topic to another.

Transitions/Topical Shifts: The social worker makes appropriate transitions from one topic to the other, or recognizes the need to pursue a different area even though the client may want to continue in an area that is not fruitful. For example, the social worker may state I know you want to tell me more about your experiences this week and hopefully we will get to it in this session. However, I feel it is important that we bring some closure to what we have previously discussed and then we can move on to other topics. However, if what the client wanted to discuss has urgency to it, then the social worker must show flexibility and give the client the opportunity to present his/her urgent concerns.

These behaviors employed by the social worker in the interviewing and helping process have been referred to interchangeably as skills and techniques. A technique implies a specific type of behavior in which the social worker has gained expertise. A skill implies the discipline use of techniques within the framework of social work knowledge, skills and values. A skill in interviewing techniques is essential for effective social work practice.

BARRIERS TO EFFECTIVE INTERVIEWING

Barriers to effective interviewing can result from a variety of sources. Such sources may be race, age, sex, social class, culture and the failure to recognize the existence of transference and countertransference phenomena. A moralistic or judgmental attitude on the part of the social worker, racist attitudes, cultural insensitivity and a lack of knowledge about the functions of his/her agency can also create barriers to effective interviewing. Effective interviewing is dependent on the worker showing honesty and integrity in his/her contacts with clients. Stereotyping clients can be equally detrimental to effective interviewing as such stereotypes initiate self-fulfilling prophecies. The social worker must recognize that at the center of the interviewing process is the client, and the client must be given the opportunity to reveal his/her story. The social worker should not attempt to penetrate client's defenses until he/she recognizes the purposes they serve and is able to replace them with behaviors that are of a more positive nature. If the social worker continually interrupts the client as he/she attempts to tell his/her story, the client may view such behavior as a sign of insensitivity on the part of the social worker and curtail his/her activity in the interview. The social worker needs to be keenly sensitive to the presence of barriers in the interviewing process and attempt to address them in a positive manner. The possibility of the existence of any of these dynamics in the interviewing process highlights the importance of self-awareness on the part of the social worker and the use of supervision and consultation in identifying the existence of barriers which negatively impact on the interviewing and helping process.

CONCLUSION

Interviewing is one of the most important skills in social work practice. The social worker brings to the interviewing process a fund of knowledge, a value system, and skills which make it possible for him to understand human behavior, the ambivalence which surrounds the seeking of professional help, and to structure interviews so that specific data can be collected. This data is useful not only in identifying the source(s) of the client's problems but also in facilitating the helping process. Through effective interviewing, the social worker is able to establish rapport with the client and to begin the process of developing the therapeutic alliance.

Interviewing is best conceptualized as being a communication process characterized by professional purpose. It is also dynamic in nature as the social worker and the client affect and are affected by the dynamic interactions which occur between them. The interview has a cyclical nature which presents itself in the process of sending, receiving, decoding and responding to messages. If the messages conveyed are unclear, then the responses to them will also be unclear and confusing. While the client must always be an active participant in the interviewing process, it is the social worker who assumes the primary responsibility for its facilitation so that its purposes are achieved. This facilitation is accomplished through the skillful use of interviewing techniques employed in a responsible manner by the social worker.

Effective interviewing is dependent on the social worker possessing knowledge of human behavior and the social environment and how it presents itself in the therapeutic context of receiving and giving help. Barriers can be erected to effective interviewing and the social worker must be sensitive to those barriers which can intrude into the helping process and hamper effective communication. The social worker must actively seek to identify barriers and to work toward their removal. While the social worker brings scientific knowledge to the interviewing process, he/she also brings a degree of creativity to it. Interviewing is truly a science and an art. The social worker should always conduct the interview in a humanistic manner and view it as a humanistic encounter between the client who seeks help and the social worker who has the responsibility of giving help. In order to do this in a professional manner, the social worker must develop an understanding of the client, his/her situation, and the conditions which are contributing to it. With this knowledge, he/she with the active involvement of the client is able to develop and implement an intervention strategy. Knowledge for effective practice is dependent on effective interviewing. The social worker should always begin where the client is and meet the client with the conviction that he/she has the potential for developing the capabilities for resolving or ameliorating the problem faced in his/her psychosocial functioning with the assistance of the social worker.

In essence this chapter may be included with information provided by Benjamin which captures the knowledge, skill and value base exemplified by the social worker in the interviewing process. He states the interviewer brings to the interviewing process, knowledge, professional experience, professional skills, information on resources at his/her command, a desire to help, a deep personal regard for others, and an understanding as much as possible of our own prejudices and values. All of these attributes are actualized during the interviewing process.

SELECTED BIBLIOGRAPHY

Benjamin, B. (1969) The helping interview. 2nd. edition (New York: Houghton-Mifflin).

Bergler, M. (1977) Working with people called patients (New York: Bruner/Mazel).

Edingberg, G., Zinberg, N. and Kelman, W. (1975) Clinical interviewing and counseling (New York: Appleton-Century-Crofts).

Kadushin, A. (1982) The social work interview, revised edition (New York: Columbia University Press).

Maloney, S. (1958) The interview in casework and group work; A comparison (New York: National Association of Social Workers).

Middleman, R. and Wood, G. (1990) Skills for direct practice in social work (New York: Columbia University Press).

Schulman, L. (1984) The skills of helping individuals and groups, 2nd. ed. (Itasca, IL: F.E. Peacock Publishers).

Stewart, C. and Cash, W. (1985) Interviewing: Principles and practice, fourth edition (Dubuque, IA: Wm. C. Brown).

ADDITIONAL REFERENCES: CLASSICAL INTERVIEWING TEXTS IN SOCIAL WORK

Garrett, A. (1984) Interviewing; Its principles and methods, fourth edition (New York: Family Service Association of America).

Schubert, M. (1982) Interviewing in social work (New York: Council on Social Work Education).

Chapter 7

THE HELPING RELATIONSHIP

Even while the social worker is interviewing the client, he/she is also in the process of developing and establishing the helping relationship which is crucial to the effective practice of social work. As discussed in the previous chapter, interviewing is of a purposeful nature and should provide the client with a positive experience which is conducive to relationship building. While the interview is characterized by the exchange of feelings and meaningful communication, the relationship will see these traits transformed into a bond, a connection between the client and the social worker. This connection builds on mutual trust, confidence and acceptance and forms the foundation of the helping relationship through which assistance will be provided to the client in addressing his/her difficulties.

Establishing the social work relationship is one of the most important skills employed by the social worker. Some social workers instead of using the term helping or social work relationship may also use the term therapeutic alliance. In this chapter, social work relationship, therapeutic alliance and the social work relationship are used interchangeably. Patterson (1973) states,

> The evidence seems to point to the establishment of a particular kind of relationship as the critical element in counseling or psychotherapy. It is a relationship characterized not so much by what techniques the therapist used as by who he is, not so much by what he does as the way he does it (pp. 535–536).

Truax and Carkhuff (1967) identify the important ingredients of the helping relationship: empathy, warmth and genuineness. They view these qualities as being interpersonal skills used by the therapist in applying techniques and expert knowledge to the counseling process (p. 31). The effectiveness of the intervention process is influenced to a large degree by the strength of the therapeutic alliance which exists between the client and the social worker. Consequently, the formation and maintenance of the therapeutic alliance is a central task for the social worker. Recognizing the importance of the helping relationship to the therapeutic process, it becomes the responsibility of the social worker to deliberately develop, nurture and maintain it throughout the life of the case. The social worker will need to be sensitive to any barrier which impedes its development and address it.

THE NATURE OF THE HELPING RELATIONSHIP

The helping relationship is formed for a particular purpose. Once, its purpose has been achieved, it is brought to a formal ending. Because it is purposefully formed, it differs from other types of relationships. It is distinguished by the fact that (1) it is deliberately and consciously developed, (2) it is time-limited, (3) it is goal-oriented, (4) is objective in nature and (5) it is the medium through which professional services are rendered. The helping relationship constitutes a means to an end. Its existence is vital and necessary if the client and social worker are to engage in meaningful interactions and work which are directed toward the achievement of specific goals. While the relationship is fused with emotions and feelings, the social worker attempts to maintain them under conscious control so that a degree of objectivity always characterizes the relationship. Relationship building and maintenance is not always a smooth process and at points it may be characterized by friction and irrational behavior. When this occurs, it is the responsibility of the social worker to address these feelings so that they do not harm the relationship indefinitely or result in the premature termination of the client from services. While the helping relationship is not in effect at the time of initial contacts with client systems, the potentialities for development of the relationship do exist. These potentialities are activated and nurtured by the social worker through his/her behavior and attitudes which are conveyed to the client. In time, the client will respond to these attributes and the therapeutic alliance is formed. Literally, the helping relationship may be viewed as a bond, a connection, or an intense involvement between the client and the social worker. This bond characterizes the joint activities of the social worker and client as they engage in the problem-solving process. Crucial to the establishment of the relationship are such attributes as warmth, accepting, the presentation of a caring attitude, honesty, integrity, genuineness and congruency.

Warmth suggests an on-going interest in the client which is revealed in the social worker's caring attitude. The social worker reveals through his/her behavior, comments, actions that he/she deeply cares about the client and his/her well-being and wants to be of assistance in the amelioration of his/her problem. Acceptance presents itself in the individualization of the client and the acceptance by the social worker of the client as he/she is without regards to sex, race, ethnicity or the nature of the problem presented. The client is not judged or labeled, and the social worker views the client as an individual with problems, but capable of dealing with his/her difficulties with the assistance of the social worker. In acceptance of the client, the social worker also seeks to instill a sense of hope in the client that his/her situation is not helpless. Acceptance is sometimes referred to as an unconditioned regard for the client with all his/her human frailties. Empathy is the capacity to feel with the client, to genuinely share his/her feelings and to see the world as the client sees it. Caring is the capacity to show concern for the client in his/her struggles and to provide nurturance and comfort as indicated. Genuineness is the capacity to be authentic, free of pretention, in the presentation of oneself to the client. Honesty is to be open and above board with the client, to accurately inform him/her of what is happening and what is expected of him/her. Trust is the capacity to show confidence in the client's ability to improve his/her situation, and congruency is to be consistent with verbal and nonverbal behaviors.

Many writers (Biestek, 1957; Northen, 1969; Kadushin, 1972; Keith-Lucas, 1972; Edinberg, Zinberg, and Kelman, 1975, and Perlman, 1982) have written about the helping relationship, its nature and its characteristics. Biestek (1957) states "The relationship permeates all aspects of the casework process and the relationship is the medium through which the help is given" (p. 239). Biestek views the relationship as being inseparable from techniques. Edinberg, Zinberg and Kelman refer to the helping relationship as being a working agreement between the therapist and the client. This working agreement identifies the working arrangements, responsibilities and roles of the participant in the change process. Their description of the qualities of the relationship resemble those features contained in the contract. These qualities also imply a conscious aspect to the relationship when in reality it develops over time and evolves from the feelings which have been engendered by the client and the social worker through the interaction process which surrounds their joint efforts. Perlman (1982) refers to the relationship as a person's feelings or emotional bonding with another," (p. 23). She states it is formed for a specific purpose, is time-bound, carries authority and is of a controlled nature. Northen (1969) states the relationship consists of "emotional responses which ebb and flow from person to person as human behavior evokes different affective responses" (p. 53). Northen views the relationship within the small group as an unique relationship with each member. Keith-Lucas defines the helping relationship as a medium offered to people with problems. Through this medium, clients are given the opportunity to make choices about receiving help and the use they will make of it (p. 47). Keith-Lucas identifies the characteristics of the helping relationship: (1) mutuality, (2) reality, (3) feelings, (4) knowledge, (5) concern for the client, (6) purpose, (7) a here-and-now focus, (8) a nonjudgmental attitude and (9) offering the promise of something new. Pincus and Minahan (1972) view the relationship as being an effective bond which exists between the social worker and the client. They identify three types of relationships: collaborative, cooperative and conflictual. According to Pincus and Minahan, the common elements of all relationships are purpose, commitment to the needs of the client, objectivity and self-awareness on the part of the social worker. Shulman (1984) perceives the small group as a network of many helping relationships as group members help each other with their problems. Anderson and Mandell (1989) view the relationship as being a central concept in social work. It is a central concept because it is viewed as being the medium through which professional help is given and which enables change to take place (p. 110). In Biestek's view, the knowledge, skills and value system of the profession are inherent parts of the relationship. He states in the casework relationship, "Knowledge of human nature, the mobilization of the capacities of the individual, the use of community resources and skills in interviewing, study, diagnosis and treatment are revealed" (p. 4). Meyers (1976) conceptualizes the helping relationship as being a tool used by the social worker in helping the client to achieve his/her goal and in facilitating the problem-solving process in the direction of goal achievement. In discussing the helping relationship, Specht (1989) states, "These relationships after all provide the acceptance, empathy, warmth, understanding and knowledge that enable the clients to use their social and personal resources in their own interests" (p. 59). For Perlman, the relationship serves a catalytic and enabling function which stimulates the client by freeing his/her energy so that he/she can actively participate in the problem-solving process.

The importance of the relationship in social work practice is obvious from the comments stated above. It is the avenue through which social work activities are carried out and stated goals are achieved. The author defines the relationship as one of the intangibles, but potent aspect of practice. It is temporary in nature and constitutes a bond established between the client and social worker for the specific purpose of assisting the client in the process of problem resolution. It is never static, but always dynamic and changing as a result of the interactions which occur between the involved participants. As it is a deliberately formed relationship, it comes to an end when the purpose for which it has been created has been achieved. However, the relationship may also be terminated for other reasons such as when little hope for realistic change exists or the client does not show sufficient motivation for continuation of contacts. Termination may also result when the client is geographically relocated, or the social worker leaves the agency. The client may also terminate the relationship on his/her own volition (unplanned termination).

PURPOSE OF THE HELPING RELATIONSHIP

According to Bergler (1977) the purpose of the therapeutic alliance is "to develop a bond of trust, caring, communicating and understanding with the objective of changing the daily functioning of the patient so that he is capable of taking care of his own life in a goal-directed fashion" (p. 93). In social work practice, similar purposes are articulated as the purpose of the helping relationship. Its primary purpose is to establish a bond between the social work and client for problem-solving efforts in addressing the client's difficulties. As a result of the helping relationship, the client finds him/herself in an accepting, nurturing, safe and secure environment in which he/she can share his/her most intimate thoughts with the social worker and not be judged. All of the activities of the profession are carried out within the confines of the helping relationship. This emotional bonding which develops between the client and the social worker forms the therapeutic foundation for the work to be accomplished. The social worker as a warm, accepting professional acting as a catalyst motivates the client to actively engage him/herself in the change process. As Biesteck has earlier stated it is through the helping relationship that the knowledge, skill and value base finds expression through the behaviors of the social worker as he/she works cooperatively with the client system in achieving stated goals.

BARRIERS TO RELATIONSHIP BUILDING

Barriers which affect effective interviewing can also have a negative impact on the establishment of the helping relationship. Inasmuch as social workers are the product of their environments, they bring to the helping process attitudes, values and prejudices. They may have accepted stereotypes about people and place moralistic values on their behavior, or they may feel certain people are inferior and incapable of benefitting from professional help. Social class itself can be a barrier if the social worker attempts to impose his/her middle class values onto clients. If the social worker possesses preconceived opinions about clients, he/she will not be able to see their strengths and will focus only on their shortcomings. The relationship is also threatened when authority is used in a punitive manner, particularly in such settings as child welfare and corrections. Race, age, sex, issues of authority, ethnocentricism and transference and countertransference phenomena may create conflict and distance between the client and the social worker which work against the establishment of the therapeutic alliance. Minority clients who have lived in a racist society which has devaluated them may enter into the therapeutic encounter with considerable mistrust and may easily vent their anger onto representatives of a system which has historically exploited and oppressed them. If the social worker lacks sensitivity toward these attitudes and the conditions under which clients live, he/she may blame the client for his/her situation and in doing so undermine the possibility of developing the therapeutic alliance. Certainly an objective of the helping relationship is that the bond established between the client and the social worker will enable them to work cooperatively together. In the absence of a helping relationship, the social worker will do the majority of the active work and the client will be a passive participant in the change process. In such situations social work practice may be imposed and not freely entered into by the client.

In attempting to address potential and actual barriers to the establishment of the helping relationship, the social worker must develop awareness of the existence of barriers and attempt to address them in a constructive manner. This is why it is so important for the social worker to possess self-awareness and to seek assistance from peers, supervisor or through psychiatric or psychological consultation in developing ways of removing obstacles to the establishment of the therapeutic alliance.

PROCESS IN DEVELOPING AND MAINTAINING THE HELPING RELATIONSHIP

Since the helping relationship is deliberately established between the client and the social worker for the purpose of assisting the client with his/her problem in psychosocial functioning, it of a necessity must involve a process. The process is initiated in beginning contacts with the client, nurtured and reinforced throughout the life of the case. In the early contacts, the social worker exhibits a concern and accepting attitude toward the client and attempts to instill in the client a sense of hope that the agency can be of assistance to him/her. The social worker shows acceptance of the client, actively involves him/her in the process of helping and proceeds at his/her pace. The helping process proceeds in an almost magical manner as the client begins to believe in the social worker, his/her interest and capacity to be of services. When the foundation for the relationship has been erected, the social worker with the active involvement of the client seeks to collect data so that he/she can more fully understand the nature of the presenting problem and the factors which motivate the client to seek assistance at this particular time. Even though the presenting problem may not be the real problem but only a symptom of it, the social worker does not jump ahead of the client. He/she follows the social work axiom of starting where the client is. The client is placed at the center of work to be accomplished. It is important to hear the client's story from the client him/herself and this involves active listening and a total focusing on the client. Relationship building is accelerated when the client and the social worker communicates on the same level and enter into active partnership in working on the client's situation. Honesty is revealed when the social worker explains to the client exactly what the helping process is and what will be the nature of the roles and responsibilities on the social worker and the client. This behavior is similar to the following skills identified by Shulman (1984): explaining the purpose of the contact, the role of the social worker and reaching for feedback from the client. If the client asks a specific question of the social worker and the social worker cannot answer it at the time, the social worker should not make false promises or give the client inaccurate information, but should inform the client that he will seek answers to these questions and hopefully will have them at the time of the next session.

The social worker must also be sensitive to the ambivalence which characterizes the early stages of seeking help and may find it necessary to articulate the unspoken messages of the client as revealed in his/her nonverbal and verbal behavior. Even while the social worker is listening with his/her ears, he/she is also observing with his/her eyes and feeling for the client with his/her heart. He/she responds to the feelings engendered in the interview so that the client is aware of the strong emotional aspects of the interview and the social worker's sensitivity to his/her unspoken messages. When the individual embraces the role of clienthood, he/she then explores with the social worker in greater detail the problems which bring him/her to the agency. The work will then proceed to that of assessment, goal formulation, contract development and intervention. All of these activities take place within the confines of the helping relationship. As these skills are being applied, the social worker reveals to the client his/her warmth, understanding, empathy and professional competencies. In essence the helping relationship is the nucleus of the helping process, the bond between the social worker and client that makes things happen. It is initiated in the beginning contacts, deliberately formed, nurtured, maintained and terminated as the change process moves through its various phases.

CONCLUSION

Establishing and maintaining the helping relationship is one of the most important skills for the social worker to master. The helping relationship is the medium through which help is given, goals are achieved, and the values, knowledge and skills of the profession find expression. Certain characteristics have been identified as being essential to the establishment of the helping relationship. Some of them have been discussed in this chapter. The importance of self-awareness is stressed. A lack of self-awareness creates a barrier to the interviewing process as well as the establishment of the helping relationship. Self-awareness is defined as the capacity of the social worker to know him/herself as an individual and his/her values so that he/she will not impose them on the client. This characteristic is of extreme importance in relationship building. The more aware we are of our values, attitudes and prejudices, the more we can guard against their expression in our contacts with clients. Ideally, this means that if the social worker feels he/she cannot work with a client as a result of his/her value system or life experience that he/she will seek to transfer the client to another worker. If the agency is small and this is not feasible, then the social worker must seek assistance in determining if these attitudes can be contained to the degree that they do not interfere with the provision of professional services. If this is not possible, then the social worker should seek employment elsewhere and also evaluate his/her suitability for the profession. The purpose of the helping relationship is not to perpetuate or to give expression to the personal values of the social worker—the social worker has no right to impose his/her values onto the client, or to attempt to transform the client into his/her image. Its purpose is always to assist the client in the amelioration or resolution of his/her problems in psychosocial functioning and it is a mean toward this end.

Honesty as a crucial dimension of the helping relationship demands that the client be informed of his/her rights and the limitations under which the social worker works. These limitations are imposed by the employing agency and sanctioned by the society which gives the organization a charter to provide specific services. Consequently the confidential nature of the contacts has its limits as well as the client's right to self-determination. The social worker cannot maintain confidentiality if he/she possesses information that the client intends to harm him/herself or to engage in destructive behavior which is viewed as being against the best interests of society. Disclosure of confidential information without the client's knowledge and permission will undoubtedly have an adverse impact on the relationship. The client should be made aware of agency's policies and procedures and able to work within these limitations. The social worker is a representative of the society in which he/she holds membership and should not actively work against its interests. However, the social worker can and should work toward the eradication of social inequalities so that a more just society can be realized.

Within the confines of the helping relationship, it is a responsibility of the social worker to set limits on the client's destructive tendencies. The social worker should inform the client about the consequences of such behavior and assist the client in reconsidering it. The social worker cannot serve as a role model if he/she covertly or openly sanctions behaviors which are in violation of societal norms. If the relationship is of a positive nature, built on acceptance, trust, honesty and confidence, then the client will respond favorably to such heedings and view them as an indication of the social worker's interest in his/her welfare. The helping relationship does not always flow smoothly, and it should not. It will be characterized by friction and differences of opinions. Hopefully these are resolved in a positive manner.

In this chapter, the author has used the terms helping relationship, the social work relationship, the casework relationship and the therapeutic alliance in an interchangeable manner. The term therapeutic alliance has gained popularity because it denotes a relationship of equality between the client and the social worker. In contrast the helping relationship is viewed as denoting subordinate and superordinate statuses in which the social worker is vested with the power to give help to the client system. In the author's view these distinctions have no real merit. All of these terms are describing the same phenomenon, the connection which develops between the client and the social worker so that a bond is established and joint efforts are realized in problem resolution. A truly professional relationship will always contain an element of authority based on the expertise of the professional who is qualified to provide the assistance requested.

SELECTED BIBLIOGRAPHY

Anderson, S. and Mandell, D. (1989) The use of self disclosure by professional social workers. SOCIAL CASEWORK, 70, 259–267.

Berger, M. (1977) Working with people called patients (New York: Bruner/Mazel).

Biestek, F. (1957) The casework relationship (Chicago: Loyola University Press).

Edingberg, G., Zinberg, N. and Kelman, W. (1975) Clinical interviewing and counseling: Principals and techniques (New York: Appleton-Century-Crofts).

Kadushin, A. (1983) The social work interview (New York: Columbia University Press).

Keith-Lucas, A. (1972) The giving and taking of help (Chapel Hill, NC: University of North Carolina Press).

Meyers, C. (1972) Social work practice: A response to the urban crisis (New York: Free Press).

Northen, H. (1969) Social work with groups (New York: Columbia University Press).

Patterson, C.H. (1973) Theories of counseling and psychotherapy, 3rd. edition (New York: Harper and Row).

Perlman, H. (1982) The helping relationship. In H. Rubenstein and M. Bloch (Eds.) Things that matter (New York: MacMillan).

Pincus, A. and Minahan, A. (1973) Social work practice: Model and Method (Itasca, IL: F.E. Peacock Publishers).

Shulman, L. (1984) The skills of helping individuals and groups (Itasca, IL: F.E. Peacock Publishers).

Specht, H. (1988) New directions for social work practice (Englewood Cliffs, NJ: Prentice-Hall).

Truax, C. and Carkhuff, R. (1976) Toward effective counseling and psychotherapy (Chicago: Aldine).

ADDITIONAL SOURCES OF INTEREST

Bramer, L. (1973) The helping relationship: Process and skills (Englewood Cliffs, NJ: Prentice-Hall).

Corey, G. (1982) Theory and practice of counseling and psychotherapy 2nd. edition (Monterey, CA: Brooks/Cole).

Egan, R. (1982) The skilled helper: Model, skills and methods (Monterey, CA: Brooks/Cole).

Perlman, H. (1979) Relationship: The heart of helping people (Chicago: University of Chicago Press).

Chapter 8

RECORDING IN SOCIAL WORK PRACTICE

Recording is a necessary and important aspect of social work practice. A considerable amount of the social worker's time is devoted to recording, preparing reports and in answering correspondence. Recording is a communication system which is of value to the social worker in providing effective services, improving his/her practice, showing accountability and in assisting the agency in meeting its responsibility in assuring that quality services are being provided to client system. Recording can also be an effective tool in improving the agency's operations. Recording may be viewed as a commitment to paper of what has transpired between the social worker and those involved in a case situation (clients, collaterals, consultants). In its presentation, recording can be of a descriptive or dynamic/analytical nature. When recording is presented with no attempts at an analysis of its contents, it is of a descriptive nature. When recording contains the social worker's thinking about the case, it is of a dynamic nature as it involves the application of knowledge to an interpretation of the meaning of the contents. While recording formats are specific to the organization in which the social worker is employed, in all recording the knowledge, skills and value base of the profession should find expression.

DEFINITION OF RECORDING

As a social work skill, recording is an analytical and reflective process in which the social worker transmit to paper the behaviors which have occurred in his/her interactions with client systems. The following aspects of the social worker's behavior and thinking are revealed at one time or another in the recording: (1) Identification of the problem, (2) referral source, (3) interviewing skills, (4) nature of the helping relationship, (4) his/her assessment of the client and his/her capacities and motivation, (5) tasks performed, (6) problems faced, (7) the established goals, (8) comments on the contract, (9) comments relative to the progress or lack of progress shown, (10) his/her assessment of the client's situation, (11) the nature of the intervention strategy and how it relates to goals and (12) future planning. To whatever possible degree, the recording should reveal brevity and clarity in its presentation.

Unfortunately, social work recording is resisted by social workers. They do not recognize the instrumental purposes which it serves in helping the social worker to improve his/her practice. Poor recording or an absence of it will lead to ineffective practice and unnecessary meander-ings on the part of the social worker in the problem-solving effort. At some point in the life of a case, the social worker must transmit his/her thinking to the record. What is contained in his/her head is of little value to the organization and is not in the best interests of the client. Recording should be evidenced throughout the life of a case though its nature may change. It reveals what the social worker is doing with his/her clients, his/her thinking about the client's situation, his/her understanding of agency's function, and the nature of the intervention strategy he/she plans to institute based on his/her assessment. Whenever dissension presents itself between the social worker and the client, admin-istration will invariably look to the record to evaluate the quality and nature of the services provided. As an essential skill in the social work process, recording is both an evaluative and an accountability tool. It also provides the social worker with the opportunity to relook and to rethink about the interpersonal dynamics which present themselves in the case. Through recording, the supervisor is able to identify the educational needs of the worker. Perhaps some of the resistance to record-ing results from social workers' lack of knowledge about the purposes it serves. Urbanowski (1974) states, "If the social worker is clear about his role, has involved the client in the problem-solving and is goal-directed he should have no difficulties in identifying results and recording these with a sense of accomplishment" (p. 552). Further Urbanowski states that research is somewhat dependent on securing its information from the client's record (p. 552). It appears to be of little value to expect social workers to be accountable for their practice unless they have developed skills in recording.

FUNCTIONS, TYPES AND CONTENTS OF SOCIAL WORK RECORDING

Beincke (1984) identifies six functions of the social work record: (1) They serve as legal documents confirming that services have been provided, and they describe the worker's activities, particularly the intervention strategy and his/her view of the client and his/her situation; (2) auditors use them in evaluating the quantity and quality of services; (3) they are used in supervision and peer review; (4) they can be used for training programs; (5) they serve as a reminder of what has occurred in past sessions and as a guide to future planning and (6) they reveal the conceptual model being employed. In the author's view, the social work record does indeed serve a variety of functions. The author will identify the functions served by the record, recognizing that some of them are similar to those identified by Beincke:

(1) Records serve as a tool for supervision, education, in-service training and the professional development of the worker;
(2) records provide data for research and identify the need for programmatic changes;
(3) records provide a picture of the quality, quantity and types of services provided by the organization;
(4) records enable social workers and supervisors to respond to requests from agencies requesting information on the client;
(5) they are used for the compilation of reports to agencies which have contractual agreements with the agencies. Also, representatives of agencies may review records to determine if services are in compliance with the contractual agreements;
(6) records insure continuity of services in event of the social worker's absence due to such conditions as illness, vacation, or resignation from the agency;
(7) records are used for the purposes of securing funding for program development based on the nature of the services requested or an increase in the number of clients served;
(8) records provide documentation for accreditation and funding bodies;
(9) records are of value to the social worker for analysis and reflective thinking on his/her practice as he/she engages in a process of self-evaluation conducive to professional growth.

While communication may be of a written or verbal nature, recording implies written information. As stated previously, social workers should guard against becoming walking records—the sole repository of what has occurred between them and the client systems. Social workers should come to view recording as being an essential part of their practice. Recording is an analytical process in the sense that the worker interprets the meaning of the written materials from his/her conceptual framework.

It is a reflective process in providing the worker with a picture of how he/she is using him/herself in the intervention process.

The contents contained in the social work record should always reflect relevancy to the agency's purpose. The contents should be kept current and provide sufficient information to reveal a description of the services being provided to the client and the nature of the interactions which occur between the client and the social worker. If agencies wish to have more effective recording systems, then it is incumbent upon them to provide guidelines as to the nature of the contents to be included. Records present a picture over time of the client's contacts with the agency. Generally, the contents of the record should reflect the following:

   (1) Referral source and reason(s) for agency's contacts,
   (2) the nature of the presenting problem and if it is the real problem,
   (3) Identification of the client's expectation of the agency,
   (4) comments on the client's motivation and capacity to use the services of the agency,
   (5) social data information and its source(s),
   (6) assessment of the client's situation,
   (7) goal identification,
   (8) specifics of the contract,
   (9) nature of the intervention strategy and how it relates to stated goals,
  (10) selected discussion of client/worker's interactions, case progress, and potential or actual obstacles to goal achievement, and
  (11) future planning.

Many types of recording exist in social work practice. The social worker will follow the recording format designated by his/her employing agency. Regardless of the type of recording used, the social worker is always guided by the principle of clarity and relevance to agency's purpose, client services and the professional development of the social worker as he/she engages in social work practice. Whenever possible, the information given in the record should be supported by facts. However, the social worker can include his/her thinking or speculations about the case contents. For the social worker, feelings are facts until proved differently. The author will briefly discuss the following types of recording in social work practice: narrative, process, summary, topical, progress notes and problem-oriented recording;

> *Narrative Recording:* This recording is similar to process recording which will be discussed below. However, it is not verbatim in nature but contents are presented in a narrative form, similar to story telling. Case activities

and the interactions which occur between the client and the social worker are highlighted.

Example: Mr. J. and I have met for several sessions. While a little progress has been shown (He is attempting to hold his temper at work, thus decreasing disagreements with his supervisor), he still encounters problems in facing and dealing with people in authority). He presents a tendency to become defensive when topics relating to his problems with authority are introduced and how this results in difficulties with his wife. However, there is evidence that the helping relationship is developing in a positive manner, and I feel in time that sensitive subjects can be introduced to him so that he may develop some understanding of the reasons for his behavior. It remains my impressions that he has strong feelings of insecurity and fear of failing and consequently acts aggressively when he feels he is being criticized. I feel he is strongly motivated and possesses the capacity to change once he is able to explore his relationship with his father and how this relationship affected him. However, he is not psychologically ready for the introduction of these areas. I intend to continue to support him, to strengthen the relationship and to gently introduce these areas when I think he is ready.

Process Recording: This form of recording is used primarily for educational purposes. It is more often used by students and beginning workers as it provides the supervisor with a tool for evaluating skills, knowledge and competencies. It is extremely useful for identification of the values of the social worker, his/her interviewing skills, his/her use of self, and the interactions which occur within the interview and how the social worker responds to them.

A misconception exists about process recording. It is not of a verbatim nature, but consists of a paraphrasing of what has occurred in the interview to the highest degree that the student can recall these events. Through process recording, the social worker is revealed in action with clients as he/she applies knowledge, skills and values in practice. It is a good educational tool to use on occasions regardless of the competencies or experience of the social worker. It follows basically a script form:

Example: I went out to greet Mr. and Mrs. J. and observed they were sitting at opposite ends of the room. This behavior was in contrast to the closeness they had shown in the past. My gut reaction was that something had gone wrong since I last saw them. Immediately, I was in a state of anxiety. When things are not well Mr. J. becomes sarcastic and critical. I didn't look forward to this session.

I greeted them. They followed me to the office. They took their seats and looked directly at me. I asked how things had gone this week. They were silent and I intuitively stated I guess things haven't gone too well.

Before I had finished, Mr. J. leaned forward, looked me squarely in the eyes and stated you better believe it. He then stated he started not to come today. Coming here has been of no help and he doesn't see why they continue to pay good money for this service when they aren't getting anything out of it. I felt he was attacking me. Instead of asking why he felt this way, I asked if he wanted to quit coming to the agency. Darn it. I know this wasn't the right thing to say. He knows how to push my buttons, to make me feel ineffective. I feel he is always challenging me, and I respond to it even though I know he is baiting me. When this happens, Mrs. J. sits by silently. I feel so sorry for her living with this kind of man.

I struggled with what to do, to say. Finally, I asked Mr. J. if he would tell me what happened this past week. Mrs. J. would still silent. I had forgotten her again. Basically, I don't like Mr. J.

While a somewhat cumbersome process, process recording remains a viable educational tool. For example, the student in the above example is finding it very difficult to cope with a critical, attacking male. She also ignores the wife and does not include her in the interview. She probably needs some assistance in learning how to deal with aggressive men, how to maintain a focus in the interview, and how to include other participants. As process recording is too lengthy to become a part of an on-going record, it will probably be done in addition to the agency's recording format. An important feature to process recording is that the social worker attempts to present as detailed a picture as possible of what has occurred in the interview. He/she focuses on content and process and his/her feelings toward the client. Its contents should be emotional, analytical, factual and descriptive. It was extensively used in the period of social investigation in social work history. While it has become somewhat modified and selectively used, it still seeks to reveal through the contents revealed as complete a picture as possible of the process employed in the interview, and how the social worker is responding to the client.

Summary Recording: This form of recording usually follows time intervals of a quarterly nature. It is usually preceded by a rather extensive intake recording. Summary recording has a descriptive and analytical quality. In it the social worker provides a summary of the progress of the case, identifies areas of particular importance and focuses on present and future work.

Example: 4/12/90–9/12/90. During this period, the F. family has maintained regular contacts. The family has been seen for a total of 12 interviews. The family has overcomed its initial resistance to services and members have actively involved themselves in the sessions. The greater amount of growth has been shown in Mrs. F. who is now more assertive and able to express her feelings. In the past, she would cry, felt no one understood her, and end up feeling sorry for herself. The husband has responded positively to this change and no longer needs to feel guilty when his wife is unhappy or to feel responsible for her situation. The children have also benefitted from this change in the parents. The home environment is more pleasant and Mr. and Mrs. F. are doing more things together. The weekly family meetings instituted by the parents have helped the children to feel more a part of the family. The parents no longer present the need to get the children's support for their positions, thereby creating alliances in the family. The school performance of the children has improved, and they too are able to speak up more freely in the family sessions as well as the interviews.

The plan is to continue to assist family members in expressing their feelings more freely. Many of the present patterns of behavior exhibited by the parents are carryovers from their families of origin. However, I do not feel a need to address the historical experiences which have influenced their present behavior. They are well motivated for change. They love each other and are open to any suggestion that might improve their situation. The family is benefiting from an educationally oriented, supportive approach. If the family continues to show progress, then I anticipate terminating with it in a short period of time.

Progress Notes: In using a progress notes format, the social worker inserts brief comments or notations in the record to illustrate case activities and progress. These notes of a succinct nature may focus on the problem, assessment, involved participants and the activities undertaken in achieving identified goals. Progress notes by their brevity help to discipline the analytical thinking of the social worker about what is happening in the case, and the manner in which his/her activities relate to goal achievement.

Topical Recording: Topical recording is distinguished by the use of headings to identify sections of the recording such as education, health, work, family history, military history. Information collected from the client is placed under various headings or topic areas. An advantage in topical recording is easy accessibility to specific areas of information. For example, if the social worker is interested in the client's education or work history, he/she would look under these headings instead of having to search the total record to find the desired information.

Problem-Oriented Recording (POR): This recording format has become popular in social work practice. The problem-oriented format contains four basic sections: (1) Establishment of a data base, (2) formulation of all problems (problem list), (3) formulation of a plan for addressing each problem, (4) a follow-up on each problem to identify the activities undertaken and the progress made in addressing the problem. Even though a problem may be addressed, it still remains on the chart. Information is collected and organized based on the problem(s) presented by the client.

SOAP is an essential format in problem-oriented recording. Data are viewed as being both of a subjective and objective nature. Data presented by the client is subjective and that presented by the social worker is objective. Assessment focuses on identification of those conditions viewed as contributing to the problem, and plan consists of those activities undertaken in the problem-solving efforts. The social worker selects from the problem list that problems which he/she will focus on. Even though a problem may be coded as inactive, it is not deleted from the record. Problem-oriented recording makes it possible for team members to look at the client' chart or record and to receive an immediate picture of what is happening or what has been done.

The problem-oriented record is a product of medicine which has utility for social work practice, particularly in the area of accountability. With its problem focus and identifications of actions implemented to address the problem area(s), it provides a tool for evaluation of accountability and practice effectiveness. It presents an account of the performance of the social worker and helps him/her to assist on selective problems than a wide array of problems. In a sense, problem-oriented recording answers the following statement made by Rosenberg and Brody (1974), "New social services that incorporate accountability must be designed to accomplish the following: (1) explication and definition of long-range goals, (2) specification of objectives to be put into operation, and (3) development of feedback mechanisms that permit the assessment of outcomes" (p. 344).

Problem-oriented recording requires that progress notes are kept current and written in a concise manner. The progress notes provide a chronological picture of the case over time and the actions that have been undertaken in addressing specific problems by team members.

TRANSFERS, BREAKS AND CLOSING SUMMARIES

While the case is closed when goals have been achieved, several other types of breaks may occur in the life of a case. Frequently, a social worker will leave the agency and will see the need to keep the case in an active status. This is accomplished through a transfer. When social workers become ill or take vacations, services are interrupted. These interruptions hold consequences for the client, particularly if the helping relationship is a strong one. While the social worker prepares the client for the transfer, he/she also has a responsibility to bring the recording up to date. This is usually accomplished through a transfer summary. In the transfer summary, the social worker records the status of the case at the time of the transfer and provides a picture of the work which has been done since the case has been assigned to him/her. This information is of importance in preparing the new worker relative to what has occurred in the case. The transfer summary should be brief, clearly written, and reflect pertinent information. It should reveal the nature of the problem which brought the client to the agency, the assessment, a picture of the client's reaction to services and the nature of the interactions which have occurred between the client and the social worker, the goals established, case progress, and the nature of the intervention strategy. The new worker should be informed of the client's reaction to the termination and the manner in which future contacts will be initiated between him/her. The client should also be given the name of a person (usually the supervisor) to contact if an emergency should occur before the case is reassigned. If possible, it is indicated that the new worker meets the client before the official transfer occurs.

The closing summary is also an important recording responsibility. It should contain basically the same information as that in the transfer summary. The social worker should be very specific about the status of the case at the time of closing and the reason(s) for it. He/she should identify if the case is being closed as a result of planned (mutual agreement) or unplanned (client's termination on own volition) termination. The client's reactions to termination should be noted and some speculative statement made as to what may bring the client back to the agency.

When the social worker takes a vacation or becomes ill, the record should also be brought up to date. Problems may continue for the client and he/she may need to become involved with the social worker's supervisor. If the information is not contained in the record, then stress may occur in the contacts with the supervisor. The client may be extremely angry over the worker's leaving him/her for vacation, and may regress or take out his/her anger on the supervisor. It is important that the social worker identifies the areas on which he/she and the client are working as the worker goes on vacation.

Many times it is necessary for the social worker to write a referral summary or to respond to a request from another agency with which the client has made contact. The referral summary or correspondence is intended basically to provide the agency to which the client is referred or the agency requesting information with some knowledge of the client's contacts with the agency, his/her problem, the activities implemented and the progress of the case at the point when contacts were terminated. It is important to identify the reasons for referral and the client' initial reactions to referral.

CONCLUSION

Recording must be viewed as being one of the most important skills employed by the social worker in his/her practice. All social workers at regular intervals should engage in the recording process as it is the record of his/her activities with the client. While it is an essential aspect of social work practice, social workers resist it. Sackheim (1974) states "All workers accept it in theory but rebel in practice. It is recognized as important and experienced as irksome" (p. 103). In the author's view effective social work practice and research undertaking are dependent on skilled recording.

Recording serves many purposes. These purposes relate to the client, the social worker and the employing organization. Sound social work practice flows from effective recording. The maintenance of adequate records increases the effectiveness of the services provided to the client and is instrumental to the professional development of the social worker as he/she reflects on the nature of his/her practice. Recording makes possible the continuity of services and makes possible the agency's capacity in evaluating the quality of the services provided by its workers.

Information about client systems which remain solely in the worker's head is of little value to the agency and may constitute a disservice to the client. While recording serves many purposes, its most important purpose is to contribute to the quality of services provided to clients. In the absence of recording, it is difficult to determine the nature of the social worker's activities with clients, his/her thinking about the case, and how he/she is progressing in his/her professional development. Talk does not replace recording. The author concludes this chapter by identifying the essential purposes of recording and how it contributes to the professional growth and development of the social worker:

- Recording is a tool for the evaluation of services and the improvement of services to the client.
- Recording helps the social worker in his/her professional development by making it possible for him/her to analyze and to evaluate his/her performance.
- Recording can be used for research purposes and the identification of unmet community needs.
- Recording insures the continuity of services in event the social worker is unavailable.
- Recording can be used for educational purposes and in-service training.
- Recording is a testimony of the social worker's contacts with client systems and therefore it has legal implications by the fact that it can be subpoenaed.

SELECTED BIBLIOGRAPHY

Beinecke, R. (1984) PORK, SOAP, STRAP AND SAP. SOCIAL CASEWORK, 65, 554–558.

Rosenberg, M. and Brody, R. (1974) The threat or challenge of accountability. SOCIAL WORK, 19, 344–50.

Sackheim, G. (1974) The practice of clinical casework (New York: Behavioral Publications).

Urbanowski, M. (1974) Recording to measure effectiveness. SOCIAL CASEWORK, 55, 546–553.

ADDITIONAL REFERENCES

Burrill, G. (1976) The problem-oriented log in social casework. SOCIAL WORK, 21, 67–68.

Dwyer, M. and Urbanowski, M. (1965) Student process recording: A plea for structure. SOCIAL CASEWORK, 46, 283–286.

Hamilton, G. (1959) Principles of social case recording (New York: Columbia University Press).

Kane, R. (1974) Look to the record. SOCIAL WORK, 19, 412–419.

Kargle, J. (1991) Social work records (Belmont, CA: Wadsworth Publishing Co.).

Martens, W. and Holmstrup, E. (1974) Problem-oriented recording. SOCIAL CASEWORK, 55, 554–561.

Weed, L. (1969) Medical records and patient care (Cleveland, OH: Case Western University Press).

Wilson, S. (1976) Recording: Guidelines for social workers (New York: The Free Press).

Chapter 9

SOCIAL STUDY OR
DATA COLLECTION PROCESS*

The social worker in seeking to arrive at an understanding of the reasons for the client's situation engages in the social study or data collection process. This process is directed at securing relevant knowledge on the nature of the client's situation. This knowledge will be analyzed and its findings will lead to an appropriate intervention strategy. The social worker applies a theoretical orientation to this analytical process. Interpersonal, interviewing, establishment of the therapeutic alliance and recording are skills which characterized data collection. The client must be influenced by the nature of the helping relationship so that he/she will reveal requested information to the social worker.

Data collection is an on-going process in the life of a case. Additional information may provide different insights into the nature of the problem faced by the client and the contributing factors to it. This chapter in discussing the contents of the social study process will focus on the intake process, the domains of data collection, internal and external verification of data, authority, and the importance of data to the assessment process. The social worker always begins his/her contacts with client systems with a fund of general knowledge about people and their situations. This knowledge becomes more specific as he/she individualizes the client. It is wise for the social worker to avoid curiosity about clients and to direct his/her line of inquiry into those areas which are viewed as being relevant to the client's problem.

MODES AND DOMAINS OF DATA COLLECTION

Data can be collected through (1) interviews, (2) observations, (3) written materials provided by clients, (3) previous records, (4) correspon-

---

*In this chapter, the terms social study and data collections are used interchangeably.

dences sent to the agency relating to the client, (5) the results of medical, psychiatric or psychological consultations and (6) contacts with collaterals. When the social worker makes use of any of these sources of data, he/she is attempting to collect and gather pertinent information as it relates to the client, always with the purpose of developing an understanding of the client, his/her problems and the conditions which contribute to it. In social work practice, the interview is the primary means through which data are collected. The client is the center of the interview and the social worker must actively listen as the client tells his/her story.

The domains of data collection are social, cultural, psychological and biological. Usually these are the areas in which the social worker will seek information in attempting to identify the various forces which may be impacting on the client singularly or in varying combinations. Social refers to the interactions which occur between people and societal institutions. These interactions can be at the interpersonal, organizational or societal levels. In collecting social data, the social worker focuses on the nature of the interactions which characterize the client as he/she interacts with his/her environment. Stress in these interactions may be revealed in interpersonal relationships or systemic strains. Cultural data refer to the value and belief systems which characterize an ethnic or racial group and influence its life style, behavioral and communication patterns and world views. Cultural data are of extreme importance in social work practice with clients who do not share the same culture as the social worker. Language and religion are also important aspects of culture. If the social worker lacks cultural sensitivity, then he/she may aggravate the client's situation by attempting to impose his/her value system onto the client. Psychological data consist of intelligence, feelings, emotions and behavior. Such information has value in helping the social worker to understand the competency level of the client, his/her feelings, and his/her emotional state. The mental health examination is useful in identifying the client's mental state. Anxiety itself is a psychological state. Biological or physiological data often provide important information on the health of the client and if injuries, illnesses or drug-dependency are conditions which impair his/her psychosocial functioning. The "sick role" often provides the client with secondary gains and enables him/her to exert a controlling influence on his/her environment as others accommodate the client due to his/her illness.

VERIFICATION OF DATA

Whenever possible the social worker should seek to confirm or validate the data presented by the client. Two types of validation are available to the social worker: external and internal. External validation consists of those facts given by the client which can be verified through contacts with external sources. For example, if the client states he/she is to be evicted, a contact with the landlord will verify if this is true. A contact with a doctor can verify an operation, and a contact with a teacher can confirm the kind of behavior being exhibited by a child in the school setting. Internal verification consists of the application of knowledge to the client's situation. Based on a knowledge base about people and their situation, in responding to information provided by the client, the social worker asks him/herself: Where have I heard this before? Is this an expected response to the situation confronting the client? Do people usually react this way in such situations? As Perls, stated previously, states, "frightened people do not smile." While clients need to be individualize, usually people respond in normative ways to particular events. While the social worker must make allowances for cultural variations, he/she must always question the real meaning of the client's statement when it is outside of the pale of normative expectations. This is why "feelings" are referred to as being facts in social work practice. Based on knowledge and previous experiences, the social worker acts on his/her feelings (internal validation) until they are shown to be without foundation. Feelings are aspects of the social worker's creativity in responding to client.

AUTHORITY IN SOCIAL WORK PRACTICE

The client is either self-referred or referred by others to the agency for services. The client may be classified as a voluntary or nonvoluntary client. The nonvoluntary referral may result from the client's involvement with a child welfare agency, corrections, or a setting such as the school making it incumbent on the parents to receive services if the child is not to be expelled or suspended from school. The nonvoluntary client may be resistive and unable to see the value of agency's services. In social work practice with nonvoluntary clients, the social worker finds it necessary to use authority in a positive and constructive sense. Social workers should not resist authority but acknowledges its presence in one form or another in their involvement with clients. Even the nonvoluntary client may exercise his/her right of self-determination, but he/she should be informed of the consequences of his/her decision.

In contacts with clients, social workers bring several kinds of authority. They possess the authority of knowledge, the authority of the profession, and the authority of the organization in which they are employed. These organizations have been chartered by society to perform specific services. As a concept authority is difficult for social workers to understand or accept as in their education they become imbued with the value of client self-determination and view it as an absolute. In this sense, they feel that authority conflicts with self-determination and that it carries a negative connotation of coerciveness which suggests a superior-inferior relationship and a negative therapeutic outcome. In the helping process, they present an uncertainty about the use of authority. In corrections and protective services, the social worker operates under an umbrella of constitutional authority which gives him/her the right to demand certain behaviors of clients or to invoke sanctions. The social worker must always exercise the use of authority in a constructive manner and not be fearful of its use when indicated. Authority becomes truly meaningful to the client when he/she accepts its presence. He/she comes to the social worker for assistance as he/she feels that the social worker possesses the authority of knowledge. If the social worker even while operating under the umbrella of societal and professional authority conveys his/her warmth to the client and the desire to be of help, in time a relationship will be developed and the client will accept his/her assistance. The social worker should never use authority in an irrational or punitive manner. While he/she respects the client's right to refuse or accept services, if the client is nonvoluntary, the social worker has a responsibility to point out to the client the consequences of his/her behavior.

THE INTAKE PROCESS

From a social system perspective, the intake process is the point of entry of the client into the organization. Michaels (1956) states,

> Intake in a social agency is the process by which the client and the agency establish a beginning contact with each other. The caseworker assesses the needs and responsiveness of the client, determines which services can meet his needs, and clarifies with him whether he feels the agency' services may prove helpful. Whether the intake process is completed in

one interview or is more extended, it provides immediate services and sets the focus of on-going help (p. 341).

The Intake process concludes with one of the following outcomes: (1) The applicant is accepted for services and then enters into the role of clienthood, (2) the case is continued as further exploration is indicated to determine if the agency can assist the client with his/her problem, (3) the applicant is rejected for agency's services as the agency's function does not relate to his/her problem area and the client is referred elsewhere or (4) the services requested by the applicant are completed during the intake process. The intake process can cover one or several sessions.

The intake process has received more attention in social work literature in the past than it presently does. However, intake is one of the most important component of a social service agency. Decisions are made at intake which determine who will and will not become an agency client. Scherz (1952) views the intake process as being an exploratory phase in which the purpose is "the achievement of an understanding between the caseworker and the client which may result in a completed service, in supplying information about another source that may be better able to serve the client, in referral of the client to another agency, or in a decision to continue exploration of the case." While these are basically the outcomes of the intake process identified above, Scherz attributes two primary purposes to intake: understanding of need and determination of how and where the need can best be met. Perlman (1960) identifies the primary emphasis in the beginning phase; this emphasis is to engage the applicant in wanting to use the services of the agency. Brown and Daniels (1968) view the intake process as having two primary purposes: (1) the determination of whether the agency is the correct setting to assist the client with his/her problem, and (2) if it is to immediately engage the client in the problem-solving process. Berliner (1977) states the purpose of intake is (1) to provide a comprehensive understanding of the person-situation configuration and (2) to provide leads to effective intervention for needed change (p. 665). Information in the intake process exists on two levels: subjective and objective. The social worker needs to be sensitive to the existence of these two informational levels. The objective level consists of the factual events presented by the client; the subjective level consists of the feelings and meanings which surround the events presented by the client. Berliner (1977) states no intake study ever captures all of the facts. However, it should provide sufficient information for determining if the agency can be of assistance to the client. A sound intake process sets the stage for the work and attitudes to follow as the client becomes involved in agency services. Considerable diagnostic work is performed at intake which is important in determining if the agency applicant will become a client.

THE FACTS GATHERING PROCESS

The client comes to the agency for assistance with a problem in psychosocial functioning which is creating distress for him/her and/or other significant people in his/her environment. In order to develop an understanding of the problem and its nature, the social worker engages in a data collection process. In this process, the social worker directs his/her attention to the following activities:

(1) Developing an understanding of the nature of the problem, identification of the referral source, and what the client wants from the agency,
(2) Identification of the duration of the problem, the reasons why the client seeks agency's help at this time, and the efforts, if any, the client has employed in attempting to deal with the problem,
(3) Identification of how the client wants the agency to assist him/her and his/her perceptions of agency's services realistic,
(4) An evaluation of the client' motivation and capacity to use the services of the agency,
(5) Identification of those stresses and strains which appear to be contributing factors to the client's situation.

Hollis and Woods (1984) state that the psychosocial process is one of observation and orderly arrangement of the information, collected and observed, about the client and his/her situation. Always, the problem confronting the client is of multicausation. The referral information reveals general information about the client's problem and the route by which he/she has reached the agency, self-referred or referred by others. Generally, a self-referred client reveals awareness of a problem and some motivation in locating help to address it. While a client referred by others may also possess awareness of a problem, he/she comes to the agency at the urging of others. While the motivation initially may not be strong, it can be strengthened as the social worker takes steps to initiate the helping relationship and to engage the client in the fact gathering process.

In the social study process, the social worker always follows the principle of starting where the client is. He/she begins with the reason for contact as stated by the client in the intake process and eventually directs his/her line of inquiry into those areas which may shed more information on the problem. Here, an understanding of the dynamics of giving and taking help is of value in recognizing the client's ambivalence, dealing with resistance, and motivating and encouraging participation in developing a bond which is conducive to meaningful communication. The social worker gives direction to this process and is prepared to answer any question that the client may have about the reasons for the information he/she is seeking. Interviewing skills are essential in moving the data gathering process forward. The social worker prepares the client for this process and informs him/her of the nature of the questions to be asked. This information makes it possible for the client to ask questions. The social worker identifies the purpose of the interview, clarifies his/her role and seeks the client's understanding of the information provided.

A first step in the data gathering process is for the social worker to communicate warmth, acceptance, and a willingness to be of services to the client, if possible. He/she encourages the client to present his/her story in his/her own words. As the client presents his/her story, the social worker listens attentively; active engagement and forward movement take place as the social worker seeks further elaboration of statements made by the client. As the client presents information, the complexity of this information may lead the social worker to believe that the presenting problem is only a symptom of other problems. However, the social worker does not refocus his/her line of inquiry with this knowledge. Rather, he/she continues to proceed at the client's pace, and earmarks these areas for possible future discussion. These behaviors occur in the beginning phase of the data collection process.

In the middle phase of this process, the social worker demonstrates his/her interviewing and interpersonal skills as he/she makes topical transitions in leading the client to discussion of other areas. In this phase, the social worker's behavior is more directive in nature. However, the client remains the center of attention and the social worker is careful not to evoke undue anxiety by focusing on those areas perceived to be anxiety-provoking and threatening to the client. The primary emphasis is on data collection and relationship building. The social worker's timing of questions is important. If the social worker jumps ahead of the client's pace, the client may become resistive, argumentative, frighten and select to terminate contacts as a result of the anxiety engendered and the feelings aroused.

While the data gathering process is on-going throughout the life of the case, each session brings its own conclusion. In bringing the data gathering process to its conclusion, following one or several sessions, the social worker assumes responsibility for summarizing and synthesizing the information that he/she has received. This knowledge is conveyed to the client for his/her participation and feedback as to its veracity and accuracy. Following this step, the social worker explains the operational procedures of the agency and the process which will be followed in assisting the client in problem-solving. The client may challenge or disagree with the information presented by the social worker. If this occurs, the client and the social worker must engage in a process of further clarification of the situation and reach some consensus on those areas to be addressed.

As a professional with the expertise of knowledge, the social worker will always collect more information than he/she may utilize. Social study information is always used in a judicious manner and only that which is assessed as being related to the client's situation is emphasized. The social worker should approach every interview with some knowledge of the type of data that he/she needs to collect. In preparing for initial contacts with clients in the data gathering stage, the social worker will give evidence of the skills, knowledge and value base of the profession. He/she seeks to prepare him/herself for addressing the possible reactions of the client to the process of seeking help. The client may be attracted to the helping process, but may also be repelled by it as he/she does not know what to expect. This behavior has been referred to as the push and pull forces which surround the behavior associated with seeking help. While the client wants to go further, fear of the unknown pulls him/her backward. It is again stated that social workers come to all contacts with clients with a fund of general knowledge about human development and the social environment, cultural influence on behavior and values, social class stratification, knowledge of the community and its resources, and social policies which have resulted in particular programs directed at achieving societal objectives. This general knowledge about people and situations, culture and class will become more specific as it is applied to the unique situation of the client. In initial contacts with clients, the social worker may engage in a process of "preparatory empathy" (Shulman, 1984) as he/she reflects over the client's situation. This process gets him/her in tune with the possible behavior that the client may present.

Additionally, the social worker is always aware of the importance of flexibility in moving away from the identified purpose of the interview to other urgent matters which may be confronting the client. Rigidity may well reflect an uncaring and insensitive attitude.

ESSENTIAL ELEMENTS IN THE DATA COLLECTION OR SOCIAL STUDY PROCESS

Several important tasks characterize this phase. These tasks are (1) the need for the social worker to identify and clarify the nature of the problem, (2) the social worker must collect facts in order to understand the reasons for the problem and (3) he/she must determine if the agency is the right place for the client. A decision may be made at intake, which also is characterized by data collection, if the applicant is to become an agency client. As these tasks are being carried out, the helping relationship is being developed and nurtured. The use of supportive techniques will characterize the data gathering process in motivating the client to talk freely. In essence, the primary objective of this process is to arrive at an understanding of the nature of the client's problem, identification of contributing factors to it, and a determination of how the agency can be of assistance. The steps which characterize the data collection of social study phase of social work practice are:

- exploration of the problem area.
- developing and maintaining the helping relationship.
- guiding the data collection process through skillful interviewing.
- determining that the agency can be of assistance to the client.
- arriving at a tentative assessment of the conditions which appear to be contributing to the problem.
- summarizing contents, sharing this information with the client, soliciting client's feedback.
- achieving consensus and moving the problem solving process to the next step.

CONCLUSION

The data gathering process, sometimes referred to as social study or data collection, is an essential skill in social work practice. If skillfully handled, the social worker will collect the necessary information for developing an understanding of the client's situation. The social worker with this knowledge will also be able to determine if the agency is the correct setting in which to address the client's problems in psychosocial functioning. The beginning phase of contacts also provides an opportunity to evaluate the motivation and capacity of the client to use the agency's help. In this phase, the helping relationship is initiated and is then built on throughout the life of the client's contacts with the agency. It is important that the social worker formulates his/her line of inquiry so that desired information is obtained; the client should be actively engaged in this process. The social worker should be prepared to answer the client's questions about the nature of the services to be provided and the roles and responsibilities of the client and the social worker in this process. Good beginnings are extremely important as they set the foundation for the problem-solving work to follow.

SELECTED BIBLIOGRAPHY

Berliner, A. (1977) Fundamentals of intake interviewing. CHILD WELFARE, LVI, 665–673.

Brown, J. and Daniels, R. (1968) Intake: A differential approach. CATHOLIC CHARITIES REVIEW, 15, 4–10.

Michaels, R. (1956) Centralized intake in a hospital service department. SOCIAL CASEWORK, 38, 341–348.

Perlman, H. (1960). Intake and some role considerations. SOCIAL CASEWORK, (April), 171–177.

Scherz, F. (1952) Intake: Concept and process. SOCIAL CASEWORK, XXXIII, 233–240.

Schulman, L. (1984) The skills of helping individuals and groups. (Itasca, IL: F.E. Peacock Publishers).

Woods, M. and Hollis, F. (1990) Casework: A psychosocial therapy. (New York: McGraw-Hill).

Chapter 10

DIAGNOSTIC FORMULATION
OR ASSESSMENT PROCESS

The author uses the terms assessment and diagnostic formulation interchangeably. Assessment is a critical skill for the social work practitioner. An assessment is the result of data analysis and the application of a particular theoretical framework to the data. Assessment attempts to locate the reasons for the difficulties faced by the client and it is the sequential step following data collection but preceding goal setting and contract formulation. In assessing the client's situation and in identifying those conditions which are felt to be contributing to it, the social worker through the theoretical orientation applied possesses a view on the nature of the world, what it should be, and what has gone wrong in the client's situation to bring about his/her problem. The view of the world is usually of a normative nature, reflecting the structure of society and its expectations for its members. Consequently assessments are value infused and always contain some notion as to what is preferred behavior. Nurakawa (1965) states, "Diagnosis is a judgment which implies whether or not treatment is necessary. Since treatment is an attempt to change behavior, diagnosis involves a value judgment as to whether the behavior should be changed, whether it is good for the individual or for society" (p. 11). Nurakawa suggests that the problem for the helping person is to make a distinction between behavior that should be encouraged, admired and valued and that which should be discouraged or changed (p. 10). In arriving at an assessment, the social worker will be influenced by the values of the profession and the society in which he/she holds membership. An assessment will identify those areas which require corrective actions if the client' situation is to be eradicated or ameliorated. The assessment process is goal and action-oriented.

DEFINITIONS OF ASSESSMENT
IN SOCIAL WORK PRACTICE

Many social workers have defined assessment. Hepworth and Larsen (1982) conceptualizes assessment as being a process engaged in by the social worker and the client. This process is characterized by cooperation in the collection of data and in prioritizing and synthesizing this data as these relate to the common needs of the client. Hollis (1958) states, "The treatment of any problem is inevitably determined in large parts by one's understanding of its nature, and that, essentially, is what diagnosis is. In casework, diagnosis is an attempt to define as accurately and fully as is necessary for casework treatment the nature of the problem, its causative factors and the person's attitude toward the problem" (p. 38). She identifies a variety of conditions which can affect the diagnostic process. These include motivation, race, ethnic background, class, occupation and education. In emphasizing the importance of these values on the diagnostic process, Hollis states, "Any caseworker must know something about the national and racial customs of the client with whom he is working, and consider to what extent are these customs affecting behavior and attitudes" (p. 47).

Walter, Pardee and Melbo (1976) view an assessment as being a precise statement which identifies the stressors impacting on the client and the areas in which these stressors are evident. They state "An assessment refers to the gathering and analysis of data about a patient or client's current functioning in both illness and wellness" (p. 19). For them, diagnosis is the statement of conclusion following the assessment. Their statement, relating to the importance of identifying the strengths and weaknesses of a client's situation, has much validity for social workers as social workers may focus entirely on the perceived weaknesses of clients while overlooking their strengths. Moxley (1989) states that assessment is an exploratory process which results in a formal statement of the client's needs (p. 26). For the author assessment is a thinking and an analytical process in which a social worker applies a theoretical framework to the data collected and draws inferences from this data analysis as to the reasons for the client's problems. In arriving at an assessment, the social worker may find it necessary to consult with other professions to gain their insights into the problem experienced by the client.

Shulman (1984) in his interactionist approach does not utilize a formal assessment process. The areas to which attention is to be directed result from a tuning-in process in which the social worker listens to involved parties, gain some understanding of their views for the reason for systemic stress and then seek to implement a work process to restore harmony to the interactions of the involved systems. Perlman (1971) in her review of Bartlett's book states that assessment may often be the product of intervention instead of its predecessor. While Perlman's statement contains a degree of truth due to the fact that the social worker initiates intervention immediately as the client's situation is too urgent and cannot wait for the formal assessment process to conclude, it is the author's conviction that the social worker must possess clear understanding of those areas into which he/she is intervening and toward what purpose. Thus, at some point the social worker must engage in a planned, formal diagnostic process.

RELATIONSHIP OF ASSESSMENT TO GOAL-SETTING, CONTRACT FORMULATION AND INTERVENTION

The social worker cannot implement sound intervention or establish feasible goals with the client unless he/she is aware of those areas into which intervention is indicated. Without a formal assessment, the social worker is unable to identify the roles or activities which will be necessary in achieving the desired changes. Consequently, goals and intervention flow out of the assessment process. Recording must accompany the assessment process. The social worker needs to deliberately and consciously transmit the facts to paper in order to think about them in a disciplined manner; he/she needs to observe the bits and pieces of information to see how they fit together in providing an understanding of what forces have impacted on the client and adversely affected his/her psychosocial functioning. The assessment process suffers if the facts remain solely in his/her mind. Assessment requires that the social worker reflects over the facts and subjects them to an analytical process. When this process is completed, the social worker will have a clearer understanding of the problem, what to do about it, what goals are feasible, and what roles and responsibilities will be assumed by him/her and the client system in the intervention.

ASSESSMENT PROCESS IN SOCIAL GROUP WORK AND FAMILY INTERVENTION

When multiple persons are involved in the client system, assessment must also be multifaceted. In social group work, the social worker makes an assessment (1) the individual group member, (2) group dynamics, (3) the stage of group development, (4) the social group worker's use of him/herself, and (5) the nature of the program to be employed in helping the group to achieve its activities. Program may also be viewed as activities implemented by the social group worker in pursuit of the goals of the helping process. Each of these variables can enhance or impair the operations of the small group. In family intervention, the social worker makes an assessment of the individual family members, the marital dyad, the nature of parent-child and sibling relations, communicational patterns, and the family as a social system. The family assessment reveals how the family members through their behaviors verbal and nonverbal contribute to the dysfunctional patterns which characterize the family and the purpose which these patterns serve in destabilizing the family. Here the social worker in arriving at an assessment is more interested in family processes than the content which the family is addressing. In individual assessments, the social worker seeks to identify external and internal stresses which are acting on the individual and contributing to his/her faulty behavioral patterns. It is stressed that in order to carry out the dual focus of social work practice, the social worker in practice with individuals, the small group and the family must give consideration to personal and environmental forces to determine the impact of each of them on the situation faced by the client.

ESSENTIAL ELEMENTS IN THE ASSESSMENT PROCESS

The social worker in the assessment process direct his/her thinking processes to developing an understanding of the reasons for the client's problem. In order to accomplish this task, he/she applies a theoretical perspective to the client's situation. Pincus and Minahan (1973) view the primary purpose of assessment as being that of assisting the social worker in understanding through a process of analysis the relevant facts in a given situation. The outcome of assessment is to serve as a guide to intervention.

In this process, the social worker should devote consideration to the following questions:

(1) What is the nature of the client's situation and how does it present itself?
(2) What is the client's attitude toward the problem?
(3) Is the client motivated and does he/she possess the capacity to work on the problem?
(4) Is the presenting problem the real problem of a symptom of other problems which the client is unaware of or unwilling to face at this point?
(5) Why does the client seek help at this time?
(6) What is the duration of the problem?
(7) What are the client's strengths and weaknesses?
(8) What has been the effectiveness of the client's problem-solving mechanisms in the past?
(9) Are the client's goals and expectations of the agency realistic?
(10) Who needs to be involved in the intervention?

TYPOLOGY OF ASSESSMENTS

In developing and formulating an assessment or diagnostic formulation, the social worker will always be limited by the amount of information available. Planned intervention probably would never occur if the social worker waited endlessly for additional information before he/she arrives at an action plan. The social worker will usually begin intervention with a preliminary, tentativeness of working assessment and modify it as additional data are received and analyzed for their contributions to an understanding of the client's situation. In reality, the social worker makes use of many different assessments and some of these will be discussed:

Preliminary or Tentative: In this type of assessment, the social worker recognizes that he/she lacks information which would make it possible for him/her to arrive at a more sound and definitive assessment. Therefore, he/she formulates a tentative or preliminary assessment which will serve as a guide for intervention while he/she seeks to secure additional information which will shed greater understanding of the situation faced by the client.

Working Assessment: This assessment is similar to the tentative or preliminary assessment. However, the social worker proceeds on the assumption that this assessment has considerable validity and intervention can proceed from it.

Etiological Assessment: This assessment is used essentially in the problem-solving and psychosocial approaches to social work practice. In the ecological assessment, the social worker identifies the origin of the client's problems. While the social worker may select not to address these etiological factors, this knowledge provides the social worker with an understanding of the earlier problems faced by the client and how these problems contribute to his/her present situation.

Dynamic Assessment: This assessment recognizes the interplay of various forces on the client, past and present, and how they contribute to the client's existing problems. The emphasis here is on current dynamics which are acting on the client and activating issues from the past which contribute to his/her present situation. For example, a man may have difficulty with authority but can accept it more readily from a man. When he is placed under the supervision of a female, his issues with authority present themselves and his job is threatened. His issues with authority may result from unresolved issues with his strong, domineering mother which find expression in his interactions with his female supervisor.

Psychosocial Assessment: This is a broad assessment which can incorporate the etiological, dynamic and clinical assessment. The social worker identifies the psychosocial and cultural forces which are impacting on the client and resulting in stress. This assessment recognizes the strengths and weaknesses in the client's situation. In this aspect, it is similar to the ecogram used in family therapy. The etiological and dynamic assessment may be located in the genogram in family therapy in which the family is traced back over several generations to reveal family dynamics and patterns in a pictorial manner.

Clinical Assessment (DSM-III-R): A clinic is viewed as a place where an individual with a disease goes to be treated. This assessment is wedded to the so-called "medical" model of social work practice. As it is viewed as adhering to a medical assessment which is pathologically-oriented and in which the individual bears the onus for his/her problem, it is an assessment which many social workers find difficult to accept. The clinical assessment narrowedly employed would not encompass the dual focus of social work practice. However, it is an assessment of which the social worker must possess knowledge; He/she must know its nature and the uses to which it is put. The social worker cannot question or challenge a clinical assessment if he/she lacks knowledge of its essence. Williams (1981) identifies a variety of reasons for the social worker to become aware of and knowledgeable about the DSM–III. She states it can serve as an educational tool of a comprehensive nature for teaching and learning about psychopathology and mental disorders, (2) it enables the social worker in mental health settings to communicate with other professionals who use it such as psychiatrists and clinical psychologists and (3) the DSM–III provides the most-up-to-date criteria for diagnosing mental disorders (p. 101).

In contrast to its two earlier editions, DSM–I and DSM–II which were heavily based with a psychoanalytical orientation, DSM–III–R is descriptive and atheoretical. The social worker in order to use it effectively must possess knowledge of what constitutes psychopathology, as its focus is on individual psychopathology and the assessment of mental disorders. The social worker should also be knowledgeable about how to conduct a mental health examination. The DSM–III–R contains many diagnostic labels which are classified under a number of broad categories such as personality disorders, disorders first evident in infancy, childhood and adolescence, psychological factors affecting physical conditions, additional codes and V codes for identifying conditions not attributed to a mental disorder for which the client is being seen at the agency.

The importance of social workers being knowledgeable about the clinical assessment is stressed. However, in the author's opinion, social worker can never depend totally on a clinical assessment in arriving at an understanding of the client's situation. It is the unique contribution of the social worker to the psychiatric setting that he/she brings an awareness of the impact of sociocultural and political influences on the problems faced by clients. His/her contribution is frequently instrumental in preventing misdiagnosing and a focus on pathologies instead of the strengths of the client.

A clinical assessment refers to a cluster(s) of behaviors exhibited by a client over a period of time which suggests a particular mental disorder or psychiatric syndrome. As stated earlier, the DSM–III–R is viewed as providing a comprehensive diagnostic approach to the study and classification of mental disorders. It consists of five axes which cover psychological, social and biological conditions. Each axis addresses a specific area which is viewed as important in arriving at a comprehensive clinical assessment. Axis I and Axis II cover essentially psychological data. On Axis I are coded clinical syndromes and other conditions for which the client seeks help which are not attributable to a mental disorder. The name of the condition and its code are recorded on Axis I and several codes may be listed. Axis II addresses personality disorders in adults and developmental disorders in children. Only these two classifications are coded on Axis

II and all others are on Axis I. If the individual has a condition coded on Axis I and Axis II, then the social worker should identify which condition is to be the primary focus on treatment. Some classifications may be given a provisional status as clarity about it has not yet been established. Axis III addresses physiological conditions and the social worker states the source of this verification (physician, client, others, or impressions of the social worker). Axis IV identifies the psychosocial stresses impacting on the client on a range of mild to catastrophic, and Axis V covers the global assessment functioning of the client during the past year on a continuum of health-sickness with a rating scale of 0 to 100. 0 represents the sickest individuals and 90–100 represents a well or superior functioning individual. These axes taken together provide a comprehensive diagnostic assessment of the client. In totality, the DSM–III–R provides a description of the behavior(s) exhibited by a client which enables the social worker to diagnose the nature of his/her mental disorder and to take into consideration other factors, social and physiological, which may be contributing to the client's difficulties. Cultural understanding is not built into the DSM–III–R. A clinician lacking this understanding may inaccurately misdiagnosed the client's behavior, as all behavior is cultural-specific. In this aspect, the social worker through his/her understanding of culture can make a great contribution to a clinical team in shedding different insights on the client's behavior.

Some social workers view the clinical assessment as a labelling device which has negative consequences for clients. While this possibility exists, the DSM–III–R as a tool should not be discredited because it is used inappropriately by some professionals. Whatever, the social worker's feelings about it, he/she to practice effectively in the mental health field and to promote the best interests of clients, particularly minorities, must be knowledgeable about its use and misuse.

Differential Assessment: The social worker is often faced with a situation in which it is difficult to arrive at a clear assessment because of the client's situation and the numerous conditions present. Therefore, he/she is called on to make a differential assessment, to explicate from a variety of conditions those which he/she identifies as having the greatest impact on the client's situation and to focus intervention on them.

DIAGNOSTIC AIDS

If the social worker encounters difficulties in formulating an assessment due to the complexity of the case, or his/her uncertainty relative to specific aspects of it, he/she may seek guidance in attempting to develop a more accurate understanding of the client's situation. Consultation with other professions with the intent of developing a more accurate picture of the psychosocial dynamics of the client's situation may be viewed as the employment of diagnostic aids. For example, the social worker may feel a need to rule out organic conditions in the client's situation and may either refer the client to a neurologist or seek clinical psychological consultation. If the social worker wants to develop an improved understanding of the client's personality and ego defenses, he/she may seek psychiatric consultation. In seeking consultation, the social worker needs to clearly identify the areas in which he/she is seeking assistance. The social worker prepares a report on his/her contacts with the client and identifies the reason(s) for which he/she is seeking consultation.

It is extremely important that the social worker possesses knowledge of the nature of psychological testing and what a particular test is designed to accomplish. Psychological tests have been validated on middle class clients and can have negative consequences for minorities. Clients who have not shared middle class experiences may do poorly on them. The social worker must be aware that intelligence is not a singular mental process. Intelligence consists of a variety of mental functions and processes which reveal how individuals cope and deal with life situations. New and unfamiliar situations may make it difficult for individuals to perform in expected manners as they lack the skill and knowledge for competent performance. It has been demonstrated that minority children can function well in their social environment, but encounters problems in the school setting. Many times they are judged as being intellectually limited and placed in special education courses. Such decisions result from faulty assumptions and misuse of the intelligence test as the test contents do not reflect the minority child's life experience. Intelligence must be viewed and evaluated within the context of the individual's life experiences and those sociopsychological conditions under which he/she lives. Generally, the processes involved in intelligence are those of the ability to learn, to reason, to cope with one's environment and to learn from experiences.

Psychological testing may focus on the following areas: intelligence, special abilities, mental retardation, and personality tests which include projective testing. Among tests used by the clinical psychologist are the Stanford Binet and Wechsler tests for children and adults, the Peabody Picture Vocabulary for special abilities, the Vineland Social Maturity

Scale for mental retardation, the Minnesota Multiphasic Personality test for personality, and the Rorschach, Thematic Apperception Test (TAT) and the Child Apperception Test (CAT) for developing an understanding of personality dynamics and affective feelings. Stanford Binet and Wechsler are used for measuring intelligence. When the social worker prepares to use diagnostic aids in developing greater understanding of the client, his/her personality dynamics, intellectual functioning and how he/she is responding to various pressures, the client should be fully involved and give his/her consent to the use of such consultation.

CONSTRUCTING THE ASSESSMENT/DIAGNOSTIC FORMULATION

It is the responsibility of the social worker to formulate the assessment. It is basically his/her statement of the reason(s) for the problems faced by the client. Following its formulation, the social worker shares his/her impressions with the client for his/her feedback and input. In presenting this information to the client, the social worker (1) identifies the nature of the problem as presented by the client, (2) presents his/her assessment, (3) identifies those areas into which intervention is indicated, (4) outlines the intervention strategy and the roles and responsibilities to be assumed by the client in the change effort. The client responds to this information; he/she either accepts it, rejects it, or adds to it. In his/her recording, the social worker may begin with the following statement:

This problem results from the following conditions . . .

He/she then proceeds to identify these conditions and how they relate to the client's situation. By following this format, the social worker is forced to think about the client's problem, the reasons for its existence, and what needs to be done to ameliorate or eradicate it.

INFORMING THE CLIENT OF THE ASSESSMENT

The client should be informed of the social worker's view of the reasons for his/her situation. As suggested above, the client may agree or disagree with the social worker's assessment; if the client disagrees, he/she may offer his/her own view of the problem and what needs to be done to deal with it. This difference of opinion reveals the need for the client and the social worker to arrive at a consensus on the problem to be addressed. If consensus is achieved, then the process of goal selection and contract formulation may commence. If consensus is not possible, then it is questionable if the social worker can ethically offer services to the client. The social worker should always possess a larger view of the problem than the client and some knowledge of what is feasible and unfeasible in the change process. If the client is unable to accept the social worker's input and steadfastly insist that things must be done in his/her way, then it may be necessary for the agency to refuse its services to the client. By his/her decision, the client expresses his/her self-determination. If the client is an involuntary one and selects not to continue with the agency, his/her decision is also accepted. However, the social worker has a responsibility to inform him/her of the consequences of the decision and that he/she must convey the decision back to the referral source.

In the author's view, it is the resistive client who will invariably challenge the social worker's assessment and insists that things go his/her way. This behavior is a part of the client's problem. However, if the beginning steps toward the establishment of the helping relationship have been sound, if interviewing skills have been demonstrated, and if the social worker through recording has gained awareness of the client's operational personality, He/she will be able to motivate the client to engage in intervention and to reevaluate its effectiveness following a trial period.

As a part of the assessment process, the social worker needs to identify those roles he/she must assume in achieving stated goals. As stated previously, social role is an interactional concept. The roles to be assumed by the social worker will be dependent on the nature of the activities to be implemented in the change process. The diagnostic formulation will shed light on the necessary roles to be assumed by the social worker in helping the client to achieve his/her goals. Specific situations may call for the social worker to assume a variety of roles in the life of a case. These roles may include those of advocate, educator, broker, mediator, and negotiator. Also, the assessment process will determine at what levels of society, micro-messo-macro singularly or in varying combination intervention needs to be directed and what target systems need to be changed. In identifying his/her role in the change process, the social worker may state:

> In assisting the client to achieve his/her goals, it will be necessary for me to assume the roles of mediator and broker. If these roles should not prove effective, then the advocate role may need to be activated.

CONCLUSION

The assessment or diagnostic process is essentially one of thinking and analysis. The social worker is called on to collect bits and pieces of information and to make some sense of them so that he/she can arrive at an understanding of the client's situation while at the same time identifying those forces which contribute to it. To accomplish this task, he/she will need to apply a theoretical perspective to the data collected. The process of making an assessment is much like putting a puzzle together. When the puzzle is completed, a design or picture emerges. It has been stated that an assessment is a design, a plan for action. Young (1956) states, "A diagnosis in casework is a conclusion, a picture, however, incomplete made up of all the facts fitted together within a particular frame of reference" (p. 275). Further, Young states, "to discover these facts, to put them together so that they yield their meaning, and to learn upon the basis of that meaning, what we can or cannot do is the process of diagnosis (p. 275). A value orientation characterizes the assessment process. A value judgment is implicit in making a decision whether the condition should be changed and if so in what manner. The *data collection* process has provided the social worker with materials for analysis. In the *assessment process*, the social worker applies a theoretical framework to this material. This theoretical framework enables the social worker to draw inferences from these facts relative to the reasons for the client situation. With this knowledge the social worker is now prepared to engage in the process of goal setting. The assessment or diagnostic formulation must be viewed as establishing the foundation for social work practice. Assessment is an essential skill for the social worker if he/she is to plan sound intervention. Assessment leads to intervention. However, before planned intervention is implemented, goal setting and contract formulation need to be completed.

SELECTED BIBLIOGRAPHY

Hepworth, D. and Larsen, J. (1982) Direct social work practice (Homewood, IL: Dorsey Press).

Hollis, F. (1958) Personality diagnosis in casework. H. Parad (Ed.) Ego psychology and dynamic casework (New York: Family Service Association of America).

Moxley, D. (1989) The practice of case management (Newbury Park, CA: Sage Publications).

Nurakawa, W. (1965) (Ed.) Human values and abnormal behavior (Atlanta, GA: Scott, Foresman).

Perlman, H. (1971) Book Review, H. Bartlett's The common base of social work practice, SOCIAL WORK, 16, 109–10.

Pincus, A. and Minahan, A. (1973) Social work practice: Method and process (Itasca, IL: F.E. Peacock Publishers).

Shulman, L. (1984) The skills of helping individuals and groups (Itasca, IL: F.E. Peacock Publishers).

Walter, J., Pardee, G. and Melbo, D. (1976) Dynamics of problem-oriented approaches to patient care and documentation (Philadelphia: J.P. Lippincott).

Williams, J. (1981) DSM–III: A comprehensive approach to diagnosis. SOCIAL WORK, 26, 101–6.

ADDITIONAL REFERENCES

American Psychiatric Association (1987). Diagnostic statistical manual of mental disorders (DSM–III–R) 3rd. ed. (Washington, D.C.: American Psychiatric Association).

Spitzer, R., Williams, J. and Skodol, A. (1980) DSM–III: The major achievements and an overview. THE AMERICAN JOURNAL OF PSYCHIATRY, 13, 151–73.

Perlman, H. (1957) Social casework: A problem-solving process (Chicago: University of Chicago Press).

Woods, M. and Hollis, F. (1990) Casework: A psychosocial therapy (New York: McGraw-Hill).

Chapter 11

GOAL SETTING IN SOCIAL WORK PRACTICE*

The effectiveness of social work practice is related to the achievement of goals mutually agreed upon by the social worker and the client. Comptom and Galaway (1989) state that goal setting provides a means of building accountability and of monitoring and measuring the effectiveness of service outcomes (p. 495). Goal setting is a complex process and is an important skill for the social worker to master. Establishing goals precedes contract formulation and the implementation of the formal intervention strategy. Goals are discussed with the client following the assessment process in which the client and the social worker have arrived at an understanding of the nature of the client's situation, the conditions which are contributing to it, and the nature of the corrective actions required to change it. If goals are not established, then intervention has no specific direction. The helping situation, then, becomes analogous to that of an individual who starts a journey with no clear destination in mind. He/she will not know where the journey ends, and thus may continue the journey indefinitely. In the absence of clearly-stated goals, the social worker too will lack understanding of which direction to take in helping the client with his/her problem. He/she will be unable to initiate a process of planned termination or to evaluate the movement of the case toward the achievement of specific ends as he/she will have no guidelines. Gottlieb and Stanley (1967) state,

> Treatment in casework should be based on goals that are consciously established and mutually agreed upon by the client and the worker, the purpose of which is to bring about constructive changes in the client's dysfunctioning and distress and personality growth (p. 471).

Specht (1988) speaks of the objectives of social work practice as goals to be achieved in developmental socialization, resocialization and contextual socialization. Barker (1987) views goal setting as "a strategy employed

---

*In this chapter goals and objectives are used interchangeably even though it is recognized that objectives are steps taken toward goal achievement.

by social workers and other professionals to help clients clarify and define the objectives they hope to achieve in the helping relationship" (p. 64). Simons and Aigner (1985) identify three benefits which result from goal-setting: (1) mutuality of goal selection, (2) facilitation of intervention planning and (3) providing an evaluative mechanism (p. 74). In the absence of goals, the social worker will not be able to identify the activities which will be necessary for their accomplishment, nor the roles that he/she will need to assume in the change process. The ability to establish goals is a necessary and inherent part of social work practice.

PROCESS IN GOAL SETTING

The activities engaged in by the client and the social worker will be influenced by the nature of the established goals. Goals are instrumental in stimulating the active involvement of the client in the change process. Through their identification, the client develops awareness of what he/she is working toward accomplishing. It is important that the client is informed that goals are subjected to renegotiation based on new information or a recognition that insurmountable obstacles may stand in the way of achieving desired outcomes. The process of goal setting must always be viewed as a negotiable one inasmuch as the client may desire more than the agency can deliver. It is the responsibility of the social worker to make clear to the client that he/she cannot guarantee goal achievement, but will lend his/her knowledge, skills and competencies in assisting the client to achieve them. It is sometimes useful to establish a hierarchy of goals on a continuum of complex to more complex. The accomplishment of small goals may imbue the client with the strength and the desire to work on more complicated issues. Goal setting will usually encompass the following steps:

(1) Identification of the client's problem(s);
(2) An assessment of the contributing factors based on application of a particular theoretical perspective to the data collected and analyzed;
(3) Identification of corrective actions indicated to address situation;
(4) Presentation of findings to client for feedback, negotiation if indicated, and identification of goals to be achieved.

It is important that the social worker gains a clear understanding of what the client wants from the agency, and if the agency can assist the client in achieving his/her objectives or if some modification is indicated. Always the client's goals must be consistent with the agency's mission.

GOAL DEFINITION

Goals essentially are the desired outcomes or expectations of the intervention process. Goals influence the nature of treatment, the roles assumed by the social worker and the client in the change process, and the type of activities to be implemented in pursuant of the desired goals. It is important for the social worker to remember that while goals are mutually agreed on by the social worker and the client sometimes they may be superimposed by other agencies if the client is a nonvoluntary one. Vinter (1967) refers to outcome goals as those conditions which we like to see following the end of a successful change effort (p. 13).

PURPOSES OF GOALS

Epstein (1980) states that goals are powerful instruments for determining the substance of interaction (p. 125). It is also important for the social worker to recognize that goals cannot be achieved in isolation, but are often related to and dependent on the participation of others in the change process (Pincus and Minahan, 1973). Goals serve a variety of purposes. They give direction to the intervention process and serve as a means of actively enlisting the client's participation in the change process. Goals provide a means for evaluating the effectiveness of the social worker's practice. Goals should always be made explicit. Clarity should surround them and they should be operationalized into behavioral outcomes. Woods (1978) states, "To set vague goals or to set them unreasonably high is to subject clients to a cruel and destructive experience in disappointment, frustration, and erosion of their confidence in their own capacities" (p. 453). When goals are explicit and agreed on by the client and the social worker, they constitute an agreement on the expected outcomes. If goals are not made explicit, then misconception over them may exist between the client and the social worker as to the reasons for their contacts. An assumption may exist that they are working toward the same objectives, when in reality they are not. Goals are also important in providing a sense of continuity and direction to the intervention. If the social worker should leave the agency or is reassigned, the new worker will possess some awareness of the nature of the activities undertaken and toward what purposes they are directed. Planned termination is always goal-related. The social worker through monitoring the progress of the case and the positive change in the client situation can make an evaluation of movement toward goal achievement and if the services of the agency are no longer required. In the absence of concerted efforts at goal achievement by the client, the social worker needs to reassess the client's situation and the goals to determine if the client is working actively toward their accomplishment, or if the goals are capable of achievement.

NATURE OF GOALS

Pincus and Minahan identify method and outcome goals. Method goals refer to the social worker's activities in attempting to bring about specific goals. The method is used as a means of goal accomplishment. Outcome goals are the product of the intervention, or as Vinter states the conditions we would like to see following a successful change effort. The goals of the client must relate to one or several functions of the profession and the mission of the organization. Since the social worker operates as a representative of society, it would constitute questionable and unethical behavior if he/she were to pursue goals with clients which are viewed as being detrimental to the well-being of the client or society. The social worker also must always consider what the client wants to achieve and what is feasible or possible to achieve. It is in this area of unreal expectations from the agency that a process of goal negotiation must take place between the client and the social worker.

Goals may be realistic or unrealistic in nature; they may be vague or clear and they may be global or partialized in nature. Partialized goals exist when the client works on smaller problems before proceeding to more complicated ones. If partialized goals are achieved, then the client may become motivated to work on other issues. Global goals are of an all encompassing nature and are almost impossible to achieve. Lack of achievement of global type goals leads to frustration not only for the client but also the social worker. The social worker should always strive to assist the client in settling on realistic or feasible goals.

The social worker must give recognition to a variety of goals which exist in any case. These goals are those of the agency, the worker, the client, and the action system. They are uniquely related and each system must carry out its intended function if the client's goals are to be achieved.

When multiple systems are involved, such as the family or the small group, multiple goals present themselves. The individual and the family may have separate goals, but the achievement of family goals is dependent on the achievement of the goals of individual family members. Similarly, in the small group, the individual group member has his/her goal, but individual goals must be submerged to group goals. However, the individual goals must be met through the group goals. If individual goals are not met within the small group—the individual enters the small group to achieve his/her goal—then group goals will face barriers to achievement.

The goals of a client may be stated, unstated or unknown. In social group work practice, these goals are referred to as avowed, unavowed, and unconscious. The social worker should be sensitive to the type of goal on which the client is operating. If any of these goals are present, they will have an influence on the client's behavior and some effect on the intervention strategy. The client's behavior will usually present clues as to which type of goal is operating. A stated or avowed goal is the verbal statement given by the client about what he/she wishes to accomplish through agency's services. An unstated or unavowed goal exists when the client desires to achieve a goal which is not stated. This goal may be the opposite of his/her stated goal. For example, the client may state a desire to save his/her marriage, but in reality he/she desires to end it. Consequently his/her involvement in intervention will be minimal or of a destructive nature. In social group work, a client's unstated goal may be to be in the same group that his/her friend is in, but the stated goal may be that he/she wants assistance with his/her problem. An unconscious or unknown goal exists when the client lacks awareness of its presence, but through his/her psychological needs such a goal may present itself in the helping process. Many times unconscious goals present themselves in authority relationship and power struggles. For example, a stated goal of a client may be the client's desire to enhance his/her self-esteem so that he/she can become more assertive in decision making. However, an unconscious goal may present itself when the client forms a dependent relationship with the social worker and gains greater satisfaction from the neurotic relationship established instead of directing his/her energies toward working on the problem. Unconscious goals may be influenced by transference and countertransference phenomena. In case work, social group work and family work, the social worker must facilitate a helping environment in which the goals of individuals within the context of larger systems are met. Systems have their goals and the client system has its goals. The agency's goals for its client are consistent with its functions as set forth in its charter. Usually these are broad goals such as strengthening family life, or contributing to the mental health of client systems.

GOAL COORDINATION

Goal coordination has always been important in social work practice. With the attention being given to case management, the coordination of goals is even more important if the client is to receive the multiplicity of services which he/she needs in a coordinated manner. Goal coordination becomes especially important when the client is involved with multiple social systems. If the organizations involved do not agree on a common goal for the client system, then they may work at cross-purposes. The existence of conflicting goals is confusing and may work against the client improving his/her situation. Conflicting goals may also result in a waste of valuable time as well as resources. To insure that all involved systems are working toward the achievement of a common goal for the client, the social worker may convene a case conference of involved agencies to clarify the objectives which are being pursued. Discussion among the various involved agencies may result in a common goal and an identification of how each agency can contribute to it. Later case conferences may focus on how the activities of all the involved systems are contributing to the achievement of the common goal.

CONCLUSION

Establishing goals is a critical and important skill in social work practice. The activities of the social worker, the client and other involved systems will be directed at goal achievement. The process of goal setting follows assessment and precedes contract formulation and the implementation of the formal intervention strategy. Goals should always be made explicit. In the absence of explicit goals which are clearly stated and free of vagueness, the social worker will not know toward what ends he/she is working or be able to identify the activities and roles necessary to accomplish a desired end. He/she works in a vacuum, will not be able to monitor case progress or to determine an appropriate time for termination. The lack of clearly specified goals to give direction to intervention constitutes a disservice to the client. It may result in the client remaining in services long after he/she has received what he/she wanted from the agency, or it may result in termination by the client without the involvement of the social worker. Goals should always be realistic, capable of attainment and within the competencies of the social worker. It is important that the client be actively involved in the process of goal setting and that the social worker and client reach consensus on the nature of the goals to be sought. The social worker also recognizes that while goals give direction to intervention, they are subjected to change based on the presentation of new data and the mutual consent of the social worker and the client. Once goals have been established, the social worker moves onto the next step in social work practice which is that of contract formulation.

SELECTED BIBLIOGRAPHY

Barker, R.L. (1987) The social work dictionary (Silver Spring, MD.: National Association of Social Workers).

Compton, B. and Galaway, B. (1989) Social work processes, 4th. edition (Belmont, CA: Wadsworth Publishing Co.).

Epstein, L. (1980) Helping people: The task-centered approach (St. Louis, MO: Mosby).

Gottlieb, W. and Stanley, J. (1967) Mutual goals and goal setting in casework, SOCIAL CASEWORK, XLVIII, 471–481.

Pincus, A. and Minahan, A. (1973) Social work practice: Model and process (Itasca, IL: F.E. Peacock Publishers).

Simons, R.L. and Aigner, S.M. (1985) Practice principles: A problem-solving approach to social work (New York: MacMillan).

Specht, H. (1988) New directions for social work practice (Englewood Cliffs, NJ: Prentice-Hall).

Vinter, R. (1967) Readings in group work practice (Ann Arbor, MI: Campus Publishers).

Woods, K. (1978) Casework effectiveness: A new look at the research evidence. SOCIAL WORK, 23, 437–459.

Chapter 12

THE CONTRACT IN SOCIAL WORK PRACTICE*

The contract is a valuable tool in social work practice. Its development constitutes an important skill for the social worker to develop and master. A contract in social work defines the perimeters of intervention, identifies the goals to be achieved and the roles and responsibilities of the participants. Its development is the result of a collaborative relationship between the client and the social worker. In the situation of a nonvoluntary client, the contract development may be characterized by conflict. In the resolution of the conflict, bargaining is an important technique for the social worker to use in helping the client to participate in the contract development. While an unwilling client will probably not benefit in a meaningful manner in the intervention or participate reluctantly because of the consequences of his/her refusal, the social worker may through the helping relationship diffuse some of the resistance so that the client will participate more meaningfully in the change process.

The nature of the contract is influenced by the goals to be achieved and the intervention strategy designed to achieve them. Essentially, it is the process of goal setting which leads to contract formulation. Gottman and Leiblum (1974) identify the importance of contract development. They state a contract specifies agreement on a goal, the methods of their achievement and the rules which will characterize the intervention. They view the contract as serving other important purposes: (1) It increases the chances of operationalizing the helping relationship between the client and the social worker, (2) the contract emphasizes active instead of passive participation on the parts of the social worker and the client in achieving stated goals and (3) it constitutes the basic link between the intervention and the goals established (p. 44). Klein, Fein and Genero (1984) state that contracts may facilitate the intervention process by

---

*In this chapter, service contract, service agreement, treatment plan, intervention plan and contract are used interchangeably.

establishing early in intervention the time span of contacts, the goals to be achieved, and the mutual expectations of the participants. It is clear that the contract serves as a tool in bring clarity to the nature of intervention, the expectations of the involved parties, and an identification of the goals to be achieved. It is a document of accountability, and frequently when intervention is not proceeding by plan, it serves as a means of review in order to focus on the agreement which was reached by the client and the social worker.

CONTRACT DEFINITION

Maluccio and Marlow (1974) define the social work contract as

The explicit agreement between the worker and the client concerning the target problems, the goals, and the strategies of social work intervention, and the roles and tasks of the participants (p. 30).

Croxton (1974) defines the contract in the following manner,

The treatment contract is an agreement between two or more persons in which there must be mutuality of understanding concerning treatment goals (products), reciprocal obligations relating to treatment means (specifications), and ultimate expectations (terminal behavior) (p. 176).

Croxton also identifies several phases in the sequence of contract development: exploratory, negotiation, preliminary, working, secondary and terminal and evaluation. Shulman (1984) views a contract as being in existence when there is a convergence of the agency's services and the client's need. Contracting is an important sequence for Schulman in the interactionist approach: Tuning in, contracting, work, and ending and transitions. Pincus and Minahan (1973) identify two types of contracts; primary and secondary. A primary contract exist between the worker and the client system. A secondary contract consists of a working agreement with others who may be involved in the change process. Others may consist of the action, target or change agent system. They view the evolution of the contract as being a continuing process, one which is subjected to renegotiation.

PROCESS IN CONTRACT FORMULATION

At some point in the life of any case, it is expected that the social worker and client will enter into a contractual agreement. This contractual agreement will identify how they will work together in the change process and the goals which they are striving to achieve. The formulation of the contract must logically follow the conclusion of the phases which have preceded it: data collection, assessment and goal identification. A central feature in contract formulation is goal identification and the work necessary to achieve them. The work to be done is goal-focused. In the absence of clearly stated goals, the contract becomes a nebulous tool as the social worker and the client will not know when its terms have been met. A formal contract is developed and implemented only when goals have been identified. Bayles (1981) views the contract as being an agreement freely arrived at as a resulting of bargaining between equals. He states as a contractual relationship, the contract contains "mutual obligations and rights, a true sharing of ethical authority and responsibility" (p. 63). Bayles identifies six general obligations which characterize the contract: honesty, candor, competence, diligence, loyalty and discretion. Discretion includes confidentiality. These essential obligations assumed by the client and the social worker reveal the reciprocal aspects of the contract. They also will be necessary for the maintenance of the therapeutic alliance and for moving the problem-solving effort forward. Goulding and Goulding (1979) state that the contract establishes the focus for treatment and determines the basis of the helping relationship. In a similar manner, Maluccio and Marlow state,

> The use of a contract can help facilitate worker-client interaction, establish mutual concerns, clarify the purposes and conditions of giving and receiving services, delineate roles and tasks, order priorities, allocate time constructively for attaining goals and access progress on an on-going basis (p. 30).

Once goals have been identified, agreed on and the contract formalized, the next step is for the social worker and client to identify and activate the tasks (units of work) and activities which are necessary for goal achievement or meeting the terms of the contract. In the author's view, a contract in social work is essentially an agreement, written or verbal, established between the social worker and the client for engaging in specific activities relative to assisting the client with his/her problem. The features of the contract provide clarity of all the behaviors and roles to be assumed by those in the change effort. The contract remains in effect until the goals are achieved. The contract can be renegotiated upon mutual consent between the social worker and the client, or it can be nullified when it is revealed that one or both parties are not performing according to contractual specifications. Implicitly contained in the contract is the belief in the competencies of the social worker. The manner in which the contract is approached, discussed and formulated is an indication of the nature of the helping relationship which has been nurtured and developed in those phases which precede contract formulation.

FEATURES OF THE CONTRACT

A contract in social work practice will usually contain the following features:

(1) The nature of the client's situation (request for services),
(2) identification of the goals to be achieved,
(3) the nature of the intervention strategy,
(4) the roles and responsibilities of the participants in the change process,
(5) the rules which will govern the contacts. This relates to the frequency of interviews, the responsibilities of the client and the social worker,
(6) identification of the fee if one is established,
(7) the duration of the contract, and
(8) the circumstances under which the contract may be renegotiated.

When these features are present, the contract becomes a document of accountability. It provides a means for the participants to evaluate if those involved are carrying out their mutual roles and responsibilities.

WRITTEN OR VERBAL CONTRACTS

The question invariably is posed whether the contract should be of a verbal or written nature. Gottman and Leiblum recommend that the contract be written and signed. It should contain specifics on goals and methods. The author also thinks that a written contract is more effective than a verbal one. A copy of it should be given to the client. When the behavior of the social worker or client does not comply with contractual obligations, then the contract can be reviewed. A review of the contract serves to reinforce in the participants' memory the reasons why it was developed. It is a guide to intervention. Whenever work stalls in a case, the contract serves to remind participants of the reasons for their contacts. A written contract is also help in addressing confusion. It serves as the document of client and social workers' activities. In contrast the verbal contract is subjected to confusion and forgetfulness and frequently requires rediscussion.

CONTRACT PHASES

Earlier, the contract phases identified by Croxton were noted. Seabury (1976) also feels that a social work contract is always in a state of continuous development and remains in this state throughout the entire social work process (p. 17). Seabury also identifies several phases through which contract development proceeds. These phases are exploration and negotiation, preliminary contract formulation, development of a working agreement and contract termination. In the exploratory and negotiation phase, the social worker and client focus on the clarification of the problem, the identification of roles and expectations, the goals to be achieved, and the activities to be implemented pursuant to goal accomplishment. In the preliminary phase, the social worker and the client have reached agreement on the goals and intervention strategy. This phase is also characterized by the social worker and client engaging in those tasks which will facilitate case movement. In the termination phase, the social worker and client reflect over activities performed to achieve specific goals and arrived at the decision that these goals have been met and the terms of the contract fulfilled. When this happens, the services of the agency are no longer required. The contract is terminated by mutual agreement. The achievement of goals is not the only reason for contract termination. A contract can be terminated when a client is transferred to another facility or as a result of a recognition that the client lacks motivation, does not involve him/herself in an active manner in the intervention, and the likelihood of achieving specified goals are limited. The contract can also be renegotiated.

TYPES OF CONTRACTS

If the social worker is active with multiple clients such as in the small group, he/she is aware that several different types of contracts may be in existence at the same time. However, these contracts evolve over a period of time. In social group work, Estes and Henry (1976) identify four different contracts which develop in the group over a period of time.

These contracts are called independent, reciprocal, mutual and inter-dependent. The independent contract is a property of the client alone; it exists in his/her mind and may not be shared with others. This contract influences the client's behavior and the goals which he/she seeks; inas-much as it is not verbalized, it may not converge with agency's functions. The client's behavior will reveal if an unspoken contract is in operation. His/her behavior may be of a self-fulfilling nature and can seriously interfere with group processes. A reciprocal contract is established between the client and the agency. It comes into existence when agreement is reached that the client's situation is appropriate to the services provided by the agency. When the reciprocal contract is established, the client moves from the role of applicant to that of clienthood. A mutual contract implies that a state of mutuality exists between group members over the goals of the group and the manner in which the group will be structured so that individual and group goals can be achieved. The interdependent contract may be viewed as a contract of faith. It comes into existence when group members recognize their inter-dependence on each other and work cooperatively together. When the interdependence contract exists, a group identity has been formed and group boundaries established. The independent and reciprocal contracts are not the property of the group as these are developed before the group comes into existence. However, they are extremely important in the screening of members for the group and for achiev-ing a match in client's problems and agency services. The goals estab-lished in them must be met as the group works to achieve its goals. The mutual and interdependent contracts are the properties of the group and any change in them must be sanctioned by the group. In a sense, these four types of contracts are also present in family work. In family work, individual and family goals must also be met. Individual family members may also possess their own goals (independent). A reciprocity must exist between the family's goals and the agency's func-tion (reciprocal). The family members must agree to work as a collectiv-ity (mutual) and the interdependent contract is evident by the manner in which the family works as a unit in addressing its problems. In social work practice with the individual, depending on the problem to be addressed, several contracts may also exist. These are the independent, the reciprocal, and contracts with participants in the action or target systems.

INTERRELATIONSHIP BETWEEN CONTRACT AND GOALS

The contract is extremely important as it establishes the terms under which intervention will be provided. The goals specify what is to be the product or outcome of intervention. Once the contract stage has been reached, a sense of mutuality should exist between the client and the social worker. The goals specified may exist on a continuum of short, intermediate or long-range. Goals should be operationalized and capable of measurement. In effect they should be realistic in nature and capable of achievement. Gottman and Lieblum recommend that the contract be signed by the social worker and the client. When one identifies the purposes of goal setting, then the relationship between goals and the contract becomes immediately evident. Cormier and Cormier (1979) view goals as being related to a specific area of the client's problem, providing direction to intervention and serving as the basis for the selection of intervention, and they provide a framework for evaluation. Until goals have been agreed on, then, the next step in planned intervention, contract formulation, cannot go forward in a planned and purposeful manner.

CONCLUSION

Contract formulation is a crucial skill for the social worker to possess. Contract development is a mutual process engaged in by the social worker and the client. It is developed around the activities which will characterize the intervention, the rules which will govern intervention, and the roles and responsibilities of the participants. The contract must be viewed as constituting an on-going process throughout the life of the case. It is subjected to renegotiation based upon mutual agreement by the participants. When obstacles present themselves to goal achievement, the contract provides a document for reviewing its terms and for holding its participants accountable. When the terms of the contract have been met, that is, the goals have been achieved, no need remains for its existence and it is no longer operative. The contract provides direction to intervention and establishes the perimeters under which help will be given. As a document, it should be periodically reviewed by the participants as a means of keeping them on track. Always, a contract is developed as a result of goal specification. Goal specification is an outcome of the assessment process and the corrective actions indicated if the client's problem is to be addressed. The contract indicates that the social worker and the client have become joined or entered into a cooperative partnership in which they will combine their resources and those of others, if indicated, in improving that condition which has brought about the client's contact with the agency.

SELECTED BIBLIOGRAPHY

Bayles, M. (1981) Professional ethics (Belmont, CA: Wadsworth Publishing Co.).

Cormier, W.H. and Cormier, L.S. (1979) Interviewing strategies for helpers: A guide to assessment, treatment and evaluation (Monterey, CA: Brooks/Cole).

Croxton, T. (1967) The therapeutic contract in social treatment, In P. Glasser, R. Sarri and R. Vinter (eds.) Individual change through the small group (New York: The Free Press).

Estes, R. and Henry, S. (1976) The therapeutic contract in social group work: A formal analysis. SOCIAL SERVICE REVIEW, 50, 611–622.

Gottman, J.M. and Leiblum, S. (1974) How to do psychotherapy and how to evaluate it (New York: Holt, Rinehart and Winston).

Goulding, M. and Goulding, R. (1979) Changing lives through redecision therapy (New York: Bruner/Mazel).

Klien, J., Fein, E. and Gerero, C. (1984) Are written or verbal contracts more effective in family therapy? SOCIAL WORK, 29, 298–300.

Maluccio, A. and Marlow, W. (1974) The case for the contract. SOCIAL WORK, 19, 28–35.

Pincus, A. and Minahan, A. (1973) Social work practice: Model and process (Itasca, IL: F.E. Peacock Publishers).

Seabury, B. (1976) The contract: Uses, abuses and limitations. SOCIAL WORK, 21, 16–22.

Schulman, L. (1984) The skills of helping individuals and groups (Itasca, IL: F.E. Peacock Publishers).

Chapter 13

INTERVENTION IN SOCIAL WORK PRACTICE

T he social worker and the client having completed the earlier stages of the social work process in which specific skills were demonstrated such as developing the therapeutic alliance, data collection, data analysis, goal setting and contract formulation now move on to the next step which is the planning and implementation of an intervention strategy which is directed at ameliorating or eradicating those conditions which are contributing to the client's discomfort. Intervention may be defined literally as the social worker coming between the client and those conditions which are adversely impacting on his/her psychosocial functioning. The values of the profession have been continuously demonstrated in the client-social worker contacts. The intervention will be guided by a theoretical framework or practice theory. Anderson (1981) states that all practice is based on theory and defines a practice theory:

> Practice theory is a more or less formalized system of propositions, hypotheses, or practice principles, including their concepts which system-atically explain the nature of, establishes our relationship to, and pro-poses our procedures for influencing observed events in practice situations (p. 134).

Practice theory and theoretical frameworks must contain techniques which can be employed by the social worker in facilitating case move-ment so that desired outcomes can be achieved. The intervention plan is always goal-directed and carried out within the specifications of the contract.

INTERRELATIONSHIP BETWEEN ASSESSMENT, GOALS, CONTRACT AND INTERVENTION

All of the previous activity engaged in by the social worker and the client (establishing relationship, data collection, data analysis, recording, goal setting and contracting) are ultimately directed toward the development of an intervention plan. The social worker collect data, draw inferences from them, and based on these inferences plan intervention strategies. In order to employ the above skills, he/she needs to possess interviewing skills, the capacity to develop and maintain the helping relationship, and the ability to encourage and support the client in telling his/her story so that facts can be collected. The social worker must engage in recording so that he/she can analyze and reflect on the information provided by the client. When these procedures have been carried out in a purposeful manner with the active participation of the client, the stage is set for the activation of the intervention. It is again stated that the processes of data collection, assessment, establishment of the helping relationship and intervention go on simultaneously with one of them being emphasized at a particular moment.

Intervention consists of those activities, procedures, skills and techniques employed by the social worker in facilitating the change process. Since intervention is designed for the achievement of specific goals, it is evident that intervention of a planned nature must follow and not precede assessment. The social worker needs to possess knowledge of what he/she is intervening into. This knowledge only results from disciplined thinking and the application of a conceptual framework to practice. The term formal intervention is employed to distinguish the intervention plan which is agreed to by the client and the social worker. It differs from informal intervention which commences from the first moment that the client and social worker meet. The social worker needs to ask him/herself the following question: Based on this problem, and my analysis of the reasons for it, what type of intervention is indicated?

SOCIAL SYSTEMS

It is useful to discuss intervention within the context of social systems. During intervention, the four basic systems in social work practice will be activated: client, worker, action and target. Since the unit of analysis of social systems is social roles, all participants involved in the intervention will assume and perform certain roles. The concept of intervention role is an important one as it provides a framework for the identification of the roles which need to be performed by the participants and the activities associated with these roles. Role assumption and the activities associated with these roles relate to the problems to be addressed and not the methods (social casework, family work, social group work) employed.

The foci of intervention may be (1) the individual, family or small group, (2) the environment which includes organizations, societal institutions, laws, and social policies or (3) the individual and the environment. When the social worker speaks of the structural components of society, he/she is referring to its structural arrangements, i.e., the manner in which it is designed and the functions which are assigned to societal institutions. These social institutions are designed to perform specific functions which are viewed as contributing to the well-being of society and the social welfare of its members. However, societal institutions do not always operate in an intended manner; they may possess latent functions which create stress for people in contact with them.

Intervention occurs at the interface where people engage in transactions with their environments. Sometimes social work functions are identified as being those of social control and social change. The social control function seeks to protect society from the behavior of its members who are viewed as violating the norms of society. Ideally, the rehabilitative focus of this function seeks to assist individuals in changing their maladaptive behaviors so that they can become functioning members of the society in which they hold membership. A high degree of coerciveness is connected with this function, particularly if the person does not follow through with the sanctions which society has imposed on him/her. The social worker is not expected to use authority in a punitive manner but to establish a helping relationship and through this relationship to help the client to see the value in working with the social worker in the amelioration or eradication of those conditions which have aroused societal concern. The social change function focuses on modification of social policy, or organizational function when these are viewed as negatively impacting on the client system. Focus can also be directed to the development of programs and the formulation of social policies which are directed at addressing human needs through the implementation of new programs. This societal focus is instrumental in bringing into existence a more just and equitable society.

APPLICATION OF THEORETICAL ORIENTATION TO INTERVENTION

Social work intervention is influenced by the theoretical orientation or conceptual practice model (psychosocial, problem-solving, systems theory, life model) employed by the social worker in his/her practice.

This framework guides the social worker's activities as he/she seeks to implement activities directed at goal achievement. This framework has also been applied in data analysis in arriving at an understanding of the reasons for the client's situation, and presents itself throughout the life of a case. It is important that a social worker be able to articulate to the client and other professionals the reasons for his/her activities and the goals the activities seek to accomplish. The social worker is only able to articulate this understanding to others when he/she is aware of how a particular framework leads him/her to view the data collected and to analyze and draw references from the data as to the reason for the client's situation and what can be done to improve it.

SKILLS, TECHNIQUES AND ACTIVITIES*

Planned intervention requires that the social worker identifies the tasks to be performed, the skills and techniques to be employed and the activities to be implemented in the pursuit of the goals of the case. Tasks may be translated into units of work, i.e., what activities must be accomplished to push the change effort forward. Cynkins (1979) remarks on the importance of activities in the change process,

> Activities, delineated and analyzed for their therapeutic potentials and used in specific and systematic ways, are the agents of change (p. XV)

In the selection of activities is the implicit assumption that they can be instrumental in goal achievement or in the reversal of the conditions which are contributing to the client's situation (Cynkins, p. 6). Skills may refer to procedures implemented and/or interpersonal skills used by the social worker in the change effort. Shulman (1984) in his interactionist approach identifies a number of interpersonal skills employed by the social worker in his/her interactions with clients. He identifies skills as those behaviors used by the social worker in the change process. Different skills may characterize the activities implemented in the beginning, middle and ending phases of practice. Middleman and Goldberg (1990) refer to skills as generic activities implemented by the social worker. They identified 63 skills used by the social worker in practice and view skills as being the "particular how of the practitioner activity" (p. 11). They define skills as "the production of specific behaviors under the

---

*Program media in social group work refers to the selection of activities which can be used in helping the group to achieve its purpose.

precise conditions designated for their use" (p. 12). Woods and Hollis (1990) identify communication procedures implemented by the social worker in facilitating the change effort. In addition to environment work, they identify six communication procedures: sustainment, direct influence, exploration-description-ventilation, reflective discussion of the person-situation configuration, reflective consideration of pattern dynamic and developmental factors. Techniques, procedures or skills may be viewed as those tools specifically selected and used by the social worker to facilitate the change process. Activities consists of a variety of actions relating to a specific task (unit of work) to be performed. They are identified, implemented and applied in specific and systematic ways as a means of accelerating or pushing the intervention forward.

In social work practice, skills in communication are essential. These communication skills are displayed in the worker's purposeful use of him/herself in communicating with client systems as he/she poses questions to the client, elicits the client's feedback and then proceeds onto other areas as indicated. Communication is a circular process, and the involved participants must be able to send, receive, decode and act on the messages transmitted. This activity is only possible when messages are clear and understood by the participants.

INTERVENTIVE ROLES

The social worker in employing specific skills, techniques and activities perform them within the context of specific roles. The purposes which the social worker seeks to accomplish will influence the nature of the role that he/she assumes. Since role is an interactional concept, any role assumed by the social worker must be performed in interactions with others. It should be mentioned that roles (broker, advocate, therapist, educator, or mediator) are not automatically assumed or activated. Adopting the wrong role in a situation can have negative consequences. If the client is hungry, homeless, ill and the social worker assumes the role of a therapist, he/she will probably alienate the client and communication will be at cross-purposes. Such a situation relating to environmental need (resources) would indicate that the social worker would in responding to the client's need assume the role of social broker. The assumption of specific roles by the social worker in intervention should result from an assessment of the role (type of behavior to be exhibited in interactions with others) required in order to push the intervention forward or to achieve a specific purpose. Role enactment is the process by which the social worker exhibits the behavioral characteristics which are associated with specific roles. For example, if the social worker performs the role of an educator, the client assumes the role of learner; if the social worker assumes the role of behavioral changer, the client assumes the role of the individual whose behavior is to be changed. If the social worker assumes the role of an advocate, he/she is advocating for the client against a specific system.

CLASSIFICATORY SYSTEMS OF
SOCIAL WORK INTERVENTION (TREATMENT)

From its early history, efforts have been made by social work theorists to develop classification systems of social work practice. These classificatory systems or typologies of social work practice are intended to provide guides to practice relative to the specific techniques to be employed as these techniques relate to the intervention classification. Richmond (1922) proposed the classification of social work treatment into direct and indirect. Direct intervention referred to those processes that took place directly between the client and the social worker, i.e., "the influence of mind upon mind." Indirect treatment referred to those activities engaged in by the social worker on behalf of the client. The classification of tangible and intangible services provides a similar classificatory system. Tangible services are concrete in nature. A primary technique employed in tangible services is that of environmental manipulation. Examples of concrete services are helping the client to locate better housing, to secure health services or financial assistance. The advocacy role can also be employed in tangible services when the social worker seeks to modify dysfunctional organizational practices in which clients are treated in an inhumane manner. Intangible services are usually of a psychological nature and involves such techniques as insight development, clarification, and providing the client with a corrective experience.

Bibring (1947), Austin (1948) and Hollis (1949) have also proposed classificatory systems. Bibring identifies five procedures used by social workers and other professionals in the counseling process: suggestion, emotional relief, immediate influence, clarification and interpretation. Hollis's classification is divided into environmental manipulation and insight development. Later, she went on to develop the six procedures (identified above) in her psychosocial model. Austin's classification is divided into supportive therapy, insight therapy and experiential therapy. In 1953 and 1958, the Family Service Association of America proposed the treatment classification of maintenance and modification of adaptive patterns. Supportive casework and the use of environmental manipulation were identified as primary techniques used by the social worker when he/she attempted to maintain the adaptive patterns of the client. Essentially in the maintenance of adaptive patterns (Patterns refer to the manner in which the individual copes with life events.), the social worker seeks to provide those services which prevent further breakdown in the client's situation. For example, a woman who is recently divorced may seek voluntary placement for her child until she reestablishes herself. If the child is not placed and child care services are unavailable she risks losing employment. Insight development, clarification, interpretation and use of the corrective relationship were identified as techniques employed in the modification of the client's adaptive patterns when these patterns have resulted in stress for the client. As an example, the client may need to recognize his/her problem with authority and how it relates to earlier unresolved issues with an authoritative, critical parent whose approval the client feels that he/she never received. A corrective relationship with a nurturing social worker who can accept the client's reaction to authority without rejecting or criticizing him/her may be instrumental in assisting the client to work out some of these feelings. Reid (1967) identifies the nature of casework intervention in contacts with clients. Techniques identified by Reid were those of exploration concerning the client's milieu and his/her reaction to it, (2) exploration concerning the client's own behavior, (3) structuring the treatment relationship, (4) reassurance, (5) advice, (6) logical discussion, (7) identifying specific reactions, (8) confrontation, (9) clarifying current intrapsychic causation and (10) clarifying developmental causation. Kadushin (1980) provides the classification system of sociotherapy and psychotherapy for child welfare practice. His classification system is built around the concept of role dysfunctioning.

While a classification system has much utility for social work practice and provides guidelines to intervention, more work needs to be done in this area. The complex problems of today confronting the social worker demands that any classification system must make possible micro-messo and macro practice. The ecological perspective accommodates this need. In social group work, community work, family work and casework, the social worker must have available a wide range of techniques which enables him/her to intervene at any level of society. Messo and macro practice attempt in some way to bring about a degree of structural change at the neighborhood and societal levels. To achieve organizational and societal change, the social worker will need to develop skill in building coalitions, influencing these coalitions to take concerted actions in their own interest in bringing about institutional change. The social worker needs to be comfortable with conflict and may used such techniques as picketing, boycotting and demonstration in attempting to bring pressures on institutions.

While existing classifications are useful in sensitizing the social worker to the use of specific techniques in working with clients on certain problem areas, the above classifications are heavily psychologically oriented and for the most part are directed at achieving individual and not neighborhood or societal change. A general principle to guide the social worker in planning intervention is that when groups of clients are involved in a problem situation, particularly as this problem relates to a program, social policy, or the manner in which they are being treated, then a structural approach to practice is indicated. The foundation of these problems may be located in dysfunctional organizational procedures, the existence of unmet social needs or the failure of society to meet its obligations for securing the welfare of all of its citizens. When the author refers to structural change, he is referring to social work intervention which seeks to bring about some modification in the social structure of society, or to pressure organizations to change their practices when these practices are viewed as being dysfunctional and against the interest of client systems. Wood and Middleman (1989) state that their structural approach to practice seeks to modify the environmental needs of individuals (p. 13), and in the application of a structural approach to practice, the social worker should first focus on structural contributions to problems faced by the client system. If structural pressures do not exist, then the social worker can shift his/her attention to the psychic life of the client.

CONCLUSION

Intervention is the process by which the social worker, the client and significant others engage in specific activities which are directed at goal achievement. The intervention strategy is identified in the contract and has been developed as a result of the assessment process which has been used to identify the goals of intervention and the nature of the activities by which these goals can be accomplished. Before the social worker implements a planned intervention strategy, he/she should have (1) identified the nature of the client's situation, (2) isolated those conditions which contribute to it, (3) assisted the client in the selection of feasible and measurable goals and (4) identified the skills, techniques and activities which will be necessary in facilitation of the change process. The contract will detail the structure of intervention, the roles and responsibilities of the participants and the desired outcomes. The helping relationship or therapeutic alliance will provide the medium through which intervention is carried out as the social worker applies his/her knowledge, skills and the values of the profession in helping the client to improve his/her situation and problems in psychosocial functioning. Cynkins states that the intervention method should be viewed as the procedures and processes by which activities are organized, integrated and administered in the therapeutic program (p. 52).

In planned intervention, it is important that the social worker selects the appropriate activity for a given purpose. It is equally important that this activity is structured and implemented in a way that it has therapeutic objectives. The task of the social worker then becomes one of insuring that the activities are performed.

Recording continues to be an important aspect of practice even while intervention is proceeding. The social worker needs to reflect on and to analyze the contents and processes which characterize the interactions which take place between him/her, the client and the other participants in the change process. Recording will be important in evaluating the progress toward goal achievement, in analyzing the interactions which occur and in the identification of obstacles which need to be addressed. Intervention must always be viewed as being a cooperative process between the client and the social worker in which each will make contributions. The theoretical framework employed by the social worker will determine his/her analysis of the problem, what must be done about it, and the nature of the skills, techniques and activities which must be used if desired outcomes are to be achieved.

The social worker should always recognize that intervention is not approached in a haphazard manner. It is guided by knowledge, is deliberately and consciously planned and carried out in a disciplined manner. A classification system may have some utility in sensitizing the social worker to practice approaches based on the nature of the client's situation and the area(s) in which the problem presents itself.

SELECTED BIBLIOGRAPHY

Anderson, J. (1981) Social work methods and processes (Belmont, CA: Wadsworth Publishing Co.).

Austin, L. (1948) Trends in differential treatment in social casework, SOCIAL CASEWORK, 29, 203–211.

Bibring, G. (1947) Psychiatry and social work. SOCIAL CASEWORK, 28, 203–211.

Cynkins, S. (1979) Occupational therapy: Toward health through activities (Boston: Little Brown and Co.).

Hollis, F. (1949) The techniques of casework. SOCIAL CASEWORK, 30, 235–244.

Kadushin, A. (1980) Child welfare services. 3rd. ed. (New York: MacMillan Co.).

Middlemann, R. and Wood, G. (1990) Skills for direct practice in social work (New York: Columbia University Press).

Methods and process in social casework (1958) (New York: Family Service Association of America).

Reid, W. (1967). Characteristics of casework intervention, WELFARE IN REVIEW, 5, 11–19.

Richmond, M. (1917) Social diagnosis (New York: Russell Sage Foundation).

Scope and methods of the family service agency (1953) (New York: Family Service Association of America).

Schulman, L. (1984) The skills of helping individuals and groups (Itasca, IL: F.E. Peacock Publishers).

Wood, G. and Middlemann, R. (1989) The structural approach to direct practice (New York: Columbia University Press).

Woods, M. and Hollis, F. (1990). Casework: A psychosocial therapy. 4th. ed. (New York: McGraw Hill).

ADDITIONAL REFERENCES

Bartlett, H. (1970) The common base of social work practice (New York: National Association of Social Workers).

Berkowitz, S. (1955) Some specific techniques of psychosocial diagnosis and treatment in family casework. SOCIAL CASEWORK, 36, 399–406.

Gilbert, N. and Specht, H. (1981). Current models of social work practice. In N. Gilbert and H. Specht (Eds.). Emergence of social welfare and social work. 2nd. ed. (Itasca, IL: F.E. Peacock Publishers).

Sheafor, B., Horejsi, G. and Horejsi, G. (1988) Techniques and guidelines of social work practice (Boston: Allyn and Bacon).

Chapter 14

ENDINGS AND BREAKS
IN SOCIAL WORK PRACTICE

I nasmuch as the helping process is deliberately formed and maintained for the achievement of a specific purpose, it is only logical that this helping process will come to an end. Usually the end centers around goal achievement, but the social worker and client can end contacts through unplanned termination or the referral of the client to another source. Goal achievement is not the only reason for a planned ending. Endings can be precipitated by the lack of progress toward goal achievement, or it is determined that the client has gone as far as he/she can go and continual contacts would yield no greater improvement in his/her situation. Unplanned termination occurs when the client terminates contacts prematurely without prior notification to the social worker. Maluccio (1979) states that when clients terminate prematurely it is usually because they felt they have received what they were looking for, or they were dissatisfied with the services they were receiving (p. 18).

In addition to formal endings, social worker also must address other interruptions in their contacts with clients. These interruptions or breaks occur due to vacations and/or illnesses. Skills in the ending process of social work practice are extremely important. If endings or breaks are not handled in a skillful and planned manner, they may have adverse effects on the helping relationship and may result in a loss of gains for the client. The social worker also must be aware of his/her feelings toward endings as they can evoke feelings within him/her which may make it difficult for him/her to terminate even though goals have been achieved.

Hartman (1960) states if breaks are not handled carefully with the client and if they are not used as an integral part of the intervention plan, they may present barriers to the helping process and may result in premature withdrawal of the client from treatment. All people over the years have gone through some type of separation. These separations may have been traumatic or handled in a positive manner. However, earlier attitudes toward endings can be reactivated when termination draws near. A poor termination can wipe out all the gains made by the client and may lead to regressive behavior. In contrast, a sound planned termination skillfully handled should be viewed as a growth process and will be instrumental in the client consolidating the gains made in treatment. As a result of this positive ending and the consolidation of gains made in treatment, the client will be able to function in a constructive manner even when the social worker is no longer a part of his/her life. Consequently good endings are as important as good beginnings in practice.

DEFINITION OF ENDING/TERMINATION

A break may be defined as an interruption in a case. At a future point in time, contacts between the client and the social worker will resume. Several social work theorists have defined termination. Northen (1969) views termination as a dynamic and vital process in which a social service is discontinued by an individual or a group (p. 222). Goldstein (1976) suggests that the ending phase is a period of appraisal and a process of evaluating the outcomes of services. In this process, the social worker and client identify those factors which have contributed to or distracted from the achievement of desired goals (p. 274). In Goldstein's view, the ending phase of practice provides an opportunity for the social worker and client to review, summarize and evaluate the progress of a case. Fischer (1978) states that when the treatment goals as established in the contract have been achieved, and no other problem that may be amenable to work remains, then the formal programs of intervention can be terminated (p. 292).

REASONS FOR TERMINATION

Several reasons exist for formal terminations in the life of a case. Termination may result from (1) goal achievement, (2) a recognition that the client has made maximum use of services even though goals have not been achieved, (3) the client is referred to another service or (4) the social worker recognizes that the client is involving him/herself in a minimal manner and is not motivated to work on his/her situation. Termination also occurs when the client no longer continues with the agency and terminates contacts on his/her own volition. Sometimes a break may occur, in addition to those reasons already cited, when the social worker and client feel that a break from services may benefit the client by providing him/her with the opportunity to think about the helping process and if he/she wants to continue with it. Another reason for termination may occur when the social worker and client agree that they can not work together because of personality clashes and the case is reassigned to another worker.

PROCESS IN TERMINATION

The ending process should always be a planned one, and should not occur in a haphazard manner. It should center on the achievement of the goals stated in the contract. The social worker and the client have participated in an on-going evaluative process relative to the movement of the case toward goal achievement and an identification of those barriers which are affecting the capacity of the client to achieve his/her goals. It is evident that the contract review is an important aspect of the ending process.

Termination, ideally, follows goal achievement. The contract may contain the following statement: "Upon the achievement of stated goals, contacts with the agency will terminate unless other terms are negotiated." The social worker should inform the client in the beginning contacts that the assistance to be provided by the agency is time limited and when goals are achieved the contacts will come to a formal ending. Clients usually indicate more of a willingness to involve themselves more actively in the change process when they are made aware that it will come to an end. It is self-defeating to a client to think that a process will go on endlessly as it makes the client's situation appears hopeless. The termination feature connotes a positive feeling that the client can be helped. It is always important that the social worker and client engage in a process of evaluation of case movement. When an on-going evaluative process is occurring, the social worker is rarely surprised by an unplanned termination. He/she becomes sensitized to difficult issues, unexpressed feelings, and possibly feelings of withdrawal by the client from agency services. When this occurs, the social worker is able to address these feelings so that active work can continue on the case. Conditions such as barriers to communication, anger, the missing of appointments, and failure to follow through on assignment present clues to the client's growing disinterest in continuing services and may be a warning of an impending unplanned ending.

Termination as a process has a beginning, middle and ending phase. Hartford (1971) in social group work practice divides termination into three phases. The author thinks that these phases are applicable to the ending process with any client system (individual, family, the small group or community groups). These phases are (1) pretermination, (2) termination and (3) posttermination. The ending process should always be initiated early enough in the helping process to provide the client and the social worker with sufficient time to resolve the feelings which may be aroused by the approaching termination. Pretermination is the initial introduction of the subject to the client. This usually is initiated about six weeks prior to termination. Termination is the actual process of terminating agency services and posttermination is a follow-up to see how the client is progressing. Through posttermination contacts, the door to the agency remains open to the client and provides the opportunity for the social worker to evaluate how well the client has consolidated and applied to his/her life the gains made in treatment.

The social worker should always be the individual to initiate the process of ending. He/she has monitored the client's progress over time, has seen changes in his/her psychosocial functioning and coping abilities, has identified the degree to which goals have been achieved, and has arrived at the decision that the services of the agency are no longer indicated. In helping the client to actively participate in this process, the social worker recapitulates the following areas with the client:

(1) He/she identifies the state of the client at the time of initial contacts and identifies what assistance the client wanted from the agency.
(2) He/she identifies the goals of the case and how they were to contribute to an improvement in the client's situation.
(3) He/she identifies the work performed by the client during his/her period of contact with the agency and the manner in which the client is now performing in his/her life. The social worker may provide examples of the client's capacity to deal more effectively with problems which were very stressful at the point of initial contacts.
(4) He/she assists the client in revealing how significant others have responded to the client's progress, and he/she reminds the client that life is a matter of problem-solving. However, it is pointed out that with the progress made in treatment that problem-solving will not be as difficult as it has been in the past. It is important that the social

worker does not convey to the client that now all is right with his/her world. Rather, he/she wants to convey to the client a sense of empowerment in addressing future problems as a result of the gains made in treatment.

(5) He/she actively encourages the client to participate in this review process.

(6) He/she seeks to actively set the stage for future problem solving on the client's part in the absence of the worker. Thus, the ending process may take on the attributes of a graduation, a commencement in which the client is expected to apply to his/her life the skills and knowledge gained in the intervention process.

(7) He/she should always encourage the client to feel free to contact the agency in the future if indicated. This information is presented as an indication of strength on the part of the client and not as a sign of failure.

In the ending process, a primary responsibility of the social worker is to assist the client in consolidating and incorporating into his/her problem-solving repetoire the knowledge and skills which he/she has gained from his/her contacts with the social worker.

REACTIONS TO ENDINGS

The social worker is aware and sensitive to the fact that endings are anxiety provoking both for him/her and the client. Each will exhibit specific reactions to termination. As stated earlier, termination should center around goal-achievement. In the absence of goals, the social worker will be ill-prepared to introduce the process of termination. Knowledge of the behavior associated with termination enables the social worker to assist the client in dealing with it in a constructive manner. When termination is introduced, the client may exhibit signs of regression, apathy, feelings of hopelessness and anger. Maholick and Turner (1979) state that termination represents an analogy as to how we have addressed the farewells of our lives (p. 103). As this time approaches, old problems may reappear or new problems emerge. The client may miss appointments and become argumentative with the social worker. He/she may challenge the competencies of the social worker, and may withdraw early from contacts as he/she desires to reject the worker before the worker rejects him/her. The client may also seek to cloak his/her feelings by denying any reactions to the ending of contacts. Themes usually emerge around termination such as uncertainty (how can I go on without you), mourning (why are you doing this to me?), anxiety (what will I do without you?) and an exaggerated dependency on the social worker may emerge. It is the knowledge of the client's reactions to termination that enables the social worker to address these feelings as a normative reaction to what is perceived by the client as a great personal loss. With the continual acceptance and support of the social worker, the client will eventually regain his/her impetus toward growth and realistically accept the fact that the social worker is not deserting him/her. In effect if the client sees the value in termination, he/she will validate the social worker's efforts and roles in bringing him/her to this point.

The social worker may be hesitant in ending the client's contacts with the agency. A review of the record will indicate that the goals have been achieved, but the social worker resists termination. Supervision, and peer consultation will be useful in alerting the social worker to his/her feelings toward termination so that he/she may not keep the client for his/her own needs past the time when contractual terms have been fulfilled.

Skills in ending and in handling breaks are an important aspect of social work practice. A skillful ending can be of importance in assisting the client to consolidate the gains which he/she has accrued from the intervention process. A poor ending may result in regressive behaviors on the part of the client and unplanned termination. Endings should be introduced in the beginning of social work contacts. They are closely related to goal achievement. When the social worker evaluates that goals have been achieved, he/she should introduce the ending process. Endings should always be planned, and the social worker may recapitulate the helping process in helping the client to see the gains that he/she has made in goal achievement.

CONCLUSION

Social work intervention with individuals, families, small group revolves around three phases:

(1) *Beginnings:* In the initial contacts with clients, the social worker engages in developing an understanding of the client's situation, developing the helping relationship, collecting and analyzing data, establishing goals, formulating a contract and planning an intervention strategy,

(2) *Middle phase:* In this phase which is essentially the treatment phase or

the implementation of the change strategy, the social worker, client and involved others resolve conflicts and work cooperatively on problem-solving tasks which are goal-directed,

(3) *Termination:* In this phase, the concluding phase of the provision of social work services, services to the client system are terminated, ideally based on goal achievement. Other reasons may also exist for termination: (1) referral to another agency, (2) reassignment within the agency which is also a form of termination in that past relationships are concluded, or (3) a lack of progress is evident which suggests that no gains will be accrued from future contacts.

The social worker should be prepared to deal with the dynamics which surround termination and to allocate sufficient time for this purpose. Termination should be introduced to the client at the beginning of contacts so that he/she may know the time constraints under which help is to be provided, the work that will characterize the helping process, and the goals which are expected to be accomplished. The social worker throughout the life of the case is continuously monitoring and evaluating the work that is performed and the progress that is being made. When the situation which brought the client to the agency has shown improvement and the client through his/her behavior is acting in a more autonomous manner and has moved away from dependency on the social worker in addressing his/her life affairs, then the social worker can feel confident that the goals of the case have been achieved and his/her assistance is no longer required.

SELECTED BIBLIOGRAPHY

Fischer, J. (1978) Effective casework practice: An eclectic approach (New York: McGraw-Hill).

Goldstein, H. (1976) Social work practice: A unitary approach (Columbia, S.C.: University of South Carolina Press).

Hartford, M. (1971) Groups in social work (New York: Columbia University Press).

Hartman, A. (1960) The use of the worker's vacation in casework treatment. SOCIAL CASEWORK, XLI, 310–313.

Maholick, L. and Turner, D. (1985) Termination: That difficult farewell. In A. Briggs and A. Agrin (Eds.) Crossroad: A reader for psychosocial occupational therapy. 4th printing (Rockville, MD.: American Occupational Therapy Association, Inc.).

Maluccio, A. (1979) Learning from clients: Interpersonal helping as viewed by clients and social workers (New York: The Free Press).

Northen, H. (1969) Social work with groups (New York: Columbia University Press).

ADDITIONAL REFERENCES

Fox, E., Nelson, M. and Bolman, W. (1963) The termination process: A neglected dimension in social work. SOCIAL WORK, 14, 53–63.

Johnson, C. (1974) Planning for termination of the group. In P. Glasser, R. Sarri and R. Vinter (Eds.) Individual change through the small group (New York: The Free Press).

Levinson, H. (1977). Termination of psychotherapy: Some salient issues. SOCIAL CASEWORK, 58, 480–498.

Moss, S. and Moss, M. (1967) When a caseworker leaves an agency: The impact on worker and client. SOCIAL CASEWORK, 48, 433–37.

Sarri, R. and Galinsky, M. (1974) A conceptual framework for group development. In P. Glasser, R. Sarri and R. Vinter (Eds.) Individual change through the small group (New York: The Free Press).

SECTION V
THE PRACTICE OF SOCIAL WORK

INTRODUCTION

S ocial work practice consists of the application of knowledge, values and skills to the problems of client system. Basically it is the social worker in action as he/she assumes certain roles and orchestrates specific activities which are directed at goal achievement. The first several parts of this book have focused on (1) the functions of social work in American society, (2) the organizations in which it is practiced, (3) the knowledge base of social work practice, (4) the skills employed by the social worker in the change process and (5) the value base of the profession which serves as a guide to ethical practice in contacts with client systems. The focus now turns to the manner in which these attributes are demonstrated in social work practice.

Social workers meet all clients with the following attributes: (1) a general fund of knowledge about people and their situations (This knowledge becomes more specific as the social worker individualizes the client); (2) the capacity to apply skills, technical and process-oriented, in his/her contacts with clients and (3) the acquisition of a value system which enables him/her to perform in an ethical and professional manner with clients.

In practice, the social worker is expected to engage in the research function both as a means of evaluating his/her practice effectiveness and in making contributions to the knowledge base of practice. Research should result in an identification of how the profession can best meet the needs of the clients it serves. The knowledge gained from research must contribute to the improvement of the practice of social work.

It is important that the social worker recognizes that knowledge is accumulative, and that what he/she learns from one case can be transferred to another case. Following is a schematic view of social work practice over time (beginning, middle and ending phases) and the contents which characterize each phase:

Route to the Agency: Self-referred, referred by others, or mandated.

Status: Voluntary or Involuntary client.

Initial Contacts
(Beginning Phase): In planning the initial contact, the social worker may engage in a process of preparatory empathy (Schulman, 1984) in which he/she attempts to sensitive him/herself to the client's situation and to imagine how the client feels about being at the agency. In preparing him/herself for the initial meeting, the social worker thinks of the purpose of the interview, the reasons for client contacts, the nature of the questions he/she needs to ask to secure information on the client's situation. He/she prepares him/herself to address the client's ambivalency and to encourage the client's full participation in the interview. The social worker will employ a theoretical orientation as a means of attempting to make sense of the client's problem (What is its nature? Why does he/she have it? What is its duration? What has the client attempted to do about it in the past? How does the client want the agency to be of services to him/her? A desired outcome of the beginning phase is that the client will move from the status of being an applicant to that of clienthood. Essential tasks to be implemented during the beginning phase are:

(1) Exploring the client's situation,
(2) Explaining the agency's function to the client,
(3) Explaining the role of the social worker,
(4) Engaging the client in the helping process and seeking client's feedback on the information given to him/her by the social worker,
(5) Establishing the helping relationship,
(6) Engaging in data collection
(7) Engaging in data analysis (assessment)
(8) Establishing mutual goals (feasible and realistic),

(9) Formulating a contract
(10) Planning Intervention.

The social worker should be cognizant of the fact that the route by which the client comes to the agency will influence the nature of his/her behavior in the beginning contacts. The involuntary client may present problems with authority, reveal a negative attitude, hostile feelings and generally present a reluctance to engage in agency's services. He/she may frequently present a lack of knowledge as to the reasons for the agency's contact. He/she does not have a problem and only comes to the agency under coercion. If the social worker has engaged in the process of "preparatory empathy" then he/she will find himself more able to deal with this behavior. The process of engaging the involuntary client may proceed from conflict to bargaining and negotiation and finally some consensus on how the client will make use of agency's services. In contrast the voluntary client comes with a recognition of the need for services and may move quickly into the development of the therapeutic alliance. However, the voluntary client may also show signs of ambivalence toward full commitment to the status of clienthood. He/she will be attracted by what the agency offers, but fearful of entering into the unknown. He/she may view coming to the agency as a sign of weakness or failure in which he/she will be called on to reveal his/her fault. The social worker must remember that in this stage he/she represents a stranger to the client and must use his/her skills in conveying his/her desire to be of help to the client. The social worker recognizes the unspoken messages which are contained in the client's verbalizations, regardless of the client's route to agency services, and articulates these statements, their feelings and meanings for the client. To ease the client's anxiety, the social worker may need to reframe them in a more positive manner. Always, the social worker should recognize the strengths shown by the client in coming to the agency. The social worker should never present a moral judgment on the client's behavior even though the behavior may be of a repulsive nature to him/her. The social worker always recognizes that it is the existence of a problem that has brought the client to the agency, and that his/her role is to assist the client in its resolution to whatever possible degree. When the client exhibits the motivation to work on his/her situation and feels that the agency's services can assist him/her, then the middle phase of practice can be initiated. The social worker may begin this phase with a tentative or working assessment of the client's situation. This tentative assessment has led to the formulation of an intervention strategy. Based on additional data, the assessment may be refined.

Middle or Work Phase:

This phase constitutes the work phase of practice. The client and the social worker engage in problem-solving strategies. It is characterized by the active involvement of the client and the social worker in those activities which are viewed as being essential to goal achievement. The four basic systems of social work practice are activated. All participants are assigned specific roles and functions to perform. Obstacles to the success of the change strategy are identified and addressed. The middle phase (formal intervention) is constantly monitored and evaluated for its effectiveness.

Always the activities implemented during this phase are goal oriented. Effective communication is vital in this stage. The social worker uses interpersonal skills in maintaining and strengthening the helping relationship, and he/she and the client work cooperatively with other systems who are involved in the change process.

Termination or Endings/ Transitions Phase:

Movement toward the termination phase is brought on by time constraints (the time allocated for contacts) or goal achievement. This phase usually has three distinctive stages: pretermination, actual termination and posttermination (follow-up). Pretermination is usually initiated at least six weeks in advance of formal termination, and at that time the formal date for termination is established. Posttermination contacts may occur several weeks following formal termination.

This phase is extremely dynamic in nature. It is characterized by the reactions of the client and the social worker to the ending process. In this phase, the social worker summarizes the work performed by him/her and the client from the beginning stage of contacts. The client is assisted in reviewing his/her progress, identifying the goals achieved, and to articulate how the goals have assisted him/her to manage his/her life affairs in a less-stressful manner. The social worker also may ask the client for examples of how he/she has applied the learning gained in counseling to his/her life situation.

The emphasis in this phase is on the growth of the client, and the preparation of the client to carry on without the active involvement of the social worker. While a formal ending or termination of agency services, this phase is best viewed as one of transition for the client. It should signal a new beginning for the client in his/her future problem solving. However, the client should be forewarned of possible set-backs and the continual availability of agency services if he/she feels the need to return. Follow-up provides the opportunity to evaluate the effectiveness of social work intervention.

OVERVIEW OF SOCIAL WORK PRACTICE

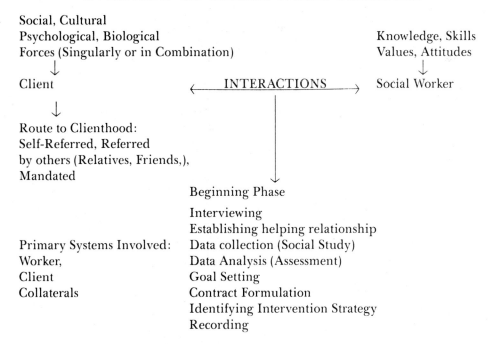

Social, Cultural
Psychological, Biological
Forces (Singularly or in Combination)   Knowledge, Skills
       Values, Attitudes
   ↓   ↓

Client   ← INTERACTIONS →   Social Worker

   ↓

Route to Clienthood:
Self-Referred, Referred
by others (Relatives, Friends,),
Mandated

                           ↓

                         Beginning Phase

                         Interviewing
                         Establishing helping relationship

Primary Systems Involved: Data collection (Social Study)
Worker,   Data Analysis (Assessment)
Client   Goal Setting
Collaterals   Contract Formulation
                         Identifying Intervention Strategy
                         Recording

$\downarrow$

Middle (Work) Phase

Implementing Intervention Strategy
(Identification of Target System

Primary Systems Involved: Implementation of Action System)
Worker   Task Identification
Client   Work Assignments
Action   Role Enactment
target   Designing and implementing goal-oriented activities
                                                  Monitoring and Evaluating Change
                                                  Strategies
                                                  Recording

$\downarrow$

Termination (Endings/Transitions)

Primary Systems
Involved   Identification of Goal Achievement
                                                  Pretermination

Worker   Termination
Client   Posttermination (Follow-up)
Action   Evaluation of Practice Effectiveness
Target*   Recording

*Worker-Client System
Terminated.
Action System Disbanded.
Target System Changed.

The client comes to the agency as a product of his/her social environment bringing with him/her personality and cultural factors. The impact of these variables have affected his/her problem solving skills and psychosocial functioning to the degree that he/she seeks help.

The social worker meets the client with a constellation of knowledge, values, skills and attitudes which taken together and applied to the client's situation constitutes social work practice.

The client and the social worker will carry out the helping process through communication procedures, interactions, the use of specific techniques and identifiable actions.

Social work practice is carried out in a planned manner and it is this planning which prevents poor or inadequate performance by the social worker.

Chapter 15

APPLICATION OF KNOWLEDGE, SKILLS, VALUES, PROCEDURES IN BEGINNING PHASE

The beginning phase of social work practice signals a process of helping which will move logically and sequentially through the middle and ending phases of contacts. A process represents a movement over time in which specific procedures directed at goal accomplishment are continuously implemented. Within this process, procedures, skills and knowledge are applied. The social worker and the client interact and work cooperatively in identifying the nature of the problem to be addressed, in developing a therapeutic bond, in identifying the goals to be achieved and the actions which can be instrumental in achieving them. Eriksen (1981) refers to the helping process as a learning experience which engages two people in problem solving through the use of the helping relationship and skills in interviewing (p. 18).

In the beginning phase, interviewing is an extremely important skill. The social worker must be involved in "listening, observing, questioning and acting." He/she must show sensitivity to the presentation of verbal and nonverbal communication as revealed in the client's clothing, posture, body movements and tone of voice as the client presents his/her story. The beginning phase commences with an exploration of the specific problem which brings the client to the agency. This exploration will focus on the present situation and the immediate past contributions to the client's stress. Cockerill et al. (1956) state "Professional practice proceeds from a clear set of principles and concepts about human being and their needs" (p. 5). According to Cockerill et al., these concepts constitute a logical justification for social work practice. In their opinion if the social worker is able to clearly explain his/her practice framework and the activities and techniques which characterize it, then the social worker will be able to explain his/her actions to others, the purposes to which they are directed and to evaluate his/her interventions for its effectiveness.

In the beginning process the social worker will direct his/her line of inquiry about the client's problem to seeking answers to several questions: (1) What is its nature? (2) How does it present itself? (3) In what general context is its present felt? This line of inquiry will generally yield sufficient data for the formulation of an assessment. The social worker also has a clear understanding of those individuals to whom he/she will be held accountable: (1) the client system, (2) his/her employing agency, (3) his/her profession which gives sanction to his/her practice and (4) the society which he/she represents.

PREPARATION

The preparation process in which the social worker engages as he/she prepares to meet the client for the first time in a series of sessions contributes greatly to the effectiveness of client contacts. Preparation prevents intervention from being performed in a haphazard manner and is characterized by several activities in which the social worker engages:

(1) The social worker examines the information presented by the client on the intake form, or contained in the case record relative to his/her service request. While the presenting problem may not be the real problem, but merely represents a symptom of a more pervasive problem in the life of the client, the social worker should be prepared to "begin where the client is" and to proceed at his/her pace. To move ahead of the client is to risk premature withdrawal from agency services. Beginning contacts should always focus specifically on the problem presented by the client or the referral source.

(2) This data should lead the social worker into a speculative process as to its meaning to the client and the manner in which he/she should present him/herself. The social worker may ponder on the nature of the information to be acquired, the type of questions to be asked (line of inquiry), the manner in which to structure the interview so that the client's anxiety will not be greatly aroused and the interview can be facilitated. The social worker may wonder about the duration of the problem and the forces which bring the client to the agency at this time. He/she may wonder about similar problems with which he/she has worked and what he/she gained from those cases that can be of value in this case. The social worker is always cognizant of the need to show flexibility in order to address the more urgent needs of the client. No prestructured plan can be strictly adhered to as it robs the interview of spontaneity and creativity and may create barriers to communication.

(3) If the client has previously been active with the agency, or if a report has been sent by the referring agency, the social worker may or may not select to review these resources in developing an understanding of what has gone on in the client's past. If the social worker elects to study these materials, he/she must guard against contamination by allowing this material to influence his/her view of the client.

(4) In applying knowledge to practice, the social worker should relate the information presented by the client to his/her stage of development in the life cycle or the family development cycle in order to identify the tasks confronting the client system. This information is of value in identifying those forces which interfere with task accomplishment.

TASKS

A task is best conceptualized as a unit of work. The beginning phase is basically a fact-gathering one in which the social worker simultaneously engages in several procedures: relationship building, data collection and data analysis. Following the completion of these tasks, he/she moves on to the tasks of goal setting, contract formulation and intervention planning. Data collection and analysis make it possible for the social worker to develop an understanding of the client system, the nature of the problem presented and to develop hypotheses as to the reasons for the problem existence. In this phase, the social worker engages in exploration of the client's situation while attempting to actively engage the client in this process. As stated previously, the social worker applies knowledge and skills in

- problem identification
- actively engaging the client in the helping process
- building the helping relationship
- securing relevant data to understand nature of client situation
- analysis of data to identify those conditions which are stress inducing and in locating points for intervention
- developing an intervention plan
- establishing mutual goals with the client system
- formulating a contract

Success in carrying out these tasks is heavily dependent on skillful interviewing, the warmth and caring attitude presented by the social worker and the use of skillful recording in which the social worker reflects over and analyzes the data that he/she has received. When these tasks are accomplished, the social worker and the client can move into the middle phase of social work practice. To a degree, social work practice is always characterize by beginnings as new information presents itself or other urgent problems may surface. Each interview itself is characterized by a beginning, middle and ending phase. Developing motivation and commitment from the client may continue for several sessions. Sometimes a goal for the social worker, which is not shared with the client, is the building of a trusting relationship with the client. Many times, this is necessary as some clients are extremely ambivalent toward agency services, are mistrustful and do not easily enter into relationships. Until a relationship is developed, these clients will not commit themselves to agency services, will constantly challenge the social worker and seeks reasons for termination. Ripple, Alexander and Polemis (1966) in one of the earliest works on client motivation found that the client's effective use of services was dependent on motivation, capacity and opportunity.

BUILDING THE THERAPEUTIC ALLIANCE

The development of the therapeutic alliance or the helping relationship is an expected outcome of the beginning phase. In its absence, little meaningful work will be accomplished and stress and mistrust will characterize the helping relationship. Parsons (1985) states the primary responsibility of the counselor in this phase is to facilitate the development of the helping relationship. In order to do this, the social worker must be able to skillfully engage the client. This objective is facilitated when the social worker demonstrates such qualities as caring, acceptance, warmth, respect, congruency, honesty, integrity and an unconditioned positive regard. The social worker must also engage in active listening and place the client at the center of attention as he/she tells her story. Crucial to the development of the therapeutic alliance and developing client's motivation is the installation of hope and a vision of what can be accomplished. The client may present an apathetic attitude and feel that his/her situation is hopeless. These feelings can be tempered by the social worker's use of the technique of universalization. In this technique, the social worker remarks on how other clients have been helped who have viewed their situations as being helpless. The expression of these qualities by the social worker is necessary if a therapeutic environment is to be created.

SKILLS

Social work theorists (Smalley, 1967; Henry, 1981; Johnson, 1986 and Schulman, 1991) use the word skills differently. Lowenberg (1977) views interviewing, engagement, communication, assessment and intervention as being core social work skills. In the author's view, skills are those actions implemented by the social worker in the change process. The use of skills implies expertise on the part of the social worker in their application. Social work skills can be categorized into several categories: interpersonal, process, technical and procedural. Essentially all social work skills can be viewed legitimately as being of an interactional, interpersonal or helping nature. Interpersonal skills characterize the interactions between the social worker and the client as they engage in the communication and helping process. These skills are interactional and affective in nature. As a result of interpersonal skills, the helping relationship is built nurtured and given direction. Communications are clarified; feelings are responded to, and the client is encouraged to actively participate in the intervention process. Schulman (1991) identifies clarifying roles, articulating the client's feelings, helping the client to manage these feelings and helping the client to manage their problems as core skills. Technical skills are basically of an analytical nature; they reveal technical expertise in such areas as data collection, data analysis, and planning and implementing intervention. Technical skills imply thinking on the part of the social worker about the client, his/her problems, the reasons for them, and what type of intervention is indicated. Process skills are also interactional in nature. They are directed at implementing and facilitating specific processes which are crucial to developing, implementing and carrying out intervention strategies. Process skills are revealed in building relationships, forming an action system, influencing client systems to mobilize and act in their own interests. Process is revealed in implementing specific actions in a logical and sequential manner. Procedural skills are those behaviors exhibited by the social worker as he/she performs certain functions which are viewed as being extremely important to the effectiveness of intervention. These procedural skills would include interviewing, goal setting, and contract formulation. Other procedural skills which are also of a technical nature are data collection, analysis, intervention and termination.

Recording is an extremely important skill in the beginning phase of social work practice. The assessment and intervention strategy are more sound if the social worker records the data, reflects over the information collected, applies a theoretical framework to it, and draws inference from the data. The social worker will find it difficult to analyze data unless the data are organized in some manner. Organization in the worker's head is difficult.

KNOWLEDGE

It has been stated that the social worker should approach all clients with a general fund of knowledge about people and their situations. It has also been stated previously that the knowledge base of social work practice generally derives from three specific areas: human behavior and the social environment, social welfare policies and social work methods. Human behavior and the social environment provide knowledge by which the social worker develops understanding of the impact of social, cultural, physiological and psychological forces on the psychosocial functioning of the client. This knowledge base enables the social worker to develop understanding of social systems, how they should work, and the forces which impact adversely on them. Social welfare policies help social workers to understand the program developed by society to address common human needs and the values which underpin them. In analyzing social welfare policies, the social worker develops understanding of societal goals and how they lead to the development of specific programs. Organizational theory helps the social worker to understand the workings of organization and the impact of organizational policies on his/her practice and the service delivery system. Methods provide the social worker with a scientific approach to problem solving. Through the application of a theoretical framework to the data collected in sequential steps from the client system, social study, diagnosis and treatment, the social worker is able to locate points for intervention so that the client's problem can be addressed.

SELECTED BIBLIOGRAPHY

Cockerill, E. et al. (1965) A conceptual framework for social casework (Pittsburg, PA.: University of Pittsburg Press).
Eriksen, K. (1981) Human services today (Reston, VA: Reston Publishing Co.).
Henry, S. (1981) Group skills in social work (Itasca, IL: F.E. Peacock Publishers).

Johnson, L. (1986) Social work practice: A generalist approach, 2nd. ed. (Newton, MA: Allyn and Bacon).

Loewenberg, F. M. (1977) Fundamentals of social intervention (New York: Columbia University Press).

Parsons, R. (1985) The counseling relationship. In R. Wicks, R. Parsons, and D. Capps (Eds.). Clinical handbook of pastoral counseling (New York: Integration Books/ Paulist Press).

Ripple, L. Alexander, E. and Polimis, B. (1964) Motivation, capacity, and opportunity (Chicago: University of Chicago press Monographs).

Schulman, L. (1991) Interactional social work practice (Itasca, IL: F.E. Peacock Publishers).

Smalley, R. (1967) Theory for social work practice (New York: Columbia University Press).

ADDITIONAL REFERENCES

Cournoyer, B. (1991) The social work skills notebook (Belmont, CA: Wadsworth Publishing Co.).

Egan, G. (1982) The skilled helper: Model, skills and methods for effective helping, 2nd. ed. (Monterey, CA: Brooks/Cole).

Chapter 16

APPLICATION OF KNOWLEDGE, SKILLS, VALUES, AND PROCEDURES IN MIDDLE PHASE

In the beginning phase of social work contacts, the social worker completes the essential work which is necessary before a formal plan of intervention is implemented. He/she has (1) identified the nature of the problem, and its impact on the client's system, (2) isolated the contributing factors, (3) discussed his/her findings with the client system, (4) engaged in goal setting and contract formulation and (5) formulated an intervention strategy. The middle or work phase of practice is characterized by the performance of specific actions on the parts of the client, the social worker, and significant others who are involved in the case. These actions are rationally planned, directed at specific targets and are goal-oriented. In this process, the social worker continues to apply knowledge, skills and values to the change process while engaging in specific procedures. In this phase, the four systems of social work practice are activated. The success of the change effort will be closely related to the competencies of the social worker in orchestrating and implementing those actions which are essential if stated goals are to be achieved. Depending on the nature of the work to be performed, the social worker may select one or several roles out of his/her role repetoire to enact: educator, social broker, advocate, mediator, negotiator, consultant or behavioral changer.

INTERVENTION STRATEGY

Social work intervention is a planned process which is directed at the modification or eradication of those conditions which are identified as having an adverse impact on the psychosocial functioning of the client. In planning intervention, the social worker must decide where its focus should be directed and at what level(s) of society: micro-messo-macro. Targets of change need to be identified, and the manner in which these targets are impacting on the client assessed. The intervention program constitutes a specific strategy which is deliberately designed and executed. It encompasses all of the activities engaged in by the participants. Basically, a strategy results from a planning process. In designing the intervention strategy, the worker gives consideration to the problem presented by the client, the characteristics of the client, the goals to be achieved, and the necessary activities that must be implemented. The outcome goals are dependent on the process goals, i.e., what must be done if goals are to be achieved.

The goals of the case and the target(s) of change heavily influence the nature of the intervention strategy. If the change program is to be effective, the client should be totally involved in its planning. The client's lack of commitment to the intervention strategy constitutes an obstacles which must be addressed. Since the intervention is a part of a process (work phase of practice) moving toward a desired outcome, it is possible that activities and strategies may need to be modified at various time intervals depending upon the presentation of new data, or a recognition that new action systems need to be composed, or that stated goals are impractical. It is important that the client is informed that intervention may hold negative consequences for him/her. The client may possess legitimate fears about engaging in specific actions which may hold negative consequences for him/her. He/she needs to be informed of this possibility. In exercising self-determination, the client may choose not to pursue a specific area of intervention, or the social worker may need to use persuasion in assisting the client to engage in the change effort.

APPLICATION OF KNOWLEDGE, SKILLS AND VALUES

In order for the intervention to move forward in a progressive manner, the social worker must guide it and not allow it to flounder. Intervention is carried forward in a desired manner through the application of knowledge, skills, procedures and techniques implemented by the social worker. The theoretical orientation employed by the social worker will influence him/her to carry out certain functions and activities. DeBlassie (1976) refers to counseling strategies and techniques as those practice and verbal and nonverbal skills used by the counselor to achieve specific goals designed to bring about desired outcomes (p. 99). Social work skills are revealed in the process of interpersonal communications between the social worker and the client such as active listening, addressing taboo areas, providing information, seeking feedback from the client on information provided, dealing with client's resistance, providing the client with support and engaging the client in problem-solving. Other skills of an interpersonal nature used by the social worker are restating, clarifying, summarizing, questioning, exploring, interpreting, reflecting feelings, confronting, empathizing, enabling, facilitating, suggesting, modeling, self-disclosing, and dealing with silence. The social worker continues to engage in such procedures as data collection, analysis, recording, and activities such as holding conferences with members of the action system, seeking and sharing information with participants, planning strategies, interviewing collaterals and when indicated holding sessions with target systems relative to negotiating, seeking conciliation and resolving conflicts.

Social work techniques or communication procedures will be directed at achieving individual and or environmental change. Environmental change or environmental manipulation is an important focus of social work practice. Grinnell and Kyte (1975) define environmental manipulation as an interventive technique which involves the provision of practical services and/or the modification of the behavior of significant others involved in interactions with the client. They divide environmental manipulation into two categories: concrete and sociopsychological. Concrete is helping the client to receive a concrete service such as housing or financial assistance. Sociopsychological techniques are directed toward achieving some change in the client's environment which relates to removing some of the pressures under which the client is functioning.

Case management is basically an environmental approach to practice. Its focus is on identifying client's needs, linking clients to resources and monitoring and evaluating these resources for their effectiveness. The objective of case management is to provide clients with multiple needs with a variety of services directed at sustaining and maintaining them in the community. In environmental work, the social worker is frequently called on to assume the role of an advocate as he/she directs his/her efforts at influencing community institutions to be responsive to client's needs.

Specific techniques can also be used in seeking to improve the client's problem solving capacities through greater awareness of his/her needs and how he/she functions. Insight development, the corrective emotional experience, clarification, reassurance and interpretation are some of the techniques which are associated with the problem solving and psychosocial approaches to practice. Many of these techniques are incorporated into the six communication procedures identified by Woods and Hollis (1990) in their psychosocial therapy. A general rule in psychosocial and problem-solving approaches is that the weaker the ego the greater the emphasis on ego-supportive techniques and environmental manipulation, and the stronger the ego strengths the greater the emphasis on the development of psychological awareness of how one's behaviors impact on people and lead to stress in interpersonal relations.

In Behavioral Social Work, the social worker may attempt to extinguish or diminish behavior viewed as being maladaptive through such techniques as token economy, assertiveness training, modeling and behavioral rehearsal. The use of these techniques is predicated on the behaviorist's basic assumption that since behavior is learned and maintained by contingencies in the environment, it can also be unlearned through the application of specific techniques. The techniques to be employed and the treatment regimen directed at bringing about change result from a behavioral analysis of the maladaptive behaviors and the environmental contingencies which maintain it.

In Client-Centered Therapy, the social worker may use the techniques of reflection, unconditioned positive regard, establishing rapport, showing genuine empathy, consistency and authenticity in helping the client to grow, to recognize his/her power in making decisions, and to self-actualize him/herself as a result of the discovery gained through the relationship. The encounters between the social worker and the client are viewed in and of themselves as growth-inducing. The social worker believes that the client knows the answers to his/her situation, and the task of the social worker is to aid the client in this discovery.

In crisis intervention, the social worker enlists the cognitive capacities of the client in problem-solving following the identification of the event (crisis) which hampers the usual problem-solving capacities of the client and places him/her in a state of crisis. The social worker is supportive, attempts to instill a sense of hope, builds on the client's ego strengths and connects the client to personal and community resources which can be instrumental in decreasing the intensity of the crisis so that it is gradually abated. In crisis intervention, the social worker provides the services within a specific time period. The objective is to restore the client to a precrisis or higher level of functioning. The social worker's behavior is active and directive, and a minimum of attention, if any, is given to historical information. The use of time in a constructive manner so that the crisis is resolved necessitates the use of a present orientation to practice in crisis intervention.

MICRO–MESSO–MACRO PRACTICE

The psychosocial, problem-solving, client-centered, behavioral modification and crisis intervention approaches are usually client or family focused approaches. They can also be used with the small group. Their desired outcome is basically of an adaptive nature as the individual is assisted to develop those competencies and skills which will enable him/her to adjust in a more adaptive manner to his/her environment. While they do accomodate the dual foci of social work practice, people in interactions with their environment, their change focus is individual in nature and directed at micro level intervention. Micro-level practice is client-centered, involves working with individuals, families, or small groups, the smallest social units of society, on interpersonal problems which are brought about by psychological stresses and pressures from the environment. Messo-level practice involves working with neighborhood organizations in the interests of families or clients who are adversely affected in some manner by their operations. In messo-level practice, the social worker stands between the client system and the organization which are involved in stressful transactions. Macro-level practice requires that the social worker directs his/her attention at the highest levels of society (city, county, state and federal government) as he/she seeks to bring about new programs to meet human need, or to bring about some change in existing policies and laws. As stated previously, social policy objectives lead to the establishment of programs which are directed at providing specific services which are consistent with certain objectives. Sometimes, these programs are not implemented according to the guidelines established by the government. The social worker's attempt to bring such programs into conformity with federal guidelines would be viewed as an example of macro and messo practice inasmuch as the mandated services are provided through organizations at the neighborhood or city and county levels.

Some social work theorists have presented practice models which can accomodate messo- and marco-level practice. Wood and Middlemann (1989) propose a structural model for direct social work practice. The basic assumption of this approach is that clients are not sick individuals; their problems are viewed as being a result of inadequate social arrangement. In contacts with clients, the social worker rules out structural contributions to the problem before focusing on the psychological difficulties of the client. The thrust of this approach is to improve the relationship which exists between people and their social environment. When structural change is accomplished, the psychosocial functioning of the client is improved and those conditions which contribute to human suffering are eradicated or modified. A focus on social development is also viewed as macro practice. Hollister (1977) identifies the core skills in social development as those of policy analysis, social planning, community organization, administration, program evaluation and social advocacy (p. 11). Hollister expresses the view that the practice of social development calls for a generalist social worker. The integrated approach to practice seeks to accomplish micro-messo and macro practice by focusing on the problem, those conditions which contribute to it, and attempting to achieve systemic change at whatever level of practice indicated.

INTERVENTIVE ROLES

The social worker will enact various roles in this phase of practice. These roles are viewed as being necessary to the success of the change effort, and they are not automatically assumed and enacted by the social worker. In the assessment process, the social worker will identify those roles that will be necessary in addressing the client's situation. He/she will eventually select one or several roles as being compatible with the change strategy and the goals to be achieved. The social worker is always cognizant of the fact that the desired outcome must be consistent with one or several of the objectives of social work practice. The roles assumed by the social worker will be employed in facilitating the intervention process, in performing specific functions, and in achieving specific objectives.

ESSENCE OF WORK PHASE

The middle phase of social work practice may be referred to as the intervention or work period. It is characterized by active interactions on the parts of the social worker, the client, and the action system. The intervention focuses on achieving some modification in the behavior of the target system. The social worker assumes specific roles, performs certain tasks and applies specific skills and techniques as he/she attempts to move the change process forward to goal achievement. The middle phase in essence is that stage of social work practice in which the social worker orchestrates specific activities which he/she, the client system and the action system implement so that the situation of the client is improved. All activities are goal-directed and deliberately and consciously planned.

SELECTED BIBLIOGRAPHY

DeBlassie, R. (1976) Counseling with Mexican-American Youth: Preconceptions and processes (Boston, MA: Teaching Resources Corporation).

Grinnell, R. and Kyte, N. (1975) Environmental modification: A study, SOCIAL WORK, 20, 313–318.

Hollister, D. (1977) Social work skills for social development, SOCIAL DEVELOPMENT ISSUES, 1, 9–20.

Wood, G. and Middlemann, R. (1989) A structural approach to direct service practice (New York: Columbia University Press).

Woods, M. and Hollis, F. (1990) Casework: A psychosocial therapy, 4th. ed. (New York: McGraw-Hill).

ADDITIONAL REFERENCES

Papell, C. and Rothman, B. (1966) Social group work models: Possession and heritage, JOURNAL OF EDUCATION FOR SOCIAL WORK, 2, 66–77.

Rothman, J. (1970) Three models of community organization practice. In F. Cox et Al. (Eds.). Strategies of community organization (Itasca, IL: F.E. Peacock Publishers).

Weisner, S. and Silver, M. (1981) Community work and social learning theory, SOCIAL WORK, 26, 146–150.

Chapter 17

APPLICATION OF KNOWLEDGE, SKILLS IN TERMINATION AND EVALUATION

Inasmuch as the purpose of the intervention is to assist the client in the modification or eradication of those conditions which are impacting on him/her and adversely affecting his/her psychosocial functioning, once stated goals have been achieved, then agency services are no longer required and the change process can be brought to a formal ending. In order for the gains made by the client to become consolidated, the termination process must be carried out in a planned manner. The types of termination have been discussed in Chapter 14. This chapter focuses on the behaviors of the social worker and the client in this final phase of social work practice. The major work for the social worker focuses on the following:

(1) He/she has evaluated the progress made by the client to determine if the goals have been achieved.
(2) He/she needs to actively engage the client in this process and be prepared to addressed the feelings which are aroused by it. The client and the social worker will have their individual feelings about termination and each must be recognized and handled.
(3) The social worker must prepare the client for the future when he/she is no longer an active participant in the client's life.

Termination does not always occur as a result of goal achievement. It may result in the absence of goal achievement. As the social worker monitors and evaluates the intervention process for its progress, he/she may arrive at the conclusion that the client has gone as far as he/she can go and no further benefits may be expected from continual contacts even though all of the stated goals have not been achieved. Consequently, the social worker explores termination with the client. It is the author's opinion that the social worker should always initiate the subject of termination. If the client initiates this topic, it suggests that the social worker has not monitored the case in a thorough manner and does not

217

possess awareness of some of the dynamics occuring in the helping relationship. Client-initiated termination suggests that the client has gone as far as he/she wishes to go with the agency. Possibly the client is not getting what he/she wants or has gotten it and the social worker is unaware of this fact. Unplanned termination or client-initiated termination can frequently be prevented if the social worker periodically asks the client if he/she feels the agency is helping him/her with the problem and if so, how.

TERMINATION

Yalom (1975) views termination as being more than an act signalling the end of the helping process. He views it as being an integral part of the therapeutic process which brings about the ending of a relationship that has been meaningful to the participants. Pincus and Minahan (1973) identify three tasks for the social worker to accomplish at termination so that the case can be brought to a successful conclusion:

(1) The social worker must evaluate the change effort for its effectiveness,
(2) The social worker must disengage from the helping relationship, and
(3) The social worker must seek to stabilize the change effort (p. 272).

They state that "Skills in terminating a planned change effort and disengaging from relationships are as necessary as skills in initiating the effort and engaging people in it" (p. 272).

When the subject of termination is presented, many emotions are aroused, sometimes of a mixed nature. The client may desire to end the helping process, but is ambivalent. He/she is concerned about his/her ability to carry on without the involvement of the social worker. Therefore, he/she may show resistance to the process of ending and may perceive it as a sign of abandonment, rejection or a significant loss. Earlier feelings surrounding traumatic separations are reactivated leading the client to exhibit anger, hostility and regressive behaviors. The social worker will also have his/her feelings toward termination. As a result of the satisfaction that he/she has received from the contacts, he/she may be reluctant to terminate the client and may continue with interviews even when goals have been achieved. Supervision and/or consultation will prove helpful in assisting the social worker to come to grips with his/her feelings toward termination.

Endings are a dynamic process. They are fused with a variety of reactions. When the client and the social worker are aware from the beginning of the time-limitation of intervention or the nature under which the agency's services will be withdrawn, then termination is viewed as being an inherent part of the change process Specific and important work characterize this final phase of contact.

STRUCTURAL ASPECTS OF TERMINATION

Termination should evolve around the three distinct stages which have been identified by Hartford (1971): pretermination, termination and posttermination. In the stage of pretermination, the client is informed usually six weeks in advance of formal termination that the time is approaching for the end of contacts based on earlier agreement and goal accomplishment. In this stage, the social worker and the client will address those feelings which are aroused by this knowledge. The client may forget appointments, develop new problems, revert back to earlier dependency, show regression in symptoms, challenge the social worker's knowledge, or be critical of the social worker's performance. He/she may also select to break contacts before he/she is rejected by the social worker. If this phase of termination is skillfully handled, then these feelings will be resolved, worked through and formal termination will ultimately be accepted by the client. Formal termination can be characterized by a celebration; it also can take place away from the agency. With a child, termination can end with the social worker giving the child a toy or token by which to remember him/her. The client may also present the social worker with a gift. Agency policy will determine if the social worker is able to accept gifts from client, and if so, what kinds of gifts.

In posttermination, the client and the social worker will arrange an appointment at some time in the future for a follow-up report on the client and how well he/she is doing in handling his/her life affairs. The primary purpose of posttermination is to evaluate if therapeutic gains have continued to find expression in the client' life. During the periods of termination and posttermination, the client may have periodic contacts with the social worker usually over the telephone for some advice or guidance. These contacts are handled without a formal reopening of the case.

Termination is also characterized by the presence of distinctive emotional feelings. These emotional states reveal themselves in the following behaviors: denial, anger, apathy, withdrawal and ultimately acceptance.

In the denial state, the client refuses to accept the reality of termination; it may go into one ear and out of the other without registering. The client may also feel that termination is too soon, that it is not indicated and may attempt to bargain with the worker in extending contacts or changing the termination dates. When the client finally accepts the reality that termination will occur, he/she may show his/her anger through regressive behaviors, or present apathetic states indicating that he/she has psychologically withdrawn from services. This apathetic period, similar to that of mourning and grieving over the loss of a meaningful relationship, is ultimately replaced by acceptance. The social worker fully aware of the dynamics of endings and termination has prepared for dealing with these reactions by allowing sufficient time (usually six weeks) for working on them. He/she reaches out to the client with warmth and understanding so that the client does not become trapped in a regressive mode and loses all of the gains that he/she has made. It is important that the social worker does not respond angrily to the client when he/she is exhibiting these behaviors. Usually they are normative reactions to a deeply felt loss. The concern expressed by the social worker is important in helping the client to master the finality of termination and to see the reasons for it. The social worker would not allow the client to terminate unless he/she felt the client was ready for it. When this acceptance occurs, the client begins progressive movements as he/actively engages in preparing for the future without the active involvement of the social worker on whom the client has come to depend. The social worker should reframe the termination experience. While it is the end of agency's services, it signals a new beginning for the client. In effect the client moves away from dependency on the social worker to greater faith in his/her ability to address his/her life situations. If the therapeutic alliance has been a meaningful one, the social worker will remain with the client in memory and when confronted with problems, the client may well reflect over what the social worker would say or how he/she would handle the situation.

REFERRAL AND TRANSFER

Contacts may be terminated between the client and the social worker as the result of a transfer or a referral to another facility. The client in these situations may exhibit similar reactions as he/she has in the termination process. The client is still losing an important relationship and will feel a deep sense of loss. The anger held by the client may be carried over to the new social worker or facility. Similar work must be performed by the social worker as has been done in the termination process. If the social worker does not adequately and capably handle these feelings so that the client will see the need to continue in the helping process, the client may prematurely end his/her contacts with the agency. The new worker should also be sensitive to the fact that he/she will not be immediately accepted by the client and will be put through a period of testing. The client may often compare the new worker with the old worker. The importance of recording and keeping the record current is especially evident at transfers and referrals. Knowledge of what has transpired between the social worker and the client will make it unnecessary for the social worker to ask questions that have already been asked and answered. It is important that the feelings which accompany referrals or transfers are addressed if future work is to be effective and the client is to be maintained in the helping process.

Many times, it is a positive move to introduce the client to the new worker before the transfer is finalized. The new worker may sit in on one of the concluding sessions.

CONTENTS OF SUMMARY RECORDING IN REFERRALS AND TRANSFERS

The worker to whom the case is transferred will have available to him/her the client's record. These records should contain recording summaries. The transfer or referral summary should be of a brief nature. It should contain the following information: (1) the reasons for the client's contacts with the agency and the referral source, (2) a description of the work performed and the progress made, (3) the reason(s) for the transfer or referral and the client's reactions to it. The information should also contain some mentioning of how the new contact is to be initiated. Is the client to contact the worker, or does the client expect for the worker to make the initial contact? Recording at the time of termination, referral, or transfer reveals the importance of agency's record in assuring that services will be of a continuous nature since it is the bridge of communication between the new worker and the client who has been transferred to him/her.

EVALUATION

A need always exist for a social worker to evaluate the effectiveness of his/her practice. Evaluation does not wait until the termination of services. It is an on-going process throughout the life of a case. Increasing attention has been focused on practice evaluation. Pincus and Minahan (1973) state two general areas need to be considered in evaluation: the outcome and the process. The focus of these two areas is on goal accomplishment. Evaluation will usually focus on the outcome of contacts with client systems (individuals, the families and small groups) or program evaluation. Evaluative instruments are the single subject design, goal achievement scales and client satisfaction questionnaires (postintervention follow up surveys) aimed at collecting the client's perception of the treatment that he/she received. The single subject design is generally used to evaluate if specific behaviors or actions have been instrumental in achieving specific outcomes. Single subject design follows basically a behavioral approach in that a baseline is established for specific behaviors; then techniques are employed to determine if the behavior is being increased or decreased based on the goals of the case. Reports from significant others involved in the client's life, such as a teacher, a minister or a spouse can also be used for evaluative purposes as they can report on changes, if any, in the client's situation which can be attributed to intervention. In the final analysis, it is the client and significant others in the client's life who are best able to evaluate the outcome of social work practice.

The lack of goal achievement cannot always be construed as an indication of intervention failure. Many intervening variables over which the social worker has no control or a lack of knowledge of may determine the outcome of a case. The author remembers many cases which had favorable outcomes for which the author was reluctant to take credit. For example, one case focused on helping neglectful parents to relinquish their children for adoption. The parents were adamant against such a decision. When the social worker decided that possibly focus should be placed on helping the parents to become better parents if they were to keep their children, the parents seemingly out of a clear blue sky decided to relinquish their children for adoption.

The client's lack of motivation may constitute a barrier which interferes with goal accomplishment. Sometimes, the clients in the middle of the intervention process may decide on a different goal than the earlier one which they have agreed to work on. The goal of a particular case was to assist the couple in saving their marriage. While this goal was operationalized into specific behaviors, following social work contacts, the husband decided that he wanted a divorce. The wife as a result of counseling was more able to accept his decision than she would have been at the beginning of contacts. No matter how well planned the intervention strategy may be, in the final analysis, clients make decisions primarily based on their own needs. The social worker must not view outcomes which are contrary to the planned ones as an indication of intervention failure.

The dual focus of social work practice requires that the social worker attempts to bring about change in the client's external environment when existing conditions are evaluated as having negative consequences for the client. As a result of organizational analysis, program evaluation, community assessment, the social worker may identify unmet needs in the community, determine that programs are ineffective, or that modification is required in service delivery systems. Mordock (1979) states, "An effective treatment program may not necessarily produce changes in an individual, but may prevent further deterioration," (p. 298). Treatment, according to Mordock, may be designed to improve environmental supports rather than to change the individual. It is inevitable that practice effectiveness must always center on determining the degree to which identified goals have been achieved by social work intervention. Accountability and practice effectiveness go hand in hand.

CONCLUSION (CHAPTERS 15, 16 AND 17)

Social work practice is characterized by a beginning, middle and ending phase. As a process, social work practice is directed toward the achievement of a particular outcome (goal). In each phase of social work practice, the social worker applies knowledge, skills, values, techniques and procedures. The social worker also assumes specific roles which are viewed as being instrumental to the change process and goal achievement.

Social work practice has a dual focus, people in interactions with their environments. Intervention may be directed at the individual, the environment or the individual and the environment. Intervention is facilitated through the helping process which is the medium through which help is provided. The communication process which characterizes the interactions which take place between the client and the social worker is of a cyclical nature as the social worker and the client send, receive, decode and respond to specific messages. In the helping process, the four basic systems of social work practice are activated.

The helping process is best viewed as being time-limited. It is deliberately formed for a specific purpose and is not intended to last forever. The goals established by the social worker and the client are written into a contract which is ratified by the social worker and client. The actions to be performed by the participants involved in the change process, the roles they are to assume, and the goals they are to pursue must be consistent with the agency function as embodied within its charter. The contract is subjected to renegotiation based upon mutual consent as the helping process moves forward. The helping process is also imbued with expressive feelings and instrumental activities. As a dynamic process, the helping relationship does not always flow smoothly and sometimes the client and social worker are called on to address those obstacles which stand in the way of goal achievement. When goals are achieved, termination signals the withdrawal of the agency services and marks the end of the client's formal contacts with the agency.

From a structural point of view, the helping process is characterized by the social worker and the client engaging in specific steps which are of a logical and sequential nature. These steps or procedures are (1) Initial contact, (2) engaging the client in using the agency's services once it is established that the agency is the appropriate place for the client to be, (3) developing and maintaining the therapeutic alliance, (4) data collection, (5) data assessment, (6) goal setting, (7) contract formulation, (8) implementing the intervention and (9) termination and evaluation.

In the preceding chapters, the author has characterized social work practice as a "constellation of knowledge, values, and skills" which are put into action by the social worker as he/she engages in contacts with client systems. Practice is goal-oriented. Whatever the focus of practice and its desired outcome, the social worker is expected to engage in practice evaluation to identify if his/her practice is effective.

SELECTED BIBLIOGRAPHY

Hartford, M. (1971) Groups in social work (New York: Columbia University Press).
Mordock, J. (1979) Evaluation in residential treatment: The conceptual dilemma. CHILD WELFARE, LVIII, 293–302.

Pincus, A. and Minahan, A. (1973) Social work practice: Model and process (Itasca, IL: F.E. Peacock Publishers).

Yalom, I. (1975) The theory and practice of group psychotherapy, 2nd. edition (New York: Basic Books).

SECTION VI
TRANSCULTURAL
SOCIAL WORK PRACTICE
WITH PEOPLE OF COLOR

INTRODUCTION

Transcultural practice is a term employed to denote social work practice with People of Color. In the United States, Blacks, Hispanics, Native Americans and Asian-Americans are members of this group. Social work has not always been sensitive to the plight of these minorities. They have been referred to as the "unmeltables" as their specific characteristics have acted as barriers to their total acceptance and assimilation into American society. These minorities have historically suffered great social injustices as a result of their race and cultures. Laws have been implemented from the judicial, executive and legislative branches of the federal government which have held negative consequences for them. While these groups have made some progress in their attempts to become a part of mainstream society, they still encounter racist practices and structural barriers which deny to them the rights which are given to the members of the dominant group. A responsibility of the social worker in a transcultural practice approach is to identify societal barriers to their progress, to act as their advocate, and to assist them in overcoming socioeconomic barriers so that they can live a satisfying life without barriers being placed in their way. A satisfying life can only be achieved for American minorities when they attain social equality and social justice.

Chapter 18

SOCIAL WORK PRACTICE
WITH PEOPLE OF COLOR*

Morales (1981) uses the term, "Third World People" to refer to the colored minorities in American society who in his view have shared a common experience of political and economic exploitation. For the social worker to practice effectively within a transcultural perspective, he/she must possess knowledge of the cultural and historical experiences of the colored minorities in American society and the tensions which exist between them and the dominant group. The social worker must be sensitive to his/her own cultural values so that he/she does not attempt to impose them on minority group members or to place them in stigmatized categories.

Culture and race influence cognitive patterns, world views, values, beliefs and communication styles. In effect culture provides a design for living. If the social worker acts in an encapsulated manner and is not sensitive to the effects of race and culture on behavior particularly in the context of race relations in the United States, he/she will be unable to individualize clients from different cultures and will view all people from his/her own cultural framework. In practice, the social worker in contacts with ethnic minorities will face an "invisible wall" which stand between him/her and the ethnic client. This wall will lead to misunderstanding and impair the development of the helping relationship. A sense of trust and mutual understanding cannot be developed when cultural barriers exist between the social worker and the client.

MINORITIES IN AMERICAN LIFE

While all ethnic groups have shared similar experiences including rejection and oppression in the process of assimilation, the colored

---

*The terms People of Color, Third World People, colored minorities, will be used interchangeably. The same applies to Anglos, white and Euro-Americans.

minorities have faced vastly different experiences than those faced by the European ethnics. In remarking on this difference, Marden and Meyer (1962) state that while linguistically different, the Germans, Scandinavians and others did not suffer the discrimination which subsequent groups encountered. These groups assimilated more rapidly because they were less visibly different; they were largely Protestant and their cultures had more affinity to the dominant Anglo-Saxon culture (p. 74). The attitude of the receiving culture toward the incoming group has a great bearing on the assimilation process and the barriers erected against the total assimilation of the incoming group. With the exception of blacks (enslaved), Mexican-Americans (annexed and conquered) and the Native Americans (conquered), all ethnic groups have come to this country on a voluntary basis. Even though Asian-Americans came voluntarily, they too eventually became victims of oppression and discrimination. Gibson (1980) states that although other groups have been targets of oppression, blacks have faced greater hostility than the European ethnics and no group has been the victim of such practices to the same extent and length of time as blacks (p. 27). As the United States was deciding its national character at the turn of the century, the nation had formed its opinion of how people of color were to be treated. They were to be excluded from the dominant society. Colored minorities could not be assimilated according to the Melting Pot. Handlin (1957) succinctly and forcibly describes the manner in which the country would deal with its colored minorities:

> By the end of the century the pattern of racist patterns and ideas seems fully developed. The Orientals were to be totally excluded; the Negroes were to live in segregated enclaves; The Indians were to be confined to reservations as permanent wards of the nation; and all whites were to assimilate as rapidly as possible to a common standard (p. 38).

This common standard was to be the Melting Pot. Since the minorities were not only viewed as being inferior but also "unmeltable" they were to be excluded in a systematic manner from mainstream American society. This exclusion was accomplished through racist practices which were supported and maintained by dominant societal institutions. In practice with People of Color, the social worker must always possess a commitment to social justice and to engage actively in changing those conditions which are viewed as being detrimental to the well-being of people and against the principles of the society in which they live.

RACISM IN AMERICAN LIFE

Racism is pervasive in American society. Unless the social worker is aware of its existence and possesses knowledge of the sociohistorical experiences of minorities in American society, he/she may encounter difficulties in seeing the need for a transcultural practice perspective. The need for innovative practice approaches with minorities results from their experiences in the United States. These experiences must receive attention in the analysis of any problem presented by the minority plan and in planning intervention.

Bullock and Rodgers (1975) state, "Racism has been a wound on American society from our earliest days" (p. 1). They identify several events as being evidence of racist practices: (1) black enslavement, (2) the attempted genocide of the American Indian, (3) the failure of the nation to follow through on its post Civil War commitment to Blacks, (4) the internment camps during World War II and (5) the economic and social oppression of Mexican-Americans. The government failed to honor the terms of the Treaty of Guadalupe-Hildago following the Mexican-American War. Hoffman (1974) states that over 400,000 Mexican aliens and their children were repatriated to Mexico during the depression years. They were blamed for the economic ills facing the country. Social workers actively assisted in these repatriation efforts. The repatriation of Mexican-Americans has been compared to the treatment of the American Indians and the relocation of Japanese during World War II. It was not until 1924 that Congress granted citizenship to the American Indian. However, the Bureau of Indian Affairs continued to claim responsibility for the American Indian and to plan for them.

As a result of the actions of the Bureau of Indian Affairs, American Indians were citizens in name only and their citizenship and its rights were not the same as those granted to Anglos. Asian-Americans have also been subjected to rejection and harsh immigration policies. The Exclusion Act of 1882 was directed against Chinese immigration. It suspended all Chinese immigration for 10 years. This Act was repeated in 1892 for ten additional years and in 1902 Chinese immigration to the United States was suspended indefinitely until 1943. The Gentlemen Agreement Act of 1907 limited the immigration of Japanese who also were treated unjustly and in an inhumane manner. Hostility directed at them was great in the State of California due to their success in agriculture. They were referred to as "Mongolians" or the "Yellow Peril." In the State of

California, the testimony of an Asian-American against white men was inadmissable in court. Segregated schools were permitted until 1946 when the State repealed that section of its Educational Code. The Supreme Court in its decision of Plessy vs. Ferguson in 1897 established the doctrine of a "separate but equal" society. As a response to this doctrine, blacks were denied admittance to societal institutions which served whites, had to fight for equality and develop parallel social institutions to serve their own. While Plessy vs. Ferguson was overturned in 1954 in Brown vs. Topeka, blacks have still had to struggle for equality of treatment in American life. Gibson (1980) views the negative attitudes of whites toward blacks as resulting from the negative stereotypes which exist about them. These stereotypes are used to justify the treatment of blacks in the social, economic and political spheres of American life.

TYPES OF RACISM

Three types of racism present themselves in American society: individual/psychological, cultural and institutional. Individual/psychological racism is personal in nature and presents itself when members of the dominant group claim superiority over minorities due to the circumstances of birth. It presents itself in the desire to prevent minorities from living in certain neighborhoods, racial harassment, the refusal to socialize with minorities on a personal basis, the assignment of minorities to menial tasks and the belief that minorities lack the skills or knowledge to perform competent work. Cultural racism is built and maintained on beliefs which provide a foundation for racist practices and differential treatment of people based on race and culture. It is cultural because it is an enduring aspect of the fibers of American society. It is located in such early beliefs as the white man' burden, manifest destiny, and the inherent deficits of minorities. Knowledge to support these beliefs is taken from a variety of sources including the Bible, and the fields of anthropology and sociology. Cultural ethnocentricism is also a form of cultural racism. It presents itself when the social worker views his/her culture as being superior to that of others. As a result of its nature, social workers find themselves more involved in addressing institutional racism. It is through institutional racism that racist practices and beliefs find expression through societal programs and the differential treatment of minorities. Institutional racism permeates the social service delivery system. It is a structural phenomenon which has been instrumental in denying minorities equitable services and in maintaining them in a status of second class citizenship. Through institutional racism, minorities have been effectively blocked in their attempts to gain total assimilation into American society.

The existence of racism as a dynamic force in American life and the insidious and systematic manner in which it presents itself necessitates that the social worker frequently assumes the role of an advocate and an organizational analyst in intervening into racist practices. In combatting racist practices, the social worker will frequently need to engage in social conflict strategies and employ social action techniques in attempting to bring about structural change. Differential assessment is extremely important. While it is evident that minorities live in stressful situations and do have interpersonal problems, it is also a fact that many of their problems result from structural inequities. Dominant group social workers do not always share the same view of the problem as does the minority client. Brown and Arevalo (1979) state,

> Minority groups generally have viewed their problems as requiring structural instead of instead of individual change, or requiring a social action focus instead of an intrapsychic one. The intrapsychic focus is viewed as adaptive, while the structural focus calls for modification of institutions and direct action to deal with substantive problems such as poverty, powerlessness, inadequate housing, unemployment, health problems and racism (p. 331).

TRANSCULTURAL SOCIAL WORK PRACTICE

Racism is only one of the reasons for a transcultural social work practice perspective. The social worker also needs to possess knowledge of different cultures and the capacity to apply this knowledge in practice. Substantive differences exist across different cultures and in practice with minorities and Anglo clients. These differences are culturally-based. It is the author's opinion that a transcultural practice approach to be effective must embrace the dynamics of race and culture.

Culture consists of values, beliefs, world views, religion and language. These traits provide the individual with a design for living and make it possible to distinguish one ethnic group from another. Ironically, minorities as a result of their race and cultures have been denied access to full equality in a country which is said to value cultural diversity. Minorities have been expected to give up their cultural heritages and to replace them with the values of the dominant group. Intervention failure is assured when the social worker and client operate out of different value frameworks and undue tension will characterize the helping relationship.

Many reasons exist for the social worker to be sensitive to the value system of other ethnic groups. Otherwise, he/she may characterize or misinterpret the behaviors of others and classify it as being of a defective or pathological nature, merely because it differs from his/her values. Here the author will discuss and identify those values which have been identified as being peculiar to Anglo society. In the sections which discuss various minorities, the value system of these groups will be discussed and contrasted with Anglo society. In this way, the social worker will receive a comparative view of values from a cross-cultural perspective.

ANGLO VALUES

Brown (1964) states, "Unless the fact of cultural difference is accepted and an attempt made to learn about and view sympathetically the beliefs and customs of other groups, great damage to intergroup relations may result" (p. 45). The following have been identified as being indicative of Anglo values:

- competitiveness
- winning
- individualism
- abstract thinking (a focusing on parts instead of wholes and a search for cause-effect relations)
- an internal locus of control
- a future orientation
- the valuing of time, thrift and cleanliness
- a distrust of authority
- a tolerance for ambiguity
- a desire to conquer nature instead of living harmoniously with it
- a tendency to brag about accomplishments
- a preference for eye to eye contact
- punctuality

Brown (1964) identifies other values which are associated with the dominant group. Some of her values are located in those identified above but stated differently:

- occupational success and achievement
- hard work and stable employment

- thrift, piety, punctuality, respectability
- monogamous marriage, marital fidelity
- educational achievement
- respect for law and order
- concern for private property and home ownership
- Protestant church membership
- membership in voluntary associations
- white skin color
- cleanliness and love of country (p. 53).

Other Anglo values are presented in an emphasis on "rugged individualism," a valuing of the nuclear family and the belief that a man's home is his castle. As a result of racism, many of these values are out of the reach of minorities. All social workers face clients with a professional and a personal value system. As a result of their personal value systems, social workers have developed views of what is proper and improper behaviors and they may attempt to impose their values onto minority client systems. For example, the Anglos value time and do not want to waste it. In beginning contacts, they may immediately want to discuss their problems. To immediately discuss a problem without some preliminary discussion of an informal and leisurely nature may prove threatening to other cultural groups.

In all aspects of the social work process, the social worker must devote some attention to a discussion of culture, race, the immigration experience and the minority experiences in the United States to determine their impact if any on the problem presented by the minority client. Brown (1964) states,

> By the time the individual reaches adulthood, he has developed a vast amount of detailed knowledge about how he should act or refrain from acting in situations similar to those in which he has grown up. He has a system of values by which he judges what is pleasant, desirable, appropriate, right or the reverse (p. 49).

If the social worker does not value the client's culture, trust cannot be developed, barriers will be erected to the building of the therapeutic alliance and the minority client may prematurely disengage from agency services.

The need for a transcultural orientation to practice is heightened by the fact that People of Color are projected as becoming the majority population in the United States in early decades of the 21st century.

EXISTING DEMOGRAPHICS

Existing demographics reveal that the United States is fast becoming less white. The 1980 Census reported that slightly more than 1 in 5 persons of the 226 million people in the United States was either black, Hispanic, Asian-Pacific Islander or Native American. These numbers include 26.5 million blacks (11.7 percent), 14.6 million Hispanics or Latinos (6.5 percent), 3.5 million Asian/Pacific Islanders (1.5 percent) and 1.4 million Native Americans, Indians, Eskimos and Aleuts (.6 percent). It is predicted that by the year 2080 that whites will no longer be the majority population in the country. These figures reveal the need for cultural sensitivity and a transcultural approach to practice. Social workers will come into contacts with different cultural groups, and they must be prepared to provide services to these clients within the context of their culture while at the same time assisting them in their adaptation to the American environment.

SOME DIMENSIONS OF
TRANSCULTURAL SOCIAL WORK PRACTICE

Race and culture constitute important dynamics in practice with minority clients. They become important variables in developing an understanding of the nature of the client's problems, the conditions contributing to them, the manner in which the client is responding to these stressors, and in planning and implementing an intervention strategy that is culturally sensitive. The client's culture will also influence relationship protocol. Social workers should develop an ease in discussing race and culture. They are facts in American society.

Intervention with minority clients must be individualized. While they have undergone similar experiences in American society, they have also undergone different experiences in their cultures of origin. Each group may operate out of a different value framework. In the data collection process, the social worker gathers data on the immigration experience, the experiences of the minority in American society, and seeks to place the client at a particular stage on the acculturation continuum: atraditional, bicultural or traditional. The traditional level of acculturation is basically the folk-culture, the value system of the culture of origin which the client has brought to the United States and steadfastly adheres to. The elderly client, first generation, is more likely to conform to this value framework. The bicultural individual, usually second generation, is equally comfortable in two cultures, is bilingual, and can operate effectively within each culture. However, he/she may present a preference for a particular culture depending on the situation. At home, he/she may show a preference for his/her culture or origin. Outside of the home, he/she may adopt dominant group values. If the individual is torn between two cultures and cannot make a firm committment to either, he/she will be viewed as a marginal individual and will face psychosocial-cultural problems in his/her social functioning. In addition, the individual will be plagued with guilt feelings. The atraditional or modern individual has moved away from the culture of origin and has fully accepted the values of the dominant group. Different family members may be at different levels of acculturation and this may also pose problems for the family, resulting in family stress and intergenerational conflicts. While the social worker must not automatically assume that all the problems of minorities are culturally-related or result from racism, it is indicated that culture and racism be reviewed to determine if they are contributing factors to the client's problems. If they are ruled out, then the problem of the minority client more likely will be the result of intrapsychic factors, faulty interpersonal relations, or problems in life transitions. The social worker also needs to be cognizant of the fact that conditions which the dominant group views as indicators of pathology may upon deeper reflection and understanding emerge as the strengths and survival techniques by which minorities have been able to survive in a hostile environment.

TRANSCULTURAL SOCIAL WORK PRACTICE WITH BLACKS

In preparation for contacts with blacks, the social worker should engage in a reflective process. He/she should think about their experiences in American society, the manner in which they may react toward the worker who represents the "system" or "the man" who is viewed as the symbol of their continuing oppression. The social worker needs to think about his/her responses to their feelings while at the same time attempting to engage them in the helping process. Initial contacts may be characterized by stress, suspicion, resistance and mistrust. The blacks constitute a heterogeneous group and the black community is stratified by social class. The value system of the upper and middle classes will approximate that of white society. Also, while the view exists that the blacks are a matriarchal society, research indicates that the black family structure is egalitarian.

BLACK SURVIVAL IN AMERICAN SOCIETY

In their survival in American society, blacks have developed unique strengths and coping mechanisms. The social worker should be aware of them. Hill (1972) identifies these strengths: (1) strong kinship bonds, (2) strong work orientation, (3) adaptability of family roles, (4) a strong religious orientation and (5) a high achievement orientation. He identifies strengths as "those traits which facilitate the ability of the family to meet the needs of its members and the demands made upon it by systems outside the family unit" (p. 2). Hill recognizes that these strengths also exist in white families but feels they are expressed differently within the black family. Other strengths have been identified as a steadfast optimism and resilient children. Peters (1981) also remarks on the adaptations that blacks have had to make in order to survive in American society. She states that blacks as a result of their life experiences have developed a life style which reflects their cultural heritage and the specific adaptations they have had to make. Some of these adaptations are (1) the need for women with younger children to be in the work force, (2) families in which each spouse is employed, (3) the assignment of care-taking responsibilities of younger children to older children while parents worked and (4) the use of friends and relatives as support systems. Generally, it has been easier for the black female to find employment and as a consequence the husband has assumed household responsibilities. The male child in the black family has been taught many of the duties which are associated with the female in the dominant society. This cultural characteristic has developed because each family member has had to do his/her part in insuring the survival of the family. Consequently, role adaptability is an important cultural traits of blacks which is unique to them. It refers to the capacity of black males and females to assume opposite gender roles without stigmatization being attached to it.

The black family is the most important institution in the black community. It is followed by the black church. Members are extremely loyal to the family, and membership in the black family includes blood and nonblood-related members. Nonblood-related members are absorbed into the family by the process of informal adoption.

THE BLACK FAMILY

The Black family may be conceptualized as an interdependent kinship system characterized by mutual aid functions and strong bonds of loyalty between its members. This mutual-aid kinship system transcends geographical boundaries and its glue is the strong sense of obligation which exists among its members. The black extended family structure includes a variety of members. Among these members are the biological parents, relatives, boyfriends, girlfriends, and quasi-kin members such as neighbors or people who live with the family and are viewed as being members of it. The elderly member is respected and accorded a position of honor within the family. Children are valued and a preference is reflected for strict discipline so that the child is respectful to elders. The child is also taught not to look adults in the eye as it is a sign of defiance and disrespect. Blacks also exhibit a tradition of sending children to live with relatives for specific periods if they are difficult to handle. The relative is expected to accept these children without argument. Usually the black child will reveal his/her feelings in a nonverbal manner in interactions with adults. He/she may look at the ground, shrug his/her shoulders or walk away. This is his/her form of communicating his/her emotions.

BLACK CULTURE

Hillard (1976) states that Blacks

(1) tend to view things in their entirety and not in isolated parts,
(2) seem to prefer inferential reasoning rather than deductive and inductive reasoning,
(3) tend to approximate space, number and time instead of aiming for complete accuracy,
(4) appear to focus more on people and their activities rather than objects,
(5) tend to prefer novelty, personal freedom and distinctiveness such as in music and styles of clothing,
(6) have a keen sense of justice and quickly perceive injustice and
(7) in general tend not to be "word-dependent" but are proficient in nonverbal as well as verbal communication.

Generally, the literature suggests that the uniqueness of Black culture derives from the fact that it is a culture which emphasizes nonverbal behavior. More emphasis is placed on performance, the experience encountered, than what is said.

In general the social worker should be aware of the following aspects of black culture:

- "Cultural paronia:" Blacks possess a suspicion of societal institutions as a result of the manner in which they have been treated. In a sense, this "cultural paranoia" is healthy a reality for blacks in American society.
- A present time orientation and an active instead of a passive orientation in relation to life events.
- A strong sense of family loyalty and a hesitation in discussing family matters with outsiders.
- Reciprocal obligations among family members and the practice of absorbing nonblood-related people into the family and treating them as family members.
- A humanistic orientation toward people and an inferential approach to behavior, i.e., blacks pick up clues from the social interaction as to how they should act in a particular context.
- An external locus of control, a fatalistic attitude and a quick response to situations.
- In counseling, blacks prefer actions instead of engaging in a process of analytical thinking that is future-oriented.
- Some blacks due to a sense of powerlessness will consult folk-healers or fortune tellers or exhibit a belief in astrology as this gives them some control over events.
- Blacks exhibit a nonverbal pattern of communication when they are unsure of the situation. However, once a sense of trust is gained, they will become more verbal and communicate in a clear, unambiguous manner.
- The Black family structure is egalitarian.
- Blacks present a great respect for the elderly, and the expectation exists that the children will care for them, and they will always occupy a place of importance in the family. As a result of their wisdom, they often participate in decision-making. Adult children usually meet as a group to determine who will assume the responsibility of the aged parent when he/she is no longer capable of independent living. An extreme reluctance exists to placing an elderly member in a hospital or nursing home as these are viewed as places in which the elderly member will not receive good care and may not leave, i.e., they are viewed as places in which people die.
- Blacks present an other-worldly view of religion, i.e., a world after death in which they will receive answers for their troubles in this

world. This belief contributes to their steadfast optimism and stoicism in the face of adversity. This faith is revealed in their beliefs that God will make a way, will give them no more trouble than they can bear, and that they have come this far by faith and faith will see them home.

- A view exists that death is both a joyous and a sad occasion. It is sad because someone is leaving loved ones behind. It is joyous in the sense that one is leaving the mortal world and will soon be united with those who have gone before. Thus, Blacks view death as being "regressive" (going home) and not as an indication of annihilation (nothingness).
- Blacks use humor in dispelling potentially tension-filled situations. Thus, laughter is also a coping device.
- Black adults prefer to be called by surnames as this is an indication of respect.

APPLICATION OF CULTURAL KNOWLEDGE IN TRANSCULTURAL PRACTICE WITH BLACKS

Gibbs (1985) states that blacks have developed certain interpersonal coping strategies as a means of addressing unfamiliar and anxiety-provoking situations. She states that blacks tend to evaluate situations relative to negative or positive feelings and proposes a five-stage interpersonal model for practice with blacks: (1) Appraisal (sizing up), (2) investigation (checking out), (3) involvement (joint interaction), (4) commitment (personal loyalty) and (5) task-involvement. In initial contacts blacks will bring a more personal than objective perspective to the interviewing situation. The personal aspects will be revealed in how they feel about the situation and the conditions which have brought about the contacts. They may not view the interview as a goal to a future outcome. It is important that the social worker be able to transcend the different expectations that will exist between him/her and the black client. He/she should have a humanistic orientation which allows him/her to focus more on the qualities and potentials of people rather than their problems. As Brown (1981) states when the minority client is referred to the social worker, the assumption exists that somehow he/she has failed and he/she expects to be criticized. The process is more important than the verbal discussions which will occur among the participant. The social worker must reveal a willingness for self-disclosure, to operate in the here-and-now, and to install a sense of hope into the client's situation. Certainly the story should be presented in the client's own words and the social worker should take cues from these words as to how he/she should react. It is necessary that the Black client comes to see the social worker as a "potential friend" rather than as a representative of a cold, aloof institution who has mistreated him/her in the past. While the method will remain the same (data collection, assessment, and intervention), the social worker must be prepared to be creative, flexible and to modify his/her techniques.

In these initial contacts, the social worker faces two important tasks: (1) He/she must reveal him/herself as an authentic person whose behavior is congruent, an individual who is genuine, caring and can relate to the situations faced by the black client. In order to do this, he/she must possess knowledge of the sociohistorical experiences of blacks in American society, and (2) the social worker must be prepared to face challenges and confrontations without retaliation and to recognize the feelings which are behind this behavior. Only when the social worker is able to meet and to carry out these tasks will the therapeutic alliance begin to take hold. With black clients, the social worker should reveal some degree of comfort in discussing race as it is a fact of life in American society. The social worker should also inquire of the client the manner in which he/she wants to be addressed and if he/she is more comfortable in being referred to as colored, Negro, black or Afro-American as these are evolutionary terms in the blacks' attempt to define themselves in American society. The elderly client will probably prefer the term Negro. It is important that the social worker show that he/she is comfortable with blacks and should have dispelled any stereotype which he/she has of them. The use of humor or laughing or sharing feelings with the client can reveal this comfortableness. While blacks prefer formality in their contacts with dominant group institutions, they are approachable. Social workers should not use their first names without their permission as this is a sign of disrespect and an affront to their dignity. It is also a sign of their identity. White Americans have frequently used impersonal terms in referring to blacks such as boy, girl, or their first names. In contrast, blacks have been expected to refer to whites by their surnames with the proper prefix (Mr., Mrs. or Miss).

The social worker needs to take time in explaining the helping process to blacks and in clarifying their roles. The client's feedback should be elicited to determine that he/she understands the process and also for him/her to make his/her contributions to it. The black client will more freely invest of him/herself in the helping process when he/she is treated in a humane and considered manner, understands the purpose of the contact, is informed how it will be of help to him/her, what his/her role will be, and feels that he/she is not being judged by the social worker. Once the social worker has passed the test of scrutiny, and the client has perceived from his/her actions that he/she is interested in him/her, then the social worker and client can focus on the client's situation and what can be accomplished through agency contacts.

It seems indicated to view the interviews between the black client and the social worker as encounters in which each will validate and authenticate the other. The social worker must be aware that black cognitive style differs from that of Anglos. Their emphasis is on feelings and emotions, and their cues to behavior result from inferences drawn from the interactions between them and the social worker. In contrast, Anglos place greater emphasis on talk and abstract thinking. The relational approach to contacts valued and expressed by blacks must be recognized, understood and accepted if the therapeutic alliance is to be formed. Inasmuch as blacks live in stress-inducing environments, they often seek immediate assistance in changing their situations when they present themselves at the agency for assistance. Crisis intervention or a task-oriented approach has great utility as a theoretical framework for practice with blacks. These time-limited, action-oriented approaches require that the social worker assumes an active role. Through this active role assumed by the social worker, the black client is able to witness the activities engaged in by the social worker in improving his/her conditions. In a very real sense, the strength of the helping relationship will rest on what the social worker does, not what he/she promises to do. In addition, a task-orientation is less ambiguous than an abstract verbal approach to intervention. An abstract approach directed at the achievement of future psychological benefit is time-consuming, meaningless, and of little importance to clients who are struggling with the need to survive and to make it from day to day in the face of ever-continuing pressures. As stated earlier, blacks prefer action in problem-solving and are rejecting of a passive approach. They seek advice, sound directions from the social worker and want to fully participate in addressing their problems. A failure to provide direct, concrete information may result in expressions of anger from the client who cannot understand why the social worker refuses to tell him/her what to do. Certainly, the social worker should not be fearful of encouraging dependency. This may be a positive sign in clients who are mistrustful. He/she should be comfortable in providing advice and guidance to black clients and in acting as an advocate when indicated. Once the client's problem has improved, he/she will assume greater responsibility in addressing his/her situation as he/she has seen the effectiveness of the social worker.

Chestang (1976) describes the "black experience" as conveying the ideas of a culture, a style and social pattern developed by blacks to cope with the life situation to which society has consigned them. Consequently social workers who practice with blacks must develop an understanding of their culture and life styles. Chestang also identifies social injustice, societal inconsistency and personal impotence as three socially determined and institutionally supported conditions that characterize the black experience. These experiences have resulted in a stigmatization of blacks and resultant feelings of powerlessness. As a result of the black experience, social work practice with blacks will require substantive differences than the practice approach used with Anglos. The Anglo value system enables them to be more responsive to intrapsychic therapies which basically are unstructured, ambiguous in nature, require a tolerance for ambiguity, seek future outcomes, and locate problems primarily within individuals instead of societal structures. The existence of racism as a dynamic force in American society and its impact on the black condition requires a transcultural practice approach and a dual focus on people in interactions with their environment. Such a practice approach must accomodate micro-mezzo and macro-level intervention. In this approach, the social worker must view the client in his/her uniqueness, validates him/her as a person with dignity who has lived under conditions of oppression, accepts and responds warmly to his/her feelings, and actively engages him/her in problem-solving, based on assessment, at the individual and/or societal level. The social worker must guard against making faculty assessment based on stereotypes and activating a self-fulfilling prophecy in his/her contacts with blacks. Certainly, the social worker must recognize the strengths which exist in the black culture and utilize them in the helping process.

TRANSCULTURAL SOCIAL WORK
PRACTICE WITH HISPANICS

For many years, the Hispanics were characterized as the forgotten minority. This description is no longer true as Hispanics have actively advocated for their rights. They too have faced racist practices based on their culture. Hispanics are a heterogeneous population and the United States is the fourth largest Spanish-speaking nation in the world. Generally, Hispanics or Latinos live in urban areas, are employed in menial type employment, are undereducated and live in conditions of poverty. They may be divided into the following groups: Mexican-Americans, Cubans, Puerto Ricans and Central and South Americans. Mexican-Americans live primarily in the southwest, Puerto Ricans in the Northeast, and Cubans in the Southeast. While cultural differences exist among Hispanics, sufficient similarities exist which make it possible to discuss specific aspects of their culture as a group. Dieppa and Montiel (1978) state, "Although there are variations among Cubans, Mexican-Americans and Puerto Ricans, there also are shared values and cultural attributes" (p. 3). Hispanics have also lived under conditions of oppression, have faced problems in attaining social mobility, and have also been unable to depend on the law for their protection. In practice with Hispanics, the social worker must possess cultural sensitivity, understand relationship protocol and the importance of the family as the cornerstone of Hispanic culture. Loyalty to the family is paramount and takes precedence over loyalty to any other social institution. Its honor is to be protected and individual family members are expected not to engage in any behavior which brings dishonor to the family.

HISPANIC VALUES

Hispanic values differ greatly from those of Anglo society. Ramirez and Castaneda (1974) identify four value clusters which are characteristic of Hispanic culture: (1) identification with the family, (2) personalization of interpersonal relationship, (3) status role definition in the family and (4) Hispanic Catholic ideology. The following also constitutes Hispanic values:

- The society is patriarchal in nature. The father possesses a role of authority and importance. He is the instrumental leader of the family, the primary decision maker and represents the family in the community. The mother performs an expressive function in the family, is devoted to it, makes sacrifices, and within the home exerts expressive leadership and is in charge of the children.
- Rigid sex-role differentiation characterizes Hispanic culture. The oldest male child is given a role of importance and leadership over the younger children. In the absence of the father, he becomes the domi-

nant male. The female is expected to defer to the male authority and to devote her career to the home and the roles of wife and mother.

- Children are loved and revered. They are socialized to show respect for adults and to understand their behaviors reflect on the image of the family.

- Hispanics have an extended family system which include the Comparadgo system or godparents. This extended support system is highly valued as a part of the family and is expected to provide assistance to the family in times of needs. Parents also consult with godparents relative to problems and how to address them. Godparents may also be expected to take responsibility for their godchildren if anything should happen to the parents. Thus, the role of Comparadzgo carries with it familial obligations.

- In the Hispanic culture extreme importance is attached to the safeguarding of the family' honor. Individualism (a dominant group value) is submerged to the welfare of the collectivity and the honor of the family. Consequently, Hispanics reveal a reluctance to discuss family matters with outsiders. Problems are expected to be resolved within the family. Only when an individual in authority such as a priest, or an intermediary who is known and respected by the family sanctions such discussions is it permissable to discuss family problems with the social worker. Permission may also occur when the social worker has gained the family's respect. Family unity and honor are important cultural values which influence the behavior of the Hispanic client.

- Within the Hispanic culture, a separation does not exist between the mind (mental) and the body (physical). They are viewed in an unitary manner. Consequently, psychological stresses are experienced as somatic complaints. A physical illness may place the individual into the "sick role" and provide secondary gains as the individual is relieved of some of his/her responsibility due to the somatization of his/her complaints.

- The Curandero (folk-healer) is important in the Hispanic culture, particularly due to their external locus of control and belief that events happen to them as a result of supernatural forces or the placement of hexes on them by an envious person. Curanderos provide a self-regulating cultural mechanism for addressing illnesses and feelings of discomfort. The external locus of control is revealed in such statements as it is God's will. The social worker should be aware of the fact that if individuals define situations as being real, then the consequences of these situations are also real (Thomas and Znaniecki, 1927). This belief indicates that social worker may often need to work with curanderos.

- In the Hispanic culture, the elderly is also highly valued and accorded a place of respect and honor within the family. They are expected to live with their children when they can no longer live independently. They are frequently the arbitrators of family problems due to their wisdom and the role which they occupy within the family. Intergenerational conflict, feelings of depression, and guilt feelings may result for the child and the elderly parent when this cultural value is rejected due to the Americanization of the child. Married children frequently visit their parents and such behavior within the context of the Hispanic culture should not be assessed as a sign of enmeshment or pathological dependency. The enduring loyalty of Hispanic children to their parents is difficult for the Anglo worker to accept as the American value emphasizes the independence of the nuclear family from the family of origin.

- Regarding children, socialization patterns within the Hispanic culture sensitizes children to be extremely sensitive to the feelings of others and to respect and obey adults. Children are also taught that eye contact with an adult is a sign of disrespect and the importance of cooperation instead of competition in their contacts with peers. Individualism is viewed as disturbing the family unity. A belief also exists that bragging or ostentatious behavior attracts attention to the individual and may arouse feelings of envy in others which may lead to negative outcomes such as "mal ojo" the evil eye or a hex being placed on the individual.

- As mentioned earlier, Hispanics see a unity in mind and body. Their primary defense mechanism is to present psychological stress as physical complaints or to project blame onto events which are perceived of as being outside of their control (external locus of control).

- The Hispanic culture places strong emphasis on such values as respect, honor, dignity and personalismo. Personalismo emphasizes the importance of personal relationships between people rather than one which is cold, aloof and impersonal. The Hispanic client prefers to relate to the social worker more as a person than as a representative of an impersonal organization. Within the Hispanic culture, relationships are personalized and the Hispanic client, in contrast to the Black client, may prefer to use first names instead of formal titles in counseling situations. Also, in the counseling situation, the value of personalismo contrast with Anglo values. Anglos prefer a formal and impersonal approach in contacts with professionals.

APPLICATION OF CULTURAL KNOWLEDGE
IN TRANSCULTURAL PRACTICE WITH HISPANICS

Carillo (1982) suggests that effective intervention with Hispanics requires (1) an appreciation of their cultural historical determinants of behavior, (2) knowledge of culturally-sanctioned normative behavior and (3) sensitivity to their personal and interpersonal conflicts resulting from changes in their cultural norms (p. 52). Effective practice with Hispanics is also predicated upon an understanding of racism and how it has impacted Hispanics in American society. The values of personalismo, respect, honor and dignity require that the social worker at all times treat the Hispanic client in a respectful manner. Initial contacts with Hispanic clients should be leisurely in nature and a relationship established before the social worker enters into the reasons for the agency contact (Aquilar, 1972).

Always, the social worker needs to present him/herself as an authentic and personable person who is comfortable with self-disclosure. A leisurely interviewing pace is consistent with the Hispanic value of personalismo as it will afford the Hispanic client the chance to get to know the social worker as a person. The acceptance of the social worker as a person will be instrumental in the development of the helping relationship. Since loss of face constitutes a severe blow to the honor of the Hispanic client, the social worker should not be confrontive or insulting, or imply to the client that he/she has failed.

In the assessment process, the social worker needs to give consideration to the impact of external systems on the client's situation. The level of acculturation, the migration patterns of the family, and the support systems which are available to it should also receive consideration. Language capacity is of extreme importance. However, if the social worker must use an interpreter, an understanding of the client's culture remains of extreme importance. The use of an intermediary, a priest or an individual whom the client respects may be useful in the engagement of the client and the facilitation of the helping process. The father' role should always be validated, and attempts made to enlist him in the intervention process from the beginning of contacts. Certainly the social worker should guard against encouraging other family members to defy the father's authority or to challenge him. Such behavior places family members in a position of dishonoring the father and the father will lose face. If this occurs, the family may feel that its dignity has been threatened and premature termination may occur.

In developing a relationship with the Hispanic client, the social worker will need to join the family and to become accepted as a friend. When the family first arrives at the agency, the social worker should make every attempt to immediately greet it. His/her approach should be informal in nature and he/she should be prepared to engage in small talk, frequently of a personal nature, until the family feels comfortable with him/her. In these initial contacts, personalismo is very important. After the social worker and client have developed some personal knowledge of each other, then the social worker can gently move into the reasons for agency contact. The social worker needs to be seen as both a professional and a friend. In family sessions, it is always necessary that the father sanctions the involvement of other family members. Adults are respected and it is viewed as dishonorable behavior for children to be critical of them or to challenge their statements. Similarly in the small group composed of young and elderly Hispanics, the young may assume an inactive role out of deference to the adults. Cultural expectations influence behaviors. If the social worker is unaware of relationship protocol in a particular culture, he/she may misinterpreted behavior and classify it as being of a pathological nature.

When the Hispanic client presents him/herself at the agency, he/she will view the social worker as an expert and will expect for the social worker to tell him/her what to do. In such instances, the social worker must be careful not to mis-diagnose the client as a dependent personality, or be fearful that a dependent relationship will develop. If the social worker does not meet this expectation, then a sense of ambiguity is introduced into the helping process and the client will not know what he/she is to do to handle the situation or what the role of the social worker is in this process. However, when the social worker meets this challenge by offering suggestions and assisting the client in selecting strategies for bringing about change, he/she will be more able to involve the Hispanic client in the intervention plan.

In order to show respect for the Hispanic client, the social worker needs to understand what is meant by the words: personalismo, respecto and dignidad. Personalismo refers to the Hispanic cultural value which connotes a preference for a humanistic and personal encounter. Respecto refers to a respect for authority, cultural traditions and the importance of the family. It means that people should be treated in specific ways.

Dignidad while closely related to respeto suggests that while differences may exist among participants, no attempts should be made to take away from an individual his/her dignity. To show disrespect to a person or to embarrass him/her in front of others is viewed as exhibiting dishonorable behavior. Machismo is also identified as a Hispanic value usually in a negative sense. In a healthy sense, machismo refers to the Hispanic male's demonstration of strength in caring for his family, in upholding its dignity and in carrying out his role. In a negative sense, it has been used to refer to male superiority and domination of females in the Hispanic culture. The social worker needs to recognize, accept and respect in practice the cultural values which distinguish the Hispanics from other cultural groups. In their emphasis on the personal and affective aspects of interpersonal relations, Hispanic values differ from the rational, detached, impersonal approach to interpersonal relationships that characterize professional contacts with Anglos.

TRANSCULTURAL SOCIAL WORK PRACTICE WITH ASIAN/PACIFIC ISLANDERS

The term Asian/Pacific Islanders is used to refer to those ethnic groups whose ancestry is traced to Asia and the Pacific Islands. Included in these groups are Chinese, Japanese, Filipinos, Koreans, Samoans and Indo-Chinese. In the United States, the Chinese is the largest Asian-American subgrouping. They are followed by the Japanese and the Filipinos. Wong (1982) states at least 32 distinctive ethnic and cultural groups may be listed under this designation. Wong also states that 98 percent of all Indo-Chinese, 90 percent of Koreans, 70 percent of Filipinos and 60 percent of all Chinese residents in the United States are newly arrived. Recent immigrants such as the Indo-Chinese have faced numerous problems in their adjustment to American society. In addition to cultural shock and posttraumatic stress, Indo-Chinese have faced communication barriers, psychological stresses and socioeconomic problems such as health, housing and unemployment. Depression, isolation, loneliness and guilt over surviving and leaving loved ones behind are also factors which influence their stressful adjustment to American society. In time, intergenerational conflicts are brought on by the Americanization of their children, the casting away of old values and their dependency on their children for their English language ability. A dependency on children for their English language proficiency often leads to a role reversal and a loss of self esteem among adults which may also contribute to a loss of face and subsequent feelings of depression.

ASIAN/PACIFIC ISLANDERS VALUES

While Asian/Pacific Islanders constitute heterogeneous ethnic groups with wide variations in culture, Toupin (1980) states that they share aspects of a common cultural heritage which make it possible to discuss them as a group. Asian/Pacific Islanders usually represent a patriarachal society which is highly stratified with rigid sex-role differentiation. The following values have been identified as existing within Asian/Pacific Islander groups:

- A deference for authority and a need for smooth relationship among its members which present itself in an emphasis on individuals' knowing at all times their place and role.
- Filial piety and ancestor worship.
- An avoidance of shame or engaging in any behaviors which reflect negatively on the family; the behavior of the individual reflects on the present family, ancestors and future generations.
- Subordination of the individual's interest in safeguarding the honor of the family.
- Emphasis on public reserve, i.e., the individual conducts him/herself appropriately in public so that no shame is brought onto the family.
- Authority is vertical usually vested in the male.
- Rigid sex-role differentiation in which males are favored over females, and the eldest male child is always viewed as a son whose first allegiance is always to his parents.
- An emphasis on high achievement especially by the male as it brings honor to the family.
- Family problems are not exposed to the outside world and are expected to be resolved within the family or independently.
- Respect for the elderly.
- A socialization process in which children are conditioned to restrain from expressing feelings and emotions as these threaten the solidarity of the family and society.
- A more situation than individual centered orientation, i.e., that Asian/Pacific Islanders are more likely to receive cues to behavior from the social situation instead of acting individually.

Shame is an important aspect of Asian-American culture and serves essentially a social control function. Inasmuch as children are reared in the company of adults, they develop greater sensitivity to proper behavior and what is expected of them. They develop sensitivity to what other people think of them and always attempt to exhibit proper behaviors in the presence of others. They become acutely aware that their behaviors reflect not only on them but also on their families. Toupin remarks on the deference of the Asian-American to others, particularly those in positions of authority, and the absence of aggression and direct expression of feelings among them. She states, "The Asian lack of assertiveness fits within its culture and is related to the Asian concept of shame. Shame in the Asian sense is guilt collectively shared by the family as well as feelings of inferiority for not reaching ideals and goals defined by others" (p. 82). Other observers of Chinese culture have remarked on the sense of shame in the Asian culture. When one is shamed, one stands exposed and becomes very much aware that he/she has not acted in an accepted manner. This fact leads to extreme feelings of self consciousness and the feelings that he/she has failed and brought some shame to the family. Since the person becomes concerned about his/her behavior in the presence of others, he/she seeks not to exhibit any behavior that is socially disapproved. Aggressive behavior among Chinese children is also discouraged, and public display of affection places the Chinese in an embarrassing situation. Generally Asian/Pacific Islanders seek to avoid conflict or draw attention to themselves except in prescribed circumstances. To draw attention to oneself indicates a lack of humility. This extreme sensibility to the reactions of others is transmitted through the socialization process in which children are frequently in the company of adults. School failure, disobedience, juvenile delinquency and mental illness constitute great sources of shame to the family (Lorenzo and Adler, 1984).

Divorces are also frowned on in the Asian/Pacific Islander cultures. According to Ho (1988) "Few Asian-American/Pacific Islanders would consider befriending a woman who had been engaged, or gone steady with another man, let alone divorced" (p. 30). While divorce constitutes a great tragedy for the female, it favors the male who may traditionally divorce a wife if she argues with parental in-laws or does not produce a son. A son is important because he carries on the male line. A divorced woman is viewed as used merchandise and she may suffer social ostracism. The fear of this social ostracism can lead to suicide if a marriage is ended by divorce or if the woman finds it unbearable but does not want to pay the price of a divorce. While the ultimate decision making power and authority rests in the hands of the husband, women are able to exert some influence in such areas as the rearing of children, the management of the home and in the handling of money.

In the Asian/Pacific Islander culture, mental illness has a stigma attached to it. Lin (1980) feels that while the individual with a mental illness may receive compassion, the condition may be attributed to an immoral act committed by ancestors and therefore the family seeks to hide it. Somatic complaints and the attribution of events to supernatural forces may be viewed as defense mechanisms employed by the Asian/Pacific Islander. However, Lin suggests that while the Chinese often turn psychological problems into somatic complaints, they do have a psychological awareness of their discomfort, and emotions have been regarded as playing an important role in both physical and psychological illnesses. As an example he cites depression as an illness with psychological precipitants which are well recognized but is not treated as a psychological condition. He states, "Excess and incongruence of seven kinds of emotions (happiness, anger, worry, desire, sadness, fear and fright) are regarded as pathogenic" (p. 101).

In Lin's view in contrast to the European tradition that stresses the value of emotional catharsis, the Chinese directs their efforts to the avoidance of excesses of emotions (p. 101). The lack of excessiveness in the expression of emotions is viewed as a psychoculturally adaptive mechanism which results from Confucianism and the teaching that maintaining "harmony in familial and other social relationships requires inhibition and avoidance of emotional expressions" (Yeh, 1971, Quoted in Lin, p. 102).

A similar foundation of mental illness is located among the Southeast Asian refugees. Muecke (1985) states that unmistakable emotional disturbance is usually attributed "to possession by spirits of malicious intent; to the bad luck of familial inheritance, or for Buddhists, to bad Karma accumulated by misdeeds of the past (p. 838). Muecke feels that because mental illness is attributed to immoral causes it is commonly feared and denied, and mentally ill people are constrained usually within the home to prevent bringing shame to the family. She also states that Southeast Asians who are suffering from emotional problems will usually present somatic complaints when they seek help. She suggests that a label that does not suggest mental illness such as "family counselor" is more acceptable to Southeast Asians than therapists.

The social worker should be knowledgeable about the suppression of feelings in the Asian/Pacific Islander culture and come to view it as a cultural trait instead of resistive or avoidance behavior. Toupin states,

> The most noticeable characteristic (based on historical and anthropological observations) of an Asian are a deference to others and verbal devaluation of self and family. The absence of verbal aggression and direct expression of one's feelings, and the avoidance of confrontation, are personal qualities that are highly esteemed virtues in Asian society (p. 82).

APPLICATION OF CULTURAL KNOWLEDGE IN TRANSCULTURAL PRACTICE WITH ASIAN/PACIFIC ISLANDERS

Initial contacts with Asian/Pacific Islanders pose problems in their engagement in the helping process. They may not understand the nature of social work intervention and will be reluctant to engage themselves in this process as they fear a loss of face and do not want to violate cultural norms by discussing any aspects of their situation with outsiders. Therefore, it is important that the social worker comes to be perceived as a family member. The title "family counselor" is helpful in this regard as it connotes a friend. The social worker should present an empathetic, warm, accepting attitude toward the family so that it will come to trust and respect him/her. The social worker should also possess awareness that the family will take cues from his/her behavior as to the appropriate manner in which to respond. As a result of the Asian/Pacific Islander's deference to authority, the social worker will be viewed as an expert who will provide the family with direct advice and suggestions about what must be done to remedy its situation. They will expect the social worker to assume a direct and authoritative role, unambiguous in nature and mixed with compassion. Asian/Pacific Islanders present little tolerance for ambiguity. The provision of tangible services is important. They are a direct indication of the social worker's interests in the family and his/her desire to be of assistance. This initial dependency on the "expert" is a cultural trait. If the social worker is unaware of this cultural expectation, then he/she may misinterpret such behavior as an indication of pathological dependency or a transference phenomenon instead of viewing it as normative behavior within the context of the client's culture. Many writers have commented on this behavior in the Asian/Pacific Islander culture. Ho states, "Some Asian/Pacific American clients may ask the therapist many personal questions about his or her family background, marital status and number of children and so on" (p. 46).

In Ho's view, the social worker needs to develop a degree of comfort in answering such questions as they are crucial to the development of rapport and the gaining of the client's trust. Ryan (1985) suggests that social workers in practice with Chinese clients may often assume the role of surrogate parents. She feels this role is an important one to accept and validate. If it is not, the client may feel hopeless and inadequate. Lee. Juan and Huan (1984) also emphasize the importance of the social worker in becoming viewed as a trusted member of the family. If the family accepts the social worker as a trusted member, the cultural taboo against discussing family matters with outsiders is removed and the implicit understanding is presented that the discussion of family matters with the social worker does not result in a loss of face or a public display of family problems. They state, "The sharing of personal information by the worker though frowned upon by classically trained therapists may be a necessary feature of the engagement process and should be understood as the equivalent of the Western handshake" (p. 41).

While the Asian/Pacific Islander may defer to authority, the authority issue is of a reciprocal nature. The client expects for the social worker to respond to him/her in well defined and expected ways. Ambiguity is avoided and structure is extremely important. Work is done in the here-and-now and the social worker should reframe the situation so that the family does not feel a loss of face. The hierarchy of the father must be respected in making unilateral decisions and in giving guidance to the discussion. Generally, the father must give permission to family members to talk to the social worker about the family situation.

An awareness that somatic complaints may cloak psychological distress is important if the social worker is to arrive at a differential assessment. Within the Asian/Pacific Islander culture, somatic complaints may be viewed as a defense mechanism as they represent an acceptable means for the expression of psychological pressures in a culture which values harmony and the prohibition of excesses of emotions.

Therapeutic intervention, in addition to the provision of tangible services, may also focus on education with the social worker assuming the roles of a social broker, a cultural broker and a teacher. Culture comes into existence in the following areas in social work practice with Asian/Pacific clients:

(1) The social worker is placed automatically in the role of an expert and an authority figure. His/her expertise is made known through his/her diploma, and the certificates which adorn the wall of his/her office.

(2) The social worker will need to engage in self-disclosure.

(3) The social worker must seek to maintain a sense of harmony in the counseling session by following the relationship protocol of the culture. This means that a recognition of the father's authority is crucial, and in the absence of the father the eldest son becomes the spokesperson for the family.

(4) The social worker engages in no action which can be viewed as being disrespectful or contributing to a loss of face by the family.

(5) The social worker joins with the family and becomes viewed as a family friend. By this acceptance, the family can discuss its problems with the social worker without risking a loss of face or being threatened by the public display of its problems.

(6) The social worker should be aware of the importance of modesty and taboo areas, particularly sexual matters. It would always be contra-indicated for a male to raise sexual matters with a female.

(7) The social worker reveals his/her interest in the client through home visits, telephone contacts, sharing information, modeling behaviors, educating the client about the norms of American society and in providing concrete assistance such as help in completing forms or in accompanying the client to a social welfare or health agency.

TRANSCULTURAL SOCIAL WORK PRACTICE WITH NATIVE AMERICANS

Native Americans have also faced a history of official and unofficial maltreatment in American society. They have been subjected to prejudices, discrimination and genocide (Hull, 1982, p. 340). Native Americans are the most deprived minority group in the United States. Edwards and Edwards (1984) state that over 480 tribes exist within the United States and each tribe has its distinctive culture, history and language. Intertribal differences exist and tribes may follow patrilineal or matrilineal lines. The identity of the Native American derives from the tribe in which he/she holds membership, and thus a person is either a Navajo, a Crow, a Zuni or a Cherokee. Tribal leadership is traditionally made up of the heads of the families. Redhorse et al. (1978) state the Indian family network is structurally open, assuming a village type characteristic and containing several households of significant relatives (p. 68). Within these networks, extended families assume important roles in governance. In contacts with Native Americans some emphasis has been placed on the social network as the unit of intervention (Atteneave, 1976).

NATIVE AMERICAN VALUES

The value system of Native Americans contrasts greatly with the values of Anglo society. Approximately a third of Native Americans live in urban areas and another third live on reservations. The remaining third may be viewed as a transitory population moving back and forth between the reservation and the city. The following have been identified as Native American values:

- Strong family and extended family ties which include shared parenting and the assignment of sibling relationships to cousins.
- The resolution of problems within the family, extended family or tribal group.
- A time orientation which emphasizes the present and follows natural phenomenon such as days, nights and years.
- An emphasis on sharing one's good fortune, particularly with members of the tribe.
- A fatalistic view of life which results from an external locus of control, a desire to live in harmony with nature and a belief in the supernatural. When a Native American is ill, he/she may attribute the illness to having done something which was out of harmony with nature, or to a curse having been placed on him/her. Within their culture, religious practices usually implemented through the medicine man are used to return him/her to a state of harmony or to remove the curse.
- An emphasis on noninterference into the affairs of others.
- A respect for the elderly and a love of children. The elderly are respected for their wisdom and are actively involved in decision-making and conflict resolution.
- Permissive child rearing patterns. However, teasing and ridicule are used as a form of social control in the socialization of children so that they will learn appropriate behaviors.
- An emphasis on noncompetitiveness except in prescribed circumstances, i.e., the Native American youth may be noncompetitive with Anglos but competitive with each other. This trait may be viewed as passivity by those who lack understanding of it within the context of the Native American culture inasmuch as the Native American may withdraw

from aggressive situations or may not exhibit assertive type behaviors in confrontations.

- An avoidance of direct eye contact as this behavior is considered to be disrespectful and a sign of aggression. It is also associated with an Indian myth referred to as "He who kills with his eyes."
- A tendency to withdraw when faced with role ambiguity and to remain silent until the individual feels comfortable and capable of responding without fear of embarrassment.
- A tendency to control emotions which does not permit passionate outbursts.
- An optimistic toughness which reveals itself in a capacity for endurance and the acceptance of hardships.
- A belief that the universe and its people function according to specific rules and purposes.

TRANSCULTURAL SOCIAL WORK PRACTICE WITH NATIVE AMERICANS

The above identified values and behaviors will influence the nature of contacts between Native Americans and social workers. The social worker must be extremely patient in developing a helping relationship with the Native American. The Native American will need to get to know him/her as a friend before he/she will confide in the social worker. Goodtracks (1973) remarks on the role of silence in the Native American culture. He states the individual placed in an uncomfortable situation will not respond until the situation is clarified and he/she has gained cues as to how to respond without risking embarrassment. This cultural trait demands that the social worker demonstrate the nature of the helping process and what it entails, even to the degree of role playing, so that the Native American develops some understanding of his/her expected behavior. In remarking on the Native American's attitude toward competition, Ablon (1971) states the Native American is often not competitive in the middle class sense and will avoid aggressive actions and competitive activities when possible. In situations of conflict, the Native American withdraws. She also remarks on the diffused and everchanging nature of power among Native Americans. She states that authority may rest in many persons on different occasions. However, family and community consensus are necessary to determine collective action. The most important cultural value is that of loyalty to one's family and the extended group.

The social worker also needs to develop awareness of the socialization pattern of Native American children. Parents use teasing, ridicule and imitation in the socialization of their children. This teasing, sometimes harsh in nature, and ridicule are not only used as social control mechanisms but also to convey to the child what type of behavior is appropriate. The permissiveness that parents show in dealing with their children relates to the value of noninterference.

In initial contacts with Native Americans, the social worker must be prepared to show respect to the client, to be authentic and to show empathy. Hull identifies the best social workers as those who are "low-keyed and nondirective," who remain clear of tribal politics and can work with the natural helping networks and the medicine men. Polacca (1973) identifies some of the approaches in working with Navajos who have not adopted Anglo values. She emphasizes the importance of speaking slowly, clearly, and using a simple vocabulary. Inasmuch as bragging and exaggeration are frowned upon culturally, the Navajo who has mastered English may revert back to his/her native language in the presence of friends so as not to embarrass them. Polacca also states that the Navajo expresses a difference of opinion in unique ways. He/she will not openly state a difference, but will indicate it in his/her behavior by leaving the room or directing his/her attention to other areas. In this manner, the Navajo is expressing his/her opinion indirectly. The social worker should guard against making unkind remarks or in being critical as these comments will remain with the individual for a long time and have an adverse impact on the relationship. Personal questions should not be asked as the Native American will resent them. However, once a relationship is established and the social worker is accepted, he/she will answer questions.

The social worker should not make promises on which he/she cannot deliver. Failure to follow through on one's words is to risk losing the confidence of the client and to be viewed as one who cannot be trusted. In visiting the "hogans" of the Navajo, it is important that the social worker feels at home and to take a seat without being directed to it. Introductions may not be required as the overuse of names is perceived of as being bad. The social worker should also be careful about his/her behavior with babies and young children due to the superstitions held by Native Americans and in addition compliments may be viewed as being insulting.

The social worker at the beginning of contacts should approach the client in an informal manner and should be comfortable in engaging in small talk. Comments should be directed to all members of the family regardless of their age. The social worker must always show patience and never attempt to push the Native American who places great value on self-reliance. The social worker should also be comfortable in self-disclosure, and attempt to provide concrete services. The provision of concrete services illustrates the social worker's interest in the client, reveals that he/she is a trustworthy and dependable person who can be trusted. This provision of concrete services also illustrates that the social worker possesses the ability to help the client. The social worker may come to be viewed as an expert. As an expert, he/she may be endowed with perfection. His/her personal appearance will be important. Native Americans feel that a person who is good, worthy and industrious will be successful and blessed with material possessions. This image is also carried over to the social worker. In contrast, if the social worker pays little attention to his/her personal appearance, he/she may be negatively evaluated.

Confrontational techniques should not be employed by the social worker as they will be viewed as indications of rude behaviors which the client will resist. In the Native American culture, if the social worker's behavior is evaluated as being intrusive and abusive, or that he/she is placing the client under pressure, then it is culturally sanctioned that the client may withdraw from such situations, or exhibit passive resistance to them (silence). Yahares et al. (1973) provide succinct examples of the differences in Anglo and Native American values. They state in situations of crisis and under pressure, the white American code says "Do something about it without specifying what." The Navajo culture suggests the opposite, instead of fighting escape and instead of action, do nothing, show passive resistance. While white Americans may seek to tame nature, Navajos seek to live with it in harmony less they be destroyed. While Americans encourage individualism, Navajos encourage cooperation and respect for the individual. In family situations, the husband and wife do not struggle to control and include children in those areas concerning them. The Navajo sees security as resulting from group respect and cooperation. This process begins with the family. To the Navajo, love of life and adherence to tradition are important (p. 150).

SUMMARY AND CONCLUSION

In transcultural social work practice, the social worker must give consideration to a number of variables. Among these variables are (1) culture, (2) racism, (3) the level of acculturation, (4) the immigration experience and (5) the nature of the minority client's psychosocial-cultural experiences in the United States. Culture provides an important and additional meaning to the understanding of human behavior. The La Barres (1965) state,

> Cultural concepts particularly as they have been integrated with psycho-analytic concepts have deepened the caseworker's awareness of the molding influences of tradition and the tribe upon the pattern of child care, the development of roles in the family and the group and social resolution of conflicts between impulses and cultural demands (p. 399).

Cultural concepts used in conjunction with social concepts have also developed our awareness of the conflicts which emerge when different cultures meet and one group may attempt to impose its own value system onto the other. Cultural clashes lead to ecological imbalances and a lack of fit in the transactions which occur between interacting sociocultural systems. Racism as a social concept also have developed the social worker's awareness of the manner in which institutional racism operates and contributes to cultural genocide and cultural annihilation.

SOCIAL WORK PROCESS IN TRANSCULTURAL PRACTICE

In practice with minority clients, cultural dynamics will reveal themselves in the beginning, middle and ending phases of practice. Culture should become included in a systematic manner in the assessment process. Some theorists have employed the term psychocultural assessment to assure that the social worker recognizes the impact of culture on behavior. The social work process does not change, nor is it modified in transcultural practice. What does change are the techniques, the relationship protocol, the social worker's presentation of him/herself and the emphasis which is placed on certain aspects of the client's situation. For example, it is unlikely that the social worker would need to be concerned about racism as a sociocultural phenomenon in contacts with middle and upper class clients.

In the beginning phase, the social worker attempts to develop an understanding of the client's situation and the factors contributing to it.

He/she is more concerned with process as a means to an end, instead of initially focusing on the problem which brings the family to the agency. He/she needs to bridge the client's culture through his/her demonstration of his/her understanding of the client's cultural values. In this beginning phase, the client may also serve as a teacher to the social worker, and the social worker should become a respected learner. The demonstration of respect characterizes this phase as the social worker and the client authenticate each other. The social worker must always guard against placing the client in a position where he/she will lose face and frequently it is necessary to reframe the problem. The social worker will need to apply cultural understanding to the data collected from the client system. Leininger (1977) defines a cultural assessment as a "systematic appraisal or examination of individuals, groups and communities as to their cultural beliefs, values, and practices within the cultural context of the people being evaluated" (pp. 86–87). Tripp-Reimer, Brink and Saunders (1986) identify (1) values, (2) beliefs, (3) customs and (4) structural components as areas which should receive attention in the cultural assessment. Under customs would be listed communication styles, verbal and nonverbal, family interactions and roles, and under social structure would be listed the structure of the family, religion, politics, education, economics, law and health and welfare institutions. The social worker should recognize that a cultural assessment will rarely necessitate that information on every cultural element be secured. However, information should always be collected and assessed on those cultural factors which are operative in the client's situation and are involved in systemic stress and faulty transactions between interacting systems.

In the middle or work phase of transcultural practice, the social worker and the client are working cooperatively on problem-resolution. Consensus has been reached on the problem to be addressed; goals have been established, a contract has been formulated and the intervention strategy has been designed and implemented. This intervention strategy is culturally sensitive; targets of change have been identified and the social worker has identified those roles he/she will assume as well as the levels of society to which intervention will be directed. In the ending or termination process, the social worker should prepare the client for the ending of contact. To the client, the social worker will retain the role of family friend. The termination process may well be put into the context of friends' parting as the situation which brought them together no longer exist, and this process may also be initiated by informal discussion which will eventually lead up to the final termination. If the social worker should find it necessary to refer the client to another source, he/she should handle this area in a very skillful manner as the client may view it as a form or rejection which reactivates earlier feeling around loss of face or the airing of family problems.

A transcultural approach to social work practice is indicated with minorities due to their history of racial and cultural oppression in the United States. If the social worker lacks knowledge of their sociohistorical experiences and their cultures, he/she will encounter problems in establishing the therapeutic alliance. As a result of their treatment in the United States, minorities will approach societal institutions with an air of suspicion, fear and mistrust. These barriers can only be overcomed and trust built when the client and the social worker understand and mutually respect each other. The adjustment of minorities to American society has been made with considerable psychological stress and social strain. This psychological stress and social strain are reasons enough for a transcultural perspective in social work practice.

Transcultural practice provides a means for the systematic inclusion of race, racism and culture into practice with minorities. This practice approach needs to follow an ecological approach as a focus must always be directed on the transactions which characterize the transactions which take place between minorities and societal institutions. The social worker needs to be knowledgeable about social policy, organizational analysis, culture and race and possess skills in micro-mezzo-macro practice. The problems of minority clients are so pressing that they will rarely yield to insight therapies. The social worker should expect to be accepted as an expert, to provide advice and guidance, and concrete services. The least complex alternative should be selected for problem resolution. The social worker will need to be comfortable in self-disclosure and to present him/herself as an authentic person, who is warm, caring and interested in the welfare of the client. Patience is extremely important in contacts with People of Color. The social worker should guarded against being critical, judgmental or pressuring clients into areas which violate their values or to which they may show resistance.

SELECTED BIBLIOGRAPHY

Ablon, J. (1971) Retention of cultural values and differential urban adaptation: Samoans and American Indians in a west coast city. SOCIAL FORCES, 49, 385–393.

Aquilar, I. (1972) Initial contacts with Mexican-American families. SOCIAL WORK, 17, 186–189.

Atteneave, C. (1976) Social networks as the unit of intervention. In P. Guerin (Ed.), Family therapy: Theory and Practice (New York: Gardner Press).

Brown, J. (1981) Parent education groups with Mexican-Americans. SOCIAL WORK IN EDUCATION, 3, 22–32.

Brown, J. and Arevalo, R. (1979) Chicanos and social group work models: Implications for social group work practice. SOCIAL WORK WITH GROUPS, 2, 331–342.

Brown, L. (1964) Newer dimensions of patient case: Patients as people (New York: Russell Sage Foundation).

Bullock, C. and Rodgers, H. (1975) Racial equality in America (Pacific Palisades, CA: Goodyear Publishing Co.).

Carillo, C. (1982) Changing norms for Hispanic families. In E. Jones and S. Korchin (Eds.), Minority mental health (New York: Praeger Publishers).

Chestang, L. (1976) Environmental influences on social functioning: The Black experience. In P. Cafferty and L. Chestang (Eds.) (New York: National Association of Social Workers).

Dieppa, I. and Montiel, M. (1978) Hispanic families: An exploration. In M. Montiel (Ed.), Hispanic families: An exploration (Washington, D.C.: National Coalition of Hispanic Mental Health and Services Organization).

Edwards, D. and Edwards, M. (1984) Group work practice with American Indians. In L. Davis (Ed.), Ethnicity and social group work (New York: Haworth Press).

Gibbs, J. (1985) Treatment relationship with Black clients: Interpersonal and instrumental strategies. In C. Germain (Ed.), Advances in clinical social work (New York: National Association of Social Workers).

Gibson, W. (1980) Family life and morality: Studies in black and white (Washington, DC: University Press of America).

Goodtracks, J. (1973) Native American non-interference. SOCIAL WORK, 18, 30–34.

Handlin, O. (1957) Race and nationality in American life (New York: Anchor/Doubleday Books).

Hill, R. (1972) The strengths of black families (New York: National Urban League).

Hillard, A. (1976) Alternative to I.Q. Testing: An approach to the identification of the gifted child: Final report to the Department of Education (Sacramento, CA: State Department of Education).

Ho, M. (1988) Family therapy with ethnic minorities (Newbury Park, CA: Sage Publications).

Hull, G. (1982) Child welfare services to Native Americans. SOCIAL CASEWORK, 63, 340–347.

Hoffman, A. (1974) Unwanted Mexican-Americans in the great depression: Repatriation pressures, 1929–39 (Tuscon, AR: University of Arizona Press).

La Barre, M. and La Barre, W. (1965) "The worm in the honeysuckle: A case study of a child's hysterical blindness. SOCIAL CASEWORK, XLVI, 399–413.

Lee, P., Juan, G. and Huan, J. (1984) Group work with Asian-Americans: A sociocultural approach. In L. Davis (Ed.), Ethnicity and social group work practice (New York: Haworth Press).

Leininger, M. (1977) Culturological assessment domains for nursing practice (New York: John Wiley and Sons).

Lin, Keh-Ming (1980) Traditional Chinese medical beliefs and their relevance for mental illness and psychiatry. In A. Kleinman and T. Lin (eds.). Normal and abnormal behavior in Chinese culture (Location unidentified: D. Rudel Publishing Co.).

Lorenzo, M. and Adler, D. (1984) Mental health services for Chinese in a community mental health center. SOCIAL CASEWORK, 65, 600–609.

Marden, C. and Meyers, G. (1962) Minorities in American society (New York: American Book Company).

Morales, A. (1981) Social work practice with third world people. SOCIAL WORK, 26, 45–51.

Muecke, M. (1985) In search of healers: Southeast Asian refugees in the American health care system: Cross-cultural indicators. WESTERN JOURNAL of MEDICINE, 139, 835–840.

Peters, M. (1981) "Making it:" Black family style, building on the strengths of black families. In N. Stinnerr et al. (Eds.), Family strengths, 3: Roots of well being (Lincoln, NE: University of Nebraska Press).

Polacca, K. (1979) Ways of working with the Navajo who have not learned the white man's ways. In A. Reinhardt and M. Quinn (Eds.), Family centered community nursing: A sociocultural framework (St. Louis, MO: C.V. Mosby).

Ramirez, M. and Castaneda, A. (1974) Cultural democracy: Bicognitive development and education (New York: Academic Press).

Redhorse, J. et al. (1978) Family behavior of urban American Indians. SOCIAL CASEWORK, 59, 67–72.

Ryan, A. (1985) Cultural factors in casework treatment with Chinese Americans. SOCIAL CASEWORK, 66, 333–339.

Thomas, W. and Znaniecki, F. (1927) The Polish peasant in Europe and America (New York: Alfred Knopf).

Tripp-Reimer, T., Brink, P. and Saunders, J. (1986) Cultural assessment: Content and Process. In B. Spradley (Ed.), Readings in community health nursing (Boston: Little Brown).

Toupin, E. (1980) Counseling Asians: Psychotherapy in the context of racism and Asian-American history. AMERICAN JOURNAL OF ORTHOPSYCHIATRY, 50, 76–86.

Wong, H. (1982) Asian and Pacific Americans. In L. Snowden (Ed.), Reaching the underserved; Mental health needs of neglected populations (Beverly Hills, CA: Sage Publications).

Yahares, H. et al. (1973) The mental health of rural America; The rural programs of the National Institute of Mental Health (Rockville, MD: Office of Program Planning and Evaluation, Alcohol, Drug abuse and Mental Health Administration).

SECTION VII
SOCIAL WORK PRACTICE
WITH INTERRACIAL FAMILIES

INTRODUCTION

Interracial families have increased in American society. While the following chapter focuses on black-white families, it has relevance for other mixed racial families. The social worker in practice with these families must employ innovative practice approaches as they present a challenge due to their unique position in American society. They are viewed as violating a societal norm and for marrying for ulterior motives. Stereotypes exist about them which may influence the social worker's attitude toward them. In the past laws prohibited such unions and it was not until 1957 that such laws were held to be unconstitutional by the Supreme Court. These families and their children in addition to facing the normative problems which may affect any family may face unique problems based on the nature of their unions. They may be targets of prejudices, bigotry and racism. Children of these unions may also face unique problems in establishing their identities and in accepting their dual heritage. Parents may attempt to protect them from the realities of American society which ill prepare them to cope with the problems they may face. The social worker must be sensitive to the problems faced by interracial families and possess practice skills, knowledge and the attitudes which will enable him/her to effectively engage these couples in treatment and to remove obstacles which prevent them and their children from functioning to their fullest capacities.

Chapter 19

SOCIAL WORK PRACTICE
WITH INTERRACIAL FAMILIES

Even though a variation of mixed-racial families may exist in the
United States, this chapter focuses on black-white unions. The content in this chapter however may also have relevance to practice with
other mixed-racial families such as Asian-white, Native-American-white,
or Hispanic-white. As the United States move toward becoming a truly
multiethnic society, interracial families will increasingly come to the
attention of social workers. Social workers will need to be sensitive to
their uniqueness if they are to successfully engage them in practice. In
addition, social workers will also need to have resolved their feelings
about such unions so that they do not intrude in a negative manner into
the helping process. While greater acceptance of black-white unions have
developed over the years, the view remains that black-white unions are
deviant in nature and have violated a strong social taboo. The view also
exists that these couples have married for ulterior motives and want to
prove something. These families are frequently the targets of racism and
prejudices.

The number of black-white couples has increased in the United States.
The 1980 census revealed that 613,000 interracial couples existed in the
United States. This number doubles that of the 310,000 interracial couples reported in the 1970 census. The March 1988 Current Population
Survey revealed that the number of marriages between black men and
white women was estimated to be 149,000 and those between white men
and black women were estimated to be 69,000. It is generally estimated
that interracial children vary from 60,000 to over 5 million (Brown,
1987). Interracial children will also be confronted with problems. They
will need to resolve identity issues and to develop survival skills for
effective coping in a society which generally devaluates them. In practice
with interracial families, the social worker should always look for the

strengths within these families and the union itself must not be viewed as a sign of pathology or instability.

It was not until 1967 in Loving vs. Virginia that the Supreme Court held that laws prohibiting black-white unions were unconstitutional and that the right to marry was a fundamental one protected by the Constitution (Fullerton, 1977). The hostility and rejection which surround black-white unions does not appear to be as strong toward other interracial unions. The child who is the product of a black-white union is always viewed as being black—a status that does not always follow children of other interracial unions. Fullerton states that,

> a de facto caste line based on race has existed in the United States . . . and to some degree remains today. It has been maintained by occupational barriers, by the prohibiting of interracial marriages, and by defining as Black all children of mixed white and Black ancestry. Even when interracial marriage has been legal, it has not been possible for the white spouse to confer his status onto the Black (p. 550).

INTERRACIAL CHILDREN

Children of black-white unions will also find themselves affected by society's attitudes toward them. They may become targets of scorn and rejection as a result of their dual racial heritage. Unless they are assisted in stabilizing their identities and in developing sound self-concepts, they may become marginal individuals, divided between the races, and unable to feel totally comfortable with either. Or, if their physical characteristics make it possible, they may elect to reject their black heritage and to pass as white. In the author's opinion, children born of black-white unions are invariably designated as being black, and it is healthy for the family to come to grips with and to accept this reality in American society. The interracial child needs to be exposed to experiences which will help him/her to gain knowledge about his/her dual heritage. He/she should be comfortable in discussing his/her racial identity with his/her family and friends. Families will do great harm if they attempt to shield the child from the realities of American society. McRoy and Freeman (1986) state, "Mixed-race adolescents who are unable to reconcile their mixed cultural background into a personal and socially acceptable coalescence will not resolve this developmental stage. Thus, the individual may exhibit neurotic behavior. Acknowledging that mixed-race children represent a potentially vulnerable population requires that school social workers be able to evaluate actual or potential problems in racial identity and work collaboratively with parents, peers and community members to alleviate the situation" (p. 166).

TRANSRACIAL ADOPTIONS

The practice of transracial adoptions also presents unique opportunities and challenges for social workers in transcultural practice. As a result of the large number of black children in foster care, white couples have been allowed to adopt black children. (Similarly, white couples have also adopted Native-Americans, Hispanics and Asian children.) The practice of transracial adoptions continues to be controversial. Research has been conducted on families involved in transracial adoptions to determine how children have adjusted. These families may also present themselves to social workers for assistance in addressing some of the problems which confront them. These problems may be those customary ones which face families at various cycles of their development or they may relate to the area of the transcultural adoption. If the family has selected not to lived in integrated neighborhoods, they may request assistance in learning how to deal with racial issues, problems in identity formation, or how to address the rejection felt by the child when he/she faces difficulties in dating. The family may face particular difficulties when the child reaches adolescence and is in the process of establishing his/her identity.

INITIAL CONTACTS WITH INTERRACIAL FAMILIES

It is important that social workers do not approach these clients with stereotypes which may lead to self-fulfilling prophecies. It is equally important that social workers do not minimize the impact of racism on the problems faced by the family. Through differential assessment, the social worker needs to determine if race contributes to the problem and if so in what manner. The social worker should present an open attitude, begin where the family is, and illustrate a capacity to learn from the family. The interracial composition of the family should not become the focus of attention. Certainly, the social worker can acknowledge the difficulties faced by an interracial union in American society. As race and racism are realities in American life, the social worker should be comfortable in discussing them and in recognizing indirect cues on the part of the clients as they respond to this discussion. Unless the social worker can convey his/her comfort to the family in this area, it may remain below the surface, but its impact will be felt in uneasiness in the therapeutic alliance.

If the social worker accepts the cultural taboo which exists about black-white unions, he/she may view these unions in a negative manner and implement a "hidden agenda" which may do harm to the family based on his/her view that such unions are unhealthy. The client's right to self-determination may be ignored. This behavior is vividly illustrated in one of the earlier cases presented in the literature involving premarital counseling with a white female who was planning marriage to a black (Mudd et al., 1958). The female's parents appealed to a marriage counselor for assistance in helping their daughter to recognize the effects of the planned marriage on them. The mother feared that the proposed union would result in the loss of friends, the impairment of mental health, and the possible need for the family to move out of the area. The parents stated the family was a happy one until this problem presented itself. The mother blamed the father for allowing the daughter to associate with blacks. While the father professed to have no objection to the marriage, his concern was that his daughter would be unhappy in such a union. Though the parents did not state what they would like for the outcome of contacts with the marriage counselor to be, it is obvious that they sought his assistance in preventing the marriage.

Interviews with the daughter were held over several sessions. The fiance was not involved in counseling. The focus of contacts was on the reactions of the parents to the planned marriage. When the daughter asked if she did not have the right to make a decision regarding her marriage, the marriage counselor did not deviate from focusing on the possible effects of the marriage on the family, particularly the mother, and directed his attention toward activating a sense of guilt in the daughter over the impact of her planned marriage on the family. Following one session, the marriage counselor asks the daughter to examine her rights when it involved the unhappiness of others. He states, "This led to a discussion of her relations to her parents, theirs to her, the interrelation of their happiness as individuals and as a family group, and whether she or they had a right to pursue their own happiness at the cost of the unhappiness of the other" (p. 400). The daughter finally made a decision not to proceed with the planned marriage. She had come to view all of its "negative aspects" and states that "The venture was too much for her and that she did not possess a pioneering spirit which such a marriage required." While we have no way of knowing the intentions of the marriage counselor, from the write-up it is obvious that in subtle, almost manipulative ways, by emphasizing one topic (effects of planned marriage on parents) and deemphasizing others (the client's right to make her own decision), he influenced the daughter's decision to abandon the planned marriage. Such a belief is further supported by the fact that the potential groom was not involved in the counseling process.

Social workers must always approach interracial families with an openness of mind; individualization is extremely important. These families should not be placed into a specific category. Apart from the interracial aspects of their marriage, they will face similar problems as all families do. As a result of the interracial aspects of their marriage, they also will face unique problems. In the author's opinion, the impact of race and racism on interracial families cannot be ignored, minimized or easily dismissed. Brown states, " . . . the issue of race in Black-white unions must be recognized and assessed for its contribution to the tensions faced by the couple in the same way as variables such as communication patterns, sexual relationships, decision-making patterns, in-law interference, child rearing patterns and economic pressures are recognized and assessed" (p. 26). Staples (1973) states, "While the motivation of an interracial marriage may or may not differ from that of an intraracial marriage, certain problems are unique to this type of marriage," (p. 125). Among these problems are those of cementing a dual heritage, the identity formation of the child, and the manner in which these families cope with racist practices, bigotry and rejection.

SOCIAL WORK PROCESS

The social work process with these families does not differ from that employed with any client system. It may consist of the sequential steps of study, diagnosis and treatment, and activities will center around beginning, middle and ending stages of contact. However, it is important that the social worker possesses a knowledge base which helps him/her to be sensitive to the problems faced by an interracial couple in a society which until recently had gone to such steps as to legally forbid such unions. McRoy and Freeman suggest that assessment in cases involving racial identity problems should incorporate two goals: (1) to identify those factors which affect the child's racial identity in a positive or negative manner, and (2) identification of the specific supports that are available in the children's environment which can be used to help the child to develop and maintain an overall positive racial identity (p. 167). The ecogram is a useful tool in assessing the nature of the supports which are available to the family. Regarding the ecogram, Hartman (1978) states, "It (the eco-map) maps in a dynamic way the ecological system, the boundaries of which encompass the person or family in the life space . . . It pictures the important nurturant or conflict laden connections between the family and the world" (p. 467). Essentially the ecogram helps the family to identify and recognize stressful points in its ecological environment. It is important to remember that the family itself is also a social system which can be stressed by the interactions which occur among its members. The genogram which traces the family over three generations and provides a picture of its patterns and significant events may have limited utility in practice with interracial families as a result of the dynamics of racism and race in American society. The interracial family will present a new picture of the family's evolution and as such previous patterns need to be seriously evaluated for their generational significance and impact on the problems being faced by the family. It is highly likely that in the majority of cases of interracial marriages that some estrangement has occurred among family members over the marriage. The marriage itself must be viewed as representing a strength since it has probably taken place under considerable pressures. However, the genogram does reveal the familial experiences of the partners and as such may yield insights into their personalities, behavioral patterns and the familial forces which have molded them.

As a result of living in American society, it is expected that children of interracial unions will encounter racist experiences. These experiences should not catch them by surprise; they should be prepared to address them. These children will also need assistance in fully integrating their dual heritage and the contrasting manner in which blacks and whites are treated. Reese (1991) states, "Children of mixed racial and ethnic parentage have unique needs, but often the professional who works with these children in day care centers, schools, social services or health care settings lacks the training or awareness to provide the best possible services, support and encouragement to these children and their families" (p. 12).

Following the initial contacts, the engagement of the family and the establishment of the therapeutic alliance, the social worker will engage in the data collection and assessment processes. A determination should be made of the degree to which the mixed-racial composition of the family contributes to the problems faced by it. Time must also be devoted to the gathering of information as to how the family itself views its situation, the manner in which the parents are rearing their children, how they have prepared their children to address possible racist encounters and the problem-solving skills evidenced by the family in addressing problems. Even though the family may state that their interracial union has not been problematic, the social worker accepts the family statement but also wonders if the family is using denial. In this aspect the social worker must be sensitive to the indirect cues provided by the family. Interracial couples and those involved in transracial adoptions probably have been warned that they have gone against existing social mores and may be resistive to acknowledging negative experiences of a racist nature. In a real sense these families provide social worker with the opportunity to engage in primary and secondary prevention. Primary intervention is possible when interracial families are educated to some of the experiences which they may encounter so that they may develop coping strategies in addressing them. Secondary prevention is possible in recognizing that these families are at risk and should be referred for some type of assistance before their problem becomes acute. Primary and secondary preventive efforts of a psychoeducational nature may precede tertiary prevention. Gibbs and Moskowitz-Sweet (1991) identify conflicts as existing in the following areas in the treatment of biracial and bicultural adolescents: (1) their dual racial or ethnic heritage, (2) their social marginality, (3) their sexuality and impulse management, (4) their separation-individuation from their parents and (5) their educational and career aspirations (p. 582). Conflicts may also exist over the manner in which these parents attempt to rear their interracial children, particularly if parents elect to live in white neighborhoods and to limit the contacts of their children with black society.

INTERVENTION

Intervention with interracial families constitutes a challenge which requires traditional and innovative practice approaches at the individual, family and small group levels. If indicated, the social worker should make use of consultation in helping him/her to clarify his/her feelings toward these families and to identify effective intervention strategies.

The black partner may be extremely sensitive to the social worker's reactions to the marriage which may reveal itself in verbal and nonverbal ways. He/she may react to the social worker in a variety of ways which include denial of a problem or challenging the social worker's understanding of the black experience. Bowles (1977) states that black clients and white workers bring to the therapeutic experience "unspoken assumptions held by each other that were shaped by myths, stereotypes, preconceptions and speculations." These unspoken assumptions must be identified, articulated and addressed if the therapeutic alliance is to move forward. Unspoken assumptions may be intensified in practice with an interracial family. It is Bowles' feeling that these obstacles can be surmounted if the worker is open, possesses the ability to listen, is able to accept different values than his/her own, presents a willingness to be self-aware and the capacity to acknowledge his/her limitations, and is able to negate stereotypes and myths" (p. 11).

In practice with interracial families, Brown introduces the notion of a parallel social structure as a viable intervention technique. This parallel social structure consists of black and white therapists who act as a team. This parallel social structure is useful in minimizing the possibility of the minority client challenging the social worker on minority experiences. Challenging social workers on their knowledge of the minority experience is frequently used as an avoidance technique or as a means of showing anger when the black client is experiencing feelings of discomfort. Interracial support groups are also valuable resources for interracial families who feel isolated. In such groups, these couples can share experiences, engage in problem-solving, and receive support from each other. The members of the support group can act as a mutual aid system in helping group members in dealing with stress. Groups may also be formed for interracial children who require some form of therapeutic intervention. Reese (1991) identifies the objectives of a support/therapy group for children of mixed heritage; (1) guide group members on a path of self-discovery, (2) foster the "I'm okay" rule to children questioning their own self-identity, (3) promote higher self and cultural esteem, (4) show support for the child's own individual uniqueness, (5) promote social network among peers with similar "crisis" and (6) encourage self exploration of child's wants and needs (p. 12).

In contacts with the interracial child who must consolidate his/her identity as a black, it is indicated that the child has access to a black social worker. If society perceives the child of the interracial unit as being black, then the child must develop some degree of comfortableness with his/her blackness. The white social worker who is working with an interracial family will need to consult with and to utilize the services of black social workers both in understanding the problems faced by the family and the child and also as a cotherapist as indicated.

CONCLUSION

As the number of interracial families increases, some of them will come to the attention of the social worker for assistance with the problems that they face. The social worker must recognize that these families face unique problems in American society. Problems for them may be related to the normative crises faced by families or to the fact that as an interracial couple they have violated a fundamental social taboo. The children of these unions as well as the minority child placed in transracial adoptions may face identity problem which lead to acting out behaviors and faulty psychosocial adjustment. To work effectively with interracial families and mixed racial children, the social worker must be sensitive to their situation in the United States and employ innovative and creative practice approaches as he/she attempts to assist these families in addressing those conditions which have contributed to the problem which brings them to the attention of the social worker.

SELECTED BIBLIOGRAPHY

Bowles, D. (1970) Treatment issues in working with black clients. SMITH COLLEGE SCHOOL FOR SOCIAL WORK JOURNAL, 4, 8–14.

Brown, J. (1987) Casework contacts with black-white couples. SOCIAL CASEWORK, 68, 24–29.

Fullerton, G. (1977) Survival in marriage (Hinsdale, IL: Dryden Press).

Gibbs, J. and Moskowitz, Sweet, G. (1991) Clinical and cultural issues in the treatment of biracial and bicultural adolescents. FAMILIES IN SOCIETY, 72, 579–591.

Hartman, A. (1978) Diagrammatic assessment of family relationships. SOCIAL CASEWORK, 59, 465–476.

McRoy, R. and Freeman, E. (1986) Racial and identity issues among mixed race children. SOCIAL WORK IN EDUCATION, 8, 164–174.

Mudd, E. et al. (1958) Case #36: Contemplated Negro-white marriage. Marriage counseling: A casebook (New York: Association Press).

Reese, R. (1991) Group therapy for children of mixed heritage. INTERRACE, 3, 12.

Staples, R. (1973) The Black woman in America (Chicago: Nelson Hall Publishers).

SUPPLEMENTARY REFERENCE

Wradle, F. (1991) Interracial children and their families: How school social workers should respond. SOCIAL WORK IN EDUCATION, 13, 215–223.

SECTION VIII
SOCIAL WORK PRACTICE
WITH APPALACHIAN
AND VERY POOR FAMILIES

INTRODUCTION

The social work practitioner comes into contacts with families and clients who possess unique characteristics which must be considered in practice with them. These characteristics which resemble a culture result from regional and class differences. These differences have resulted in rural and poor clients possessing a world view, life style, and value system which distinguish them from other clients. Some of these differences have been identified as existing in minority clients. Possibly this results from the fact that many minority clients are also poor. It is important that the social worker be able to distinguish between class and cultural differences. The social worker needs to be sensitive to the unique characteristics of rural and poor clients, and possess specific knowledge and skills if he/she is to work effectively with them. The social worker also needs to show flexibility and creativity in his/her practice with Appalachian and poor families.

Chapter 20

SOCIAL WORK PRACTICE
WITH APPALACHIAN
AND VERY POOR FAMILIES

In practice with Appalachian and very poor families, the social worker must be sensitive to the impact of class and region on their behavior. These clients have also been stereotyped, and labeled as being unmotivated, unworkable and resistive to services. Gould (1967) suggests that "The differences between middle and low classes as revealed in personality types and life styles are largely a result of the differences in sociocultural and economic backgrounds" (p. 79). In addition to being a class society, the United States is also divided by regions, rural and urban, with their own value systems and life styles. The differences in behaviors between rural and urban populations may be classified as culture. Knowledge of culture, values, life styles, and relationship protocol is equally as important as cultural knowledge is in practice with People of Color. If the social worker is to successfully engage poor and Appalachian families in intervention, he/she must be knowledgeable about their culture, values, life styles and their interactions with institutions of the dominant society.

SOCIAL CLASS

A knowledge of social class provides the social worker with a general fund of knowledge about the socioeconomic conditions under which people and the impact of these conditions on their life styles. Kerbo (1983) identifies 5 class divisions in the United States: (1) upper, (2) corporate, (3) middle, (4) working, and (5) lower. He states, "A system of social stratification helps shape how people live, their opportunities for a better life, their mental health and life expectancy" (p. 3). Specific characteristics have been attributed to poor families on the community, family and individual levels. According to Kerbo at the community level, the poor is viewed as being nonparticipants in the institutional life of the community except when they get into difficulties with various institutions such as the law and welfare systems. At the family level, the poor are distinguished by having "an absence of a long childhood, an early initiation into sex, involvement in consensual marriages, female-centered families and a high desertion rate of wives and children." At the individual level, the poor are identified as presenting the following characteristics: "strong feelings of marginality, feelings of helplessness, dependence and inferiority." They are also viewed as possessing weak egos, poor impulse control, a fatalistic attitude toward life, a present time orientation, an inability to defer gratification so that they can engage in future planning, a belief in male superiority, and a high tolerance for psychopathology (Kerbo, p. 306).

Hodges (1968) suggests that the lower the family is on the class level, the more it will be burdened with mental health problems, marital stress, infant mortality, economic pressures and other problems such as poor housing and unemployment. Chilman (1965) also identifies behaviors located in very poor families:

- a present time orientation
- an authoritarian, rigid family structure
- inconsistent and harsh punishment of children
- an alienation from societal institutions and a distrustful approach to society
- a paucity of life experiences, a low self-esteem, and a belief that life is unpredictable and its events beyond their control
- a tendency to evaluate behavior and to respond to it based on the feelings that the behavior evokes in them

In middle class families, Chilman located the following behaviors:

- extensive verbal communication
- high self-esteem
- emphasis on education and success
- individualization of children
- a belief in one's own coping abilities and a view that human behavior is impacted by a variety of factors

Mayer and Timms (1969) conducted a study to identify some of the dynamics involved in contacts with working class clients. They wanted to determine if the working class lack understanding of the therapeutic process, if they attribute personal difficulties to external conditions, and if they expected the therapist to provide them with concrete advice and to assume an active role in the intervention. They state,

> Our interviews with the clients enabled us to see or at least suggest that the so-called inadequacies in the problem-solving thinking of working class persons are actually by-products or derivation of a different system. In other words, the behavior of these clients when viewed in its proper context and not by middle class standards become more understandable and in many ways more reasonable (p. 169).

MIDDLE CLASS VALUES

The imposition of middle class values on poor families leads to a number of difficulties in the helping process. Among these difficulties are communication barriers, erroneous interpretations of behavior, an expectation that poor clients can embrace middle class values when the route to social mobility remains closed to them, tensions in establishing the helping relationship, a lack of recognition of the continual energies expended by these clients in daily survival, a tendency to blame clients for their problems, and a failure to see how external institutions impact on the psychosocial functioning of these clients. Poor clients have been labeled as "multiproblem," "poverty stricken," "deprived" and "antisocial." Social workers face problems in practice with them due to their acceptance of the stereotypes which exist about them, their rigidity which prevents flexibility and creativity in addressing their needs, and the frustration which results when their therapeutic techniques prove ineffective with very poor clients. It is this lack of success that contributes to the negative views held about the poor.

Frequently, the poor family stands more in need of habilitation than rehabilitation. Minuchin (1981) speaks to the tendency of professionals to negatively label the poor family and to blame it for its problems. He states, "The poverty stricken family (a term that covers about 20 million people whose strengths and problems are bewilderingly diverse) is conceptualized as an entity that must be sick. The poverty stricken family is seen as a locus of pathology" (p. 87). If social workers are cognizant of their middle class values, resist in imposing them on poor clients, and possess understanding of the client's life style and those conditions which have contributed to it, then it is possible not only to engage them in services but also to provide these services in a manner that is acceptable and understandable to them. Hollis (1965) states, "There are indeed differences between casework with the poorly educated client and case-work with the average middle income well educated client. But these are differences in specific techniques and emphasis rather than the basic casework methods" (p. 470). It is Hollis' opinion that the caseworker in practice with impoverished clients needs the skills and diagnosis he/she needs in practice with other types of families, but also needs to be resourceful, to possess ingenuity and to be flexible and patient.

APPALACHIAN FAMILIES

Appalachian clients have been viewed in a similar manner as have poor families, and social workers have attributed similar labels to them. The social worker has also encountered problems in engaging them in the therapeutic process. Appalachian clients also have their world view, values, beliefs and codes of behavior. They are also estranged from the dominant institutions of society, mistrust them, and view themselves as self-reliant people with a disdain for the welfare system. They too have suffered oppression and exploitation. Ruel (1969) states, "Originally, the Southern Appalachian area was settled by families who wanted no part of life among the eastern seacoast. Some had been indentured servants and they carried into the wilds of the mountain a deep hatred for their masters. Many had known religious persecution. They moved into the mountain asking only to be left alone with their belief in God" (p. 63). Following the discovery of coal, these families suffered exploitation as large corporations took away their land, and as a result of these experiences they develop a deep suspicion and resentment of the outsider.

Appalachian families have also been identified as possessing behavioral traits and attitudes which are similar to those located in very poor families. Jennings (1990) identifies the following traits as existing in rural communities:

- sense of basic trust and friendliness
- isolation and resistance to change
- suspicion of newcomers and outsiders
- independence of spirt but vulnerable
- financial and experiential poverty
- reliance on informal and natural helping systems
- reserved behavior and concrete thinking

Humphrey (1980) states religion is a key to the understanding of the Appalachian culture. He states among the Appalachian people it is not unusual to find several generations in the same household as a strong sense of interdependency exists. Appalachian people are self-reliant, possess a stubborn pride, pride themselves on taking care of their own and children born out of wedlock are incorporated into the family without shame. Appalachian people are extremely religious, put their faith in God and it is Humphrey's view if the social worker is indifferent or insensitive to the value of religion in the Appalachian culture he/she will face resentment, hostility and a lack of cooperation. The social worker must be patient, get to know the Appalachian client and be accepted by him/her if he/she is to develop a therapeutic alliance with him/her. Social work in Appalachia is extremely complex in nature. The social worker is called on to provide a variety of roles, carry out a variety of functions, and interface with clients on a professional and private level in the rural context. He/she must work through formal and informal systems in providing services to clients.

Rural clients face a variety of problems with limited resources available to them. Heffernan, Shuttlesworth and Ambrosino (1992) state, "In general, however, organized social services in rural areas are not as well developed, well organized, or efficiently staffed as those that serve urban population," (p 307). Bruxton (1976) states, "No other environment compares with rural practice in carrying out the dictum of the "total individual" in the "total environment." The rural social worker by her or himself must often provide the rural dweller with services, support, and hope while simultaneously helping to change the environment" (p. 32).

SOCIAL WORK PROCESS

The social work process remains the same in practice with Appalachian and poor families. It may be divided into beginning, middle and ending phases or study, diagnosis and treatment. The techniques employed by the social worker will require some modification as they will be employed in a different manner than they are with middle class clients. As an example, in practice with middle class clients, the social worker may assume a more passive, introspective approach. In practice with poor and Appalachian clients, the social worker's approach will be more action-oriented, direct and extrospective. The social worker will also need to present sensitivity to and understanding of their life styles as well as creativity and flexibility in contacts with them. Gould identifies several characteristics which are viewed as being important in contacts with poor clients: (1) immediate accessibility, (2) continuity of contacts, (3) permissive attitude toward missed appointments and (4) the need to allow the patient to define his own crisis points or problems. The social worker should follow the axiom of social work and this is to begin where the client is. This means also that the social worker must be prepared to view the client in his/her unique situation and not to impose middle class values onto him/her. Education also looms as an important technique as these clients may need to be educated to their rights and responsibilities as parents and citizens. The social worker also needs to reject the stereotypes which exist about these families and engage in a search for their strengths. Even though the mechanisms of survival may not be consistent with middle class expectations, survival in a hostile environment must be viewed as a strength.

Initial Contacts, Beginnings

In initial contacts, the social worker must be aware of his/her role, and the purpose of the contact. The approach should be leisurely and low-keyed in nature. He/she should not attempt to exert pressures on the client or to assume an authoritative attitude. Always, he/she should present him/herself as an authentic person, sincerely interested in the client's welfare; to whatever degree possible, the client should be engaged in the process. The social worker should not expect an immediate accepting response from the client relative to his/her services. He/she will need to pass the tests which the client will devise before the client will accept his/her sincerity. Gaining the trust and confidence of the client is a time-consuming process in which the social worker exhibits considerable patience as he/she moves at the client's pace. Patience, perseverance and a nonjudgmental attitude are important characteristics for the social worker to display in developing a therapeutic alliance. Often, the social worker may need to enlist the aid of an intermediary—someone who is known and trusted by the client—before the client becomes involved with him/her.

A tuning-in process is extremely important in the beginning stage as the social worker seeks to sensitize him/herself to the client's situation. The fact that these clients live in conditions of poverty, are involved in a struggle for daily survival, and may present marked apathy toward help as well as a suspicious attitude toward the social worker alerts the social worker to the counterindications of an intrapsychic approach or to engage too much in the data collection process. The social worker is always cognizant of the need to focus on "the least complex alternative" in helping poor and Appalachian clients to work on their problems. They need indications of tangible results and do not afford the social worker the luxury of time which middle class clients may.

Assessment

The assessment process, following an ecological approach, will focus on the client in transactions with his/her environment and seek to identify those transactions which are stress-inducing. The social worker in this stage may also compose an ecogram. In rural social work practice and in practice with poor families, it is important to know the environmental supports which are positive and negative. In rural social work practice, knowledge of informal and formal networks are extremely important based on the Appalachian's belief in self-reliance. The social worker in a rural setting also needs to gain understanding of the historical dynamics which characterize the region. For example, some families may have engaged in family feuds over generations or may hold negative attitudes toward specific institutions. The social worker must also value the religious faith of the people as this will present his/her understanding of their culture and the importance of religion in their lives. Ginsberg (1976) states, "A smaller scale of life does not imply simplicity. Rural communities are often as socially complicated as cities. Many of the things that happen may be based upon little-remembered but enduringly important family conflicts, church schisms and crimes" (p. 7). In learning about the rural community, the social worker must not appear to be prying; this knowledge will come to him/her usually in an informal manner once he/she has gained acceptance and is no longer viewed entirely as an outsider.

Intervention

Chilman strongly emphasizes that the mutual focus of the social worker and the client should be on the immediate concrete situation facing the client. She states, "A tendency of the 'hard-core multi-problem poor' to swing hopelessly from crisis to crisis demands not only a focus on the immediate situation but also a firm competency on the part of the caseworker in joining with the client to resolve the present crisis and to take steps to prevent the next one" (p. 20).

Crisis intervention is an important intervention modality in practice with clients who live in constant situations of crises. The social worker needs to respond quickly to their needs with a variety of services while at the same time attempting to instill a degree of hope into their situations. The objective is that crisis intervention will enable them to become more skilled in problem solving and with sustained assistance during this period, they will gain the skills and knowledge to address future situations before they reach crisis proportion. Crisis abatement may influence them to work on other problems with the assistance of the social worker. It is important that the social worker joins with these clients in their struggles and offer them assistance as they attempt to locate and receive needed services. The social worker must not impose middle class values onto these clients or blame them for their conditions. He/she following an ecological perspective within a crisis intervention framework attempts to identify those conditions which contribute to stressful transactions between the clients and the systems with which they are involved. He/she then plans and implements an intervention strategy based on an identification of the "least complex alternative."

Endings

The social worker is satisfied with limited goals. Movement toward goal achievement prepares the social worker to initiate the ending or termination process in advance of the formal point of termination when the services of the agency are withdrawn. In practice with poor and Appalachian clients, it is extremely important that termination is skillfully handled so that it is not viewed as desertion or abandonment. Having entered into the relationship, these clients now fear its ending and wonder if their improvement will continue without the assistance of the social worker. In some cases these clients will transfer many of their unmet dependency needs onto the worker; no counterindication exists to the extension of termination if this extension is viewed as being in the interest of the client and is a step toward the stabilization of improved functioning on the part of the client. However, interviews can be spaced for greater lengths of time as the clients continue their forward movements toward growth.

The social worker will need to recapitulate the helping process, and identify and discuss the actions which have been undertaken and their outcomes. He/she acts as an educator in identifying concrete changes in the client's situation. The social worker also makes known his/her continual interest in the welfare of the client and his/her availability if the client should feel the need for his/her assistance at a later time. If intervention has been successful, then changes will be reflected in the client's life and his/her feelings of apathy will be replaced with feelings of hope for the future.

CONCLUSION

Effective social work practice with poor and Appalachian families is predicated on an understanding of their culture, life styles and value systems. While the social work methods or processes do not require modification, techniques and the social worker's use of him/herself will undergo some modification. The social worker should divest him/herself of middle class values so that he/she does not impose them on the client systems and in doing so arrive at a faulty assessment. If the social worker is sensitive to the life styles of poor families and Appalachian clients, and provide them services in a manner that they understand, then the chances are good of engaging and maintaining them in services. The social worker also needs to distinguish between class culture and culture of origin. In some situation, both types of cultures will be present.

Intervention should follow an ecological perspective and a crisis intervention framework. A dual focus should always be instituted so that the social worker is able to identify those conditions which contribute to systemic stress. Intervention should be focused on transactions and not totally on internal processes within the client.

The attributes associated with Appalachian and poor families are also associated with minority groups in American society: present time orientation, external locus of control, a fatalistic attitude toward life, an authoritarian family structure and rigid definition of sexual roles. However, there are differences. In minority groups, these traits are viewed as being healthy and a part of the minority's historical past. In Appalachian and poor families, these traits are viewed as a result of living in extreme poverty and are more reflective of class than an indigenous culture. However, the approach and the intervention strategies with minorities and poor and Appalachian clients are very similar. These include the need for a personal approach, self-disclosure, an action-oriented stance on the part of the social worker, a here and now focus, an absence of ambiguity in the relationship, the giving of direct advice, and a joining with the family so that the social worker is viewed as a "family friend." The social worker is only able to build bridges of understanding with clients when he/she develops an understanding of their culture and life styles and attempts to engage them in a manner consistent with their life styles and belief systems.

SELECTED BIBLIOGRAPHY

Bruxton, E. (1976) Delivering social services in rural areas. Social work in rural communities: A book of readings (Ed.), L. Ginsberg, (New York: Council on Social Work Education).

Chilman, C. (1965) Social work practice with very poor families. WELFARE IN REVIEW, 4, 31–21.

Ginsberg, L. (1976) An overview of social work education for rural areas. Social work in rural communities: A book of readings (Ed.), L. Ginsberg (New York: Council on Social Work Education).

Gould, R. (1967) Dr. Strangehold: Or how I stopped worrying about the theory and began treating the blue-collar worker. AMERICAN JOURNAL OF ORTHO-PSYCHIATRY, 38, 78–86.

Hefferman, J., Shuttlesworth, G. and Ambrosini, R. (1992) Social work and social welfare: An introduction (St. Paul, MN: West Publishing Co.).

Hodges, H. (1968) Social stratification: Class in America (Cambridge, MA: Schenkman Publishers).

Hollis, F. (1965) Casework and social class. SOCIAL CASEWORK, 46, 463–471.

Humphrey, R. (1980) Religion in Appalachia: Implication for social work practice. JOURNAL OF HUMANICS, 8, 4–18.

Jennings, M. (1990) Community mobilization, Presentation made to the National Association of Rural Mental Health Workers, Lubbock, TX.

Kerbo, H. (1983) Social stratification and inequality: Class conflict in the United States (New York: McGraw-Hill).

Mayer, J. and Timms, N. (1969) Clash in perspective between worker and client. SOCIAL CASEWORK, 50, 32–40.

Minuchin, S. (1981) The plight of the poverty stricken family in the United States. In P. Sinanoglu and A. Maluccio (Eds.), Parents of children in placement: Perspectives and Programs (New York: Child Welfare League of America).

Ruel, M. (1990) Deprivation and abundance: Implication for social work practice. In Changing services for changing clients (New York: National Association of Social Workers).

SECTION IX
SOCIAL WORK PRACTICE
WITH VULNERABLE POPULATIONS:
WOMEN, GAYS, LESBIANS AND
PEOPLE WITH AIDS (PWAs)

INTRODUCTION

Many groups, children, the aged, rape victims, the mentally retarded and the developmental disabled, may be viewed as being vulnerable populations. Vulnerability suggests an openness to attack, criticism or differential treatment based on particular characteristics possessed by the client group. This vulnerability can lead to discriminatory practices, exploitation, oppression, physical injuries and assaults. Women, gays, lesbians, and people with AIDS are by this definition vulnerable groups. As a result of these characteristics, they are treated differently, often in an inhumane manner and placed in a stigmatized category. These characteristics also make it possible for society to rationalize its treatment of them. These populations need to be empowered so that they can feel better about themselves and gain the competencies to more effectively address and combat those conditions which maintain them in stigmatized categories. Homophobia and sexism have been used to maintain these groups in subordinate statuses.

Client empowerment must be viewed as a major objective in practice with vulnerable groups. As it was revealed in the discussion of society's treatment of People of Color and interracial families, American society rationalizes its treatment of these population through misinterpreting social, psychological, physiological and theological knowledge. As a result of this misinterpretation, attitudes become deeply embedded and ingrained in American society and results in particular fears and beliefs such as homophobia and the subordinate status of women. Acts of wife beating and gay bashing are frequently committed on these groups as members of society react angrily to them because of their sex or sexual preferences. Wife beating in the past has been supported by the belief that a man's home is his castle, within it he can do as he pleases, that his wife and children are his property and the state should not intervene into what goes on in the sanctity of the home.

In American society, women have traditionally been viewed as being inferior to men, have been placed in a subordinate status and assigned specific roles which carry with them the expectation of specific behaviors. To exhibit behavior which is not consistent with societal expectation is to risk criticism, ostracism and pressures to return to the expected behaviors associated with roles of wife and daughter. Sexism is the term used to explain the treatment of American women. As a practice, it is systematic and invidious in nature. Sexism is defined by Zastrow and Kirth-Ashman (1989) as "prejudice, discrimination and stereotyping based on gender" (p. 516). Kagan (1964) refers to sexism as the holding of "publicly shared beliefs regarding the appropriate characteristics for males and females" (p. 144). These shared beliefs and views influence the manner in which women are treated in all spheres of American life including the home and the workplace.

Lesbians, gays and, more recently, people with AIDS have also faced discrimination, inhumane treatment and oppression. The treatment of these groups can be attributed to their sexual preference and the illness, AIDS, which have become associated with a particular life style. These groups also find themselves in a stigmatized status. AIDS victims are particularly vulnerable because of the devastating nature of their illness, the reaction of society to it, and its ultimate effect on their biopsychosocial functioning. The value code of the social work profession demands that social workers assume an instrumental role in assisting these individuals to overcome societal obstacles which maintain them in their victimized status and deny to them the equality and rights which are the heritage of all Americans.

It is extremely important that social workers possess awareness of how discrimination, inequality, exploitation and oppression impact on the lives of these vulnerable groups. Social workers also need to possess specialized knowledge and skills in practice with them, and to move beyond the characteristics they present to assisting them with the problem in biopsychosocial functioning which brings them to the attention of the social worker. Equally important, social workers should have explored their own values so that they are not imposed on these clients. The author has selected to focus on these groups and to exclude from this discussion, the aged, children, rape victims, and others who may be viewed as constituting vulnerable populations. Considerable literature is available on these groups, and therefore they are not the subjects of this section.

Chapter 21

SOCIAL WORK PRACTICE
WITH VULNERABLE POPULATIONS:
WOMEN, GAYS, LESBIANS AND
PEOPLE WITH AIDS

WOMEN

In American society, women are assigned specific roles based on sex-role differentiation. They are expected to derive their identities from their husbands and in their roles as daughter, wife and mother. From childhood onward, they are socialized into exhibiting behaviors which are associated with their sex. They are not expected to be successful in the workplace, to out perform men, to show aggression, use foul language or to act in an independent manner. Qualities associated with women are passivility, dependency, emotionality, warmth, understanding, the capacity to nurture, gentleness and an absence of logical thinking. Their primary occupation is that of housewives whose careers are in the home where they are expected to perform household duties, rear children, and to be totally dependent on their husbands. The institutionalization of sexism has had negative consequences for the mental health and self-esteem of women and has prevented them from engaging in a process of self-developmental and actualization. They are viewed as being victims.

Curlee and Raymond (1978) identify four areas in which research relating to sexual bias has been conducted: (1) the fostering of traditional roles, (2) the adherence to bias expectations and devaluating concepts of women, (3) the social application of psychoanalytic theory and (4) women as sexual objects. They also identify three categories of roles, family, sex and rival, to which women are assigned. Family roles include those of mother, daughter, homemaker and hostess. The sex roles include those of tease, a piece, a lover, a sex-object or a baby-maker, and rival roles present themselves when women are viewed as being in a competitive position with men. In these rival roles, women are categorized as being bitchy, castrating or a dumb-broad. These roles usually present themselves in work situations in which a woman is placed in an administrative position. It is readily seen that women are placed in specific roles as they interact with men. As a result of these role assignments, women are not allowed to be creative or to escape from them without risking censure, criticism or pressures to return to their expected roles and behaviors.

Feminist Therapy

Sexism has both cultural and structural components. Institutional sexism is analogous to institutional racism. Feminist therapy has evolved as a means of assisting women to develop understanding of the oppressive conditions under which they live so that they may become liberated from their bondage. Society is blamed for the status accorded to women. The task of the feminist therapist is to serve as a liberating force for women so that they may become more independent and not have decisions about their lives imposed on them by men. Consciousness-raising groups have been instrumental in helping women to become more aware of the oppression under which they live in American society. Salzman (1978) states, " . . . when the oppressed refuses to identify with the oppressor, the oppressed ceases to believe that victimization is justified and begins to fight for redress" (p. 273).

In American society, roles are given different values relative to their importance. If a role is devaluated, this devaluation may lead to feelings of low self-esteem, self-hatred and depression. The role assigned to women has resulted in their developing an attitude of dependency on men which is referred to as "learned helplessness. It has also contributed to the phenomenon referred to as "the feminization of poverty." Even though women in the work force perform the same work as men, they are paid less. Inasmuch as women are expected to derive their identities from their husbands, they do not prepare themselves for a career outside of the home, and may find themselves lacking in job skills if the husband should pass away. While making a home has been their primary career, the skills gained in this type of employment are not easily transferred to the work place. Since men define the physical characteristics of a woman which are viewed as being attractive, it is also possible that an association may be located between bulimia and anorexia and the view of what society holds to be attractive features in women. Through these behaviors women may seek to develop those characteristics which they think men value.

While women live under oppressive conditions, many women are satisfied with their lives and the roles assigned to them. They have no need for liberation. For others the oppression under which they live has resulted in feelings of anger and possibly repressed rage over their conditions and inability to do anything about them. Berlin and Kravitz (1981) state, "The majority of social work clients are women who continue to live out cultural mandates that prescribe economic powerlessness and sexual exploitation" (p. 449). When women seek professional help, they may encounter social workers who encourage them to maintain the status quo even when they may live under dangerous conditions. They seek to identify in women reasons for the behavior of men toward them by suggesting that something they have done provoked the male. An unhappy marriage may be perceived as being the woman's destiny as she has married for life, and if she were to somehow change, then the marriage would be different.

Social workers need to be aware of the pervasive presence of sexism in American society and to assist women in the process of liberation so that their self-esteems may be enhanced. In order to do this, social worker must divest themselves of sex-role stereotypes and see women as individuals who must be able to make decisions about their own lives. Frequently, they may be called on to advocate for women when conditions of oppression seek to retain them in a subordinate status against their wishes.

GAYS

Gays have been ostracized and oppressed due to their sexual orientation. The fear of homophobia has placed gays in a stigmatized category. Traditional therapeutic approaches, particularly psychoanalysis, have treated homosexuality as a disease, and the focus of intervention was directed at the elimination of the homosexual orientation. In 1973, homosexuality was removed from the index of mental disorders and recognized as a sexual orientation. While it now viewed as unethical behavior on the part of the professional to attempt to treat homosexuality as a pathological disorder, some professionals continue to view it as an illness in their attempts to eradicate same-sex feelings.

Antigay feelings are of a systematic and insidious nature. Negative feelings toward gays run deep. They are viewed as being a threat to the social order and frequently they are the victims of violence which is referred to as gay-bashing. Generally it is estimated that gays constitute at least 10 percent of the population. The individual who openly acknowledges his homosexuality frequently finds himself a victim of discrimination, faces ostracism from family and friends, and confronts rejection and derision in the work place and from society in general. Theology lends support to the stereotypes which exist about gays. Their behavior is viewed as being sinful as well as unnatural. Homosexuals have faced problems in a number of areas in society's attempts to isolate them. They have faced problems in attaining jobs in the teaching profession, have been denied permission to enter the armed services, and have faced problems in the areas of becoming foster or adoptive parents and in cases of child custody. In all areas of American life in which the dominant society freely participates, gays have faced obstacles.

Gay adolescents also can benefit from social work intervention as they struggle to accept their sexual identity in the face of tremendous pressures to adapt to a heterosexual life style. Antigay feelings may be so great that the individual develops feelings of "self-hatred," depression and suicidal ideation. In the past, parents have brought adolescents with a gay orientation to the social worker with the objective that the social worker would be instrumental in assisting the child to give up the gay orientation and to adapt to a heterosexual life. Literature and research findings strongly suggest that gays are functioning members of society and do not exhibit any greater psychological disturbances than their heterosexual counterparts. Research also reveals that the majority of gays are emotionally stable individuals who are involved in stable, productive, satisfying and fulfilling relationships. If the social worker is able to get past the sexual orientation, he/she will discover that gays face the same or similar problems other clients face.

The gay individual who is a person of color faces pressures from a variety of sources. These sources include the dominant society, his family, his ethnic/racial group and dominant group gays. These pressures can result in confusion over sexuality and the loss of vital support systems. Generally, it may be stated that all gays face some kind of oppression. It is very important that the social worker confronts and resolves his/her feelings towards gays and move beyond his/her sexual orientation. Only when feelings toward gays have been addressed and resolved will the social worker be able to offer them professional services and to assist them in resolving those issues which have necessitated social work intervention.

LESBIANS

Lesbians have been referred to as the "invisible minority." They face similar problems as gays. Generally a lesbian is defined as a woman who is attracted sexually to other women. This attraction may or may not result in sexual relations. Lesbianism carries a stigma and is frowned upon by society. Lesbians are also victims of discrimination, oppression and rejection, and may become targets of verbal and physical abuse. Lesbians in effect face double jeopardy; they are oppressed because of their sex and sexual orientation. Once, lesbianism is known, a woman may lose the support of her family, face discrimination on the job, and encounter discriminatory practices in locating housing and in situations of child custody as she will be frequently viewed as being an unfit mother. Myths also exist about lesbians. One myth in particular is that they are unfit mothers and pose a threat to children. As a result of this myth, a belief exists that lesbians should not be able to work in child-related occupations. The societal taboo against lesbianism is so great that they find themselves isolated and the only support that they receive is from the lesbian community.

Research reveals that a third of all lesbians in the United States are mothers who became aware of their sexual orientation following marriage and motherhood. Studies have also shown that children of lesbian parents are no more homosexually-oriented than are children of heterosexual parents. Lesbian mothers face similar problems as other single mothers. These problems include the need to work, to receive an education, to secure affordable child care services, to find affordable housing, and to upgrade job skills. Professionally, their sexual orientation is no longer viewed as being pathological in nature. However, some professionals and the society at large may still interpret lesbianism as pathological behavior.

PEOPLE WITH AIDS

The AIDS patient faces a number of biopsychosocial problems. As the disease progresses, these problems will become even more acute. AIDS (acquired immunodeficiency syndrome) is an illness of catastrophic proportions. It constitutes a crisis of a life threatening nature for the individual and seriously impacts his/her interpersonal relationships as well as his/her biopsychosocial functioning through its progressive devastation of the physical and mental capacities of the client. This disease has reached epidemic proportion in the United States and has become a primary objective of attention among public health and the health disciplines. It has been reported that presently the accumulated number of AIDS victims in the United States exceeds 100,000. This number is shortly expected to increase within the next several years to an excess of 300,000 to 400,000. It is also estimated that 1.5 million people in the United States are affected with HIV (human immuno-deficiency virus) and this number continues to grow.

While the majority of AIDS patients have been gay white males, a disproportionately high number of AIDS patients have been blacks and Hispanics (Rogers and Williams, 1987). Rogers and Williams identified 25 percent of AIDS patients as Blacks and 14 percent as Hispanics. Among women with AIDS, blacks and Hispanics list the higher numbers. Seventy-three percent of the women and 79 percent of the children with AIDS are Blacks or Hispanics. These women and children live in the inner city where the source of HIV infection is attributed primarily to intravenous drug use. Certainly, the sociomedical cost of treating AIDS patients will be costly, creating an enormous drain on the financial, health and social resources of the community.

AIDS is caused by a virus called the human immunodeficiency virus and is transmitted in several ways: sexually, intraveneously (an exposure to blood or blood products that have been contaminated by the AIDS virus as in such situations as sharing needles or receiving a blood transfusion that has been tainted with the AIDS virus) and from infected mothers who transmit it to their babies during pregnancy, at time of delivery, or through breast feeding following birth (Rogers and Williams). In addition to the health problems faced by the AIDS victim, he/she is also confronted with numerous psychosocial stressors. As the illness progresses, these stressors become more acute. If the gay male has not previously acknowledged his homosexuality, AIDS forces him to acknowledge it openly. As a consequence, he may be rejected by family, friends and face discrimination and ostracism at his place of employment. Some people have lost their jobs when it has become known that they are AIDS infected.

The AIDS victim becomes placed in a stigmatized category, may find social support systems unavailable, and may confront problems in identifying and locating medical institutions willing to provide him/her with quality medical care. In time as the illness progresses, cognitive impairment begins to become evident, physical health decreases, and the individual is called on to face his/her impending death and confronts the task of putting his/her life in order. In the final stages of the disease, the individual may totally become dependent on others for subsistence as he/she becomes more and more dependent and helpless. Society has responded in an inhumane manner to the plight of people with AIDS. Religious people may view the disease as a punishment for the homosexual life style. "Selective inattention" may be given to their needs. The helping professional may present fear in working with AIDS victims, feeling somehow that the disease may be transmitted to him/her.

The value base of the profession demands that social workers actively involve themselves with individuals who have been placed in stigmatized categories and deny access to those services which are vital to their well being. Women, gays, lesbians and those with AIDS have been denied social justice and are often treated in a discriminatory manner when they interface with the institutions of society.

APPLICATION OF KNOWLEDGE, SKILLS AND VALUES IN PRACTICE WITH VULNERABLE POPULATIONS

Effective social work practice with vulnerable population requires that the social worker has worked out his/her attitudes and values as they relate to these populations. Otherwise, he/she may attempt to impose them onto the client. The imposition of dominant group values on these populations is both unethical and contraindicated as these clients have a right to self-determination, their behavior is not of a pathological nature, and the social worker should not attempt to create undue stress for them. For the most part, these groups will require a variety of services; intervention may be directed toward the micro-mezzo and macro levels of society, and the social worker will be called on to assume a variety of roles. Social and organizational policy may need to be impacted so that necessary programs are implemented for these groups and carried out in an intended manner. Impacting social and organizational policies is an important task of the social worker as he/she practices with victims of AIDS. Case management becomes a crucial method for identifying needs, referring clients to organizations which can meet these needs and for monitoring and evaluating the effectiveness of the services being provided to the client. Through case management, the social worker may also recognize unmet needs and implement strategies to mobilize the community in meeting these unmet needs. With the victims of AIDS, it is highly indicated that the social worker assumes a variety of roles such as those of broker, mediator, educator, policy analyst, organizational analyst and advocate. The social worker will need to know how to work with volunteers, as the needs of AIDS patients are great, and all of these needs are not currently being met by societal institutions.

The social work processes of beginning, middle and ending or the method steps of study, diagnosis and treatment remains essentially unchanged. Again the social worker will need to be creative, flexible and innovative as he/she works with these groups. Certainly, the social worker needs to be sensitive to the plight of these groups in the United States and to possess an understanding of those attitudes, values and conditions which seek to maintain these population in vulnerable states. Women are maintained in a subordinate status due to their sex and the views which exist about their place and roles in American society. Gays, lesbians and people with AIDS are viewed as violating societal norms. Their behaviors are viewed as being of a pathological nature which threatens society. Biblical knowledge is employed to rationalize the treatment which they receive. Inasmuch as these attitudes are deeply embedded in American society, the social worker should always embrace an ecological perspective in practice with these groups; he/she must identify the manner in which societal structures seek to maintain these groups in a stigmatized status, and guard against blaming the victim.

In the beginning phase, the social worker will start where the client is, proceed at the client's pace, and present him/herself to the client as an authentic person who does not sit in judgment of the client, but whose function is to assist the client with his/her problems. He/she moves beyond the client's characteristics or sexual orientation and actively engages the client in identifying the nature of his/her problem and what he/she wants from the agency. Once the social worker and the client reach agreement on the problem to be addressed, then goals are established, a contract is formulated, and an intervention plan is implemented. With gay, lesbian and women clients the social worker must guard against possessing a "hidden agenda" in which without the client's knowledge or involvement, he/she seeks to influence the client to adjust to and adapt behaviors which society has designated as being proper.

In the work phase, the social worker and the client engage in the problem-solving process directed at the resolution to whatever degree possible of the difficulty which has brought the client to the agency. In this phase of practice, particularly with vulnerable groups, the social worker may find it necessary to assume the role of an advocate, to implement social action strategies, and to face and mediate conflict as he/she seeks to help the client in goal achievement and also to bring about more humane behaviors in those institutions on which the client is dependent for services. In this phase, the methods of casework, group work, community organization and family therapy may find expression.

When goal achievement appears imminent, the social worker prepares the client for the ending of contacts and the formal withdrawal of the services of the agency. Termination with AIDS victims may be brought on by their untimely deaths. Termination with women, gays and lesbians will follow the usual pattern of termination in social work and the social worker will need to address the feelings and behaviors which will characterize this process. Because these groups will continue to be vulnerable populations, the social worker should attempt to connect them with support groups so that a continual source of support will be available to them.

CONCLUSION

Women, gays, lesbians and people with AIDS are identified as constituting vulnerable populations who face discrimination and oppression as a result of their sex, sexual orientation, and their infliction with a catastrophic disease of a progressive and life threatening nature. It is important that these groups be empowered so that they can engage in a self-actualizing process which will enable them to enhance their self-esteem and to develop the necessary skills so that they can effectively address those conditions and beliefs which consign them to a stigmatized status.

The social worker in order to be of maximum assistance to these groups must have come to terms with his/her attitudes toward them. In order to do this effectively, he/she needs to actively engage in a process of self-awareness and to be able to move beyond sex, sexual orientation and catastrophic illness to assist them with the problems which they are encountering in living. Services should be provided free of any moralistic stance. The social worker will find him/herself identifying societal obstacles to the self-fulfillment of these groups and will find it frequently necessary to assume the role of an advocate. He/she will also find it necessary to engage in multidimensional practice which encompasses the use of a variety of methods and the assumption of various roles, including those of policy and organizational analyst, as he/she directs intervention at the micro-messo and macro levels of society in the interest of improving the quality of life for these groups.

SELECTED BIBLIOGRAPHY

Berlin, S. and Kravitz, D. (1981) Editorial Page: Women as victims: A feminist social work perspective. SOCIAL WORK, 26, 447–449.

Curlee, M. and Raymond, F. (1978) The female administrator: Who is she? ADMINISTRATION IN SOCIAL WORK, 2, 307–318.

Kagan, J. (1964). Acquisition and significance of sex-typing and sex-role identity. In L. Hoffman and M. Hoffman (Eds.), Review of child development research (New York: Russell Sage).

Rogers, M. and Williams, W. (1987) AIDS in blacks and Hispanics: Implication for prevention. ISSUES IN SCIENCE AND TECHNOLOGY (Spring).

Saltzman, K. (1978) Women and victimization: The aftermath. In J. Chapman and R. Gates (Eds.), The victimization of women (Beverly Hills, CA: Sage Publications).

Zastrow, C. and Kirth-Ashman, K. (1989) Understanding human behavior and the social environment (Chicago: Nelson-Hall Publishers).

SECTION X
PREVENTION IN SOCIAL WORK PRACTICE

INTRODUCTION

As a profession, social work historically has been interested in prevention, but has faced problems in applying a preventive approach to practice. Possibly, some of this difficulty results from the view that social work is a problem-solving profession which addresses problems in psychosocial functioning. In the 1980s the profession presented considerable interest in prevention and many publications focused on preventive practice. As the profession approaches the decade of the 1990s, interest in prevention appears to have waned and few social work publications focus on it. It is the author's opinion that prevention has a place in social work practice. In effect, social work has always engaged in tertiary prevention as it offered services to clients who were involved not only in family problems but also other problems such as child abuse, drugs, teenage pregnancies and school failure. Prevention can be directed at the individual and community levels. The task ahead for social workers is how to engage in secondary and primary prevention and receive organizational and community support for engaging in such activities.

Chapter 22

PREVENTION IN SOCIAL WORK PRACTICE

In the decade of the 1980s, social work focused its attention on preventive social work. This practice orientation was viewed as "an idea whose time has come." Problems have presented themselves in the field's total embrace of prevention in practice. A major problem results from the fact that many agencies of employment for social workers provide remedial treatment to clients who face problems in psychosocial functioning. It is more easy to identify and measure services provided to clients with problems than to measure the outcomes of preventive efforts. In the past social work was primarily engaged in remedial prevention. The social workers felt if the problems of a family was effectively addressed then other family members, particularly children, would not repeat family problems in the future. The preventive thrust of today essentially follows the public health model and seeks to implement primary, secondary and tertiary prevention programs. The focus of prevention is directed at individuals, families and populations which are viewed as being at risk.

DEFINITION OF PREVENTION

Common definitions of prevention, especially primary prevention, are not easily located in the literature. Bloom (1982) conceptualizes primary prevention as those scientific procedures which seek to prevent predictable physical, psychological and/or social problems in individuals or at-risk populations (p. 38). Signell (1983) defines prevention as the promotion of health in the community (p. 146). The activities employed in the preventive program are directed at enhancing or optimizing human development, independent of pathology. D'Andrea (1984) views primary prevention as programmatic strategies designed to do something before something of a debilitating nature happens to people. Lofquist (1985) defines prevention as "an active, assertive process of creating conditions and/or personal attributes that promotes the well-being of people." Caplan (1961) views primary prevention as a community process which seeks to lower the rate of new cases of mental disorders in a population over a period of time. The incidence of new cases is lowered as a result of the prevention program and its activities which are directed at counteracting harmful circumstances before they have an opportunity to negatively impact on people or to produce noxious effects.

SOCIAL WORK AND PREVENTION

When the social worker engages in prevention, he/she is involved in specific programs and activities which are designed to come between a specific process which may, if left unchecked, produce negative outcomes for client systems. Sundel and Homan (1979) remark that advocates of prevention feel it has the potential of reducing social problems by altering environmental forces (p. 501). The social worker practices in many settings which lend themselves to prevention activities, particularly the school. From a developmental perspective, the family also provides an excellent setting for prevention. The family goes through developmental stages and each stage presents it with a task which must be successfully mastered if the family is to perform its intended functions in American life. Through family life education programs, families can become better equipped with knowledge and skills for handling family crises before they emerge. Other problems which lend themselves to intervention in social work practice are child abuse, teenage pregnancies, drug abuse and school drop-outs.

THE PUBLIC HEALTH MODEL IN PREVENTION

The public health model has been widely used to clarify the concept of prevention and the various levels at which it can occur. The three levels are primary, secondary and tertiary prevention. Primary prevention seeks to prevent a situation from occurring, for example a program on AIDS education, parent education or family life education. In primary prevention, a general population has been identified which presents no sign of this condition but could become susceptible to it if it engages in a specific kind of behavior. In secondary prevention, a population is identified as being at risk. This population presents characteristics which suggest that it will fall prey to specific circumstances which could result in specific behaviors and outcomes. Through early recognition, this group can be involved in services which will minimize the effects of these conditions on the at-risk population. Counseling, outreach programs, health and mental health services are examples of secondary prevention. Early screening, diagnosis and intervention are characteristics of a secondary prevention program. In tertiary prevention, the focus is on remedial and rehabilitative services since the client system has already been affected by the condition to the degree that psychosocial functioning is severely impaired and a social problem is evident. According to the National Association of Mental Health (quoted in Sundell and Homan) all primary prevention activities should contain the following elements:

(1) A condition that can be observed and recorded in precise terms,
(2) An identified population at risk for the condition,
(3) A measure of the incidence of the condition in the population,
(4) A measurement of the incidence following the intervention (p. 518).

In a very broad sense, the author agrees with Weinberg (1974) who states that any strain between people and their environments which have a negative impact on the population is a significant condition for denoting such a situation as a social problem. Prevention activities should be directed at any situation which has the potential of becoming a social problem if not addressed.

KNOWLEDGE AND SKILL BASE
FOR PREVENTIVE SOCIAL WORK PRACTICE

Many of the problems which require remedial or tertiary prevention could probably have been prevented or minimized through primary and secondary prevention. While the social worker may direct prevention activities at the individual or a population, the general consensus is that prevention requires work with groups. The social worker needs to possess analytical and interactional skills in motivating clients to participate in prevention programs and in influencing his/her agencies to engage in preventive practice. Analytically the social worker engages in a problem-solving process in which he/she has determined such a program is indicated. He/she then engages in the planning process. In this process, the social worker may have to mediate differences, resolve conflicts and influence client systems. Obstacles to implementation of the program should be addressed. The social worker should be able to articulate the need for the program, and this need identification results from the research function. The problem to be prevented, the programmatic elements which will constitute the programs and the manner in which its effectiveness will be measured will occupy the attention of the social worker in the planning process.

While intervention may be directed at an individual or a population, the social worker will engage in more activities if the group is used. The individual approach is basically a case by case approach. In planning and implementing the program, the social worker may engage in the following activities: education, consultation, program development, collaboration and advocacy. Johnson (1987) identifies some community organization strategies which the social worker may employ. They are innovation and partialization. Innovation focuses on achieving acceptance from the community for a new program. Partialization occurs when an innovative program is presented on a trial basis. She feels a program presented on a trial basis, somewhat similar to a demonstration program, may gain greater acceptance as its benefits are revealed. In contrast, a long-range program implemented without a trial may face opposition as opponents gain momentum in resisting it. Cowan (1984) identifies the overall objective of any primary prevention program. Its goal is the enhancement of the adjustment of those who are exposed to these programs. According to Cowan pathways to the achievement of this goal are (1) providing people with skills, competencies and conditions that facilitate effective adaptation and ward off noxious agents before they occur, (2) developing intervention to short-circuit the psychological reactions of those who have experienced risk-augmenting life situations or stressful life events.

FOCUS OF PREVENTION

Prevention programs may deal with developmental or situational crises. In the developmental approach, the social worker follows an ecological perspective in identifying those conditions, internal and/or external to individuals which can result in their developing behaviors of a maladaptive nature. The social worker needs to identify the needs of people, the conditions under which they live, the crisis which they face during life transitions, and based on this understanding to develop and implement primary and secondary prevention programs. The situational crisis will call for secondary prevention programs in which the social worker through a variety of specific activities will seek to minimize the effects of the situation on the psychosocial functioning of the client system.

The Family as a Target of Preventive Intervention

The family is a basic societal unit. It has been given specific functions to perform which are viewed as being crucial to the maintenance of an orderly society. The family at various stages of its developmental cycle will face normative or situational crises which may have a negative impact on its capacity to perform its functions in a healthy manner. Problems may occur for the family as a result of internal and/or external forces. If the family possesses knowledge of these family cycle events they may be more able to address them in a healthy manner. A family life education program can serve this purpose. The tasks which families face at each stage of their development, the roles assigned to family members, and the conditions which impact adversely on the abilities of family members to perform in an expected manner can become the content of family life education. This knowledge may enhance the problem-solving capacity of the family.

CONCLUSION

Prevention in social work is directed at the early intervention into situations which may result in negative consequences for client systems. It may be directed at the primary, secondary and tertiary levels. In practice, the social worker works in many settings and encounters many problems which provide opportunities for preventive practice. The implication of prevention has not been an easy task in social work, and the primary emphasis has been placed on tertiary prevention. The social worker needs to embrace the philosophy of prevention and to possess knowledge and skills which will enable him/her to engage in prevention practice.

SELECTED BIBLIOGRAPHY

Bloom, M. (1982) Introducing primary prevention in human behavior courses. In J. Bowker (Ed.), Education for primary prevention in social work (New York: Council on Social Work Education).

Caplan, G. (1964) Principles of preventive psychiatry (New York: Basic Books).

Cowan, E. (1984) A general structure for primary prevention in mental health. THE PERSONNEL AND GUIDANCE JOURNAL, 62, 549–553.

D'Andrea, M. (1984) Primary prevention in high risk populations. PERSONNEL AND GUIDANCE JOURNAL, 62, 554–557.

Johnson, B. (1987) Sexual abuse prevention: A rural interdisciplinary approach. CHILD WELFARE, LXVI.

Lofquist, W. (1985) Discovering the meaning of prevention (Tuscon, AR: AYD Publications).

Signell, K. (1983) Starting prevention work. COMMUNITY MENTAL HEALTH JOURNAL, 62, 144–163.

Sundel, M. and Homan, C. (1979) Prevention in child welfare: A Framework for management and practice. CHILD WELFARE, LVIII, 510–521.

Weinberg, C. (1974) Education and social problems (New York: Free Press).

SECTION XI
INDIRECT METHODS IN
SOCIAL WORK PRACTICE:
CONSULTATION AND SUPERVISION

INTRODUCTION

Social work practice is divided into direct and indirect methods. Consultation, supervision, research and administration are identified as indirect methods. When the social worker employs these methods, face-to-face contact does not always occur with client systems. However, the client is to be the beneficiary of the activities involved in these methods. This section focuses on consultation and supervision. An abundance of information is available in the literature on research and administration in social work practice.

Social work practice has been conceptualized as consisting of the activities implemented and the roles assumed by the social worker in interactions with the client system in the change process. These activities and roles are directed toward the achievement of mutually-agreed on goals. The achievement of client goals often necessitates the use of consultation and supervision. Indeed due to the ever-changing complexity of society, the variety of problems, particularly substance abuse, which are being presented by client systems, and the changing demographics which reveal that the United States is truly becoming a multiethnic society, consultation may emerge as a dominant social work method in the future.

Chapter 23

CONSULTATION AND SUPERVISION IN SOCIAL WORK PRACTICE

CONSULTATION

In performing his/her professional responsibility, the social worker often finds it necessary to engage in consultation in gaining a better understanding of how to address a particular or several aspects of the client's situation. Consultation is conceptualized as a problem-solving process in which a consultant and a consultee analyze a client's situation and determine how the consultee can best approach those areas of concern which were instrumental in the request for consultation. The social worker is a receiver and a provider of consultation. He/she possesses special knowledge which qualifies him/her as an expert in problem-solving, particularly when social and cultural factors are involved in a particular situation. The growing complexity of American society will provide occasions for the social worker to act as a consultant in identifying the manner in which internal and/or external dynamics impact on psychosocial functioning. Through the process of consultation, participants receive knowledge, insights and skills which make it possible for them to improve their services to client systems so that problems may be resolved and movement accelerated toward goal achievement. Sackheim (1974) states,

> "When the social worker seeks consultation, the consultant's primary responsibility is to extend the worker's knowledge about his client and to help him sharpen his skills in application of that knowledge" (p. 199).

Similarly, it may be stated when the social worker provides consultation, his/her purpose is to extend the consultee's knowledge about a particular area of concern in the client's situation and to identify ways in which the consultee can apply that knowledge to the client's situation. Inasmuch as the consultant is the third party in the consultation triangle, third party consultation is often used to describe this process. Consultation is usually of an advisory nature, and the social worker may or may not elect to

315

make use of the information gained from this process. In some areas, it becomes a responsibility of the social worker as a consultee to educate the consultant in areas in which the consultant may lack knowledge or appears to be misinterpreting the data. Transcultural knowledge provides such as example if it is perceived that the consultant lacks cultural knowledge or sensitivity to the problems of the ethnic client. A consultation may last for one session or several sessions, depending on purpose. Frequently, it is necessary to follow up on consultation to determine if recommendations, following implementation, are being successful, or to look at new dynamics which may have presented themselves in the case situation.

TYPES OF CONSULTATION

Consultation may be provided in any social work setting or field of practice in which it is determined that the services of an expert are required in addressing a specific area of concern. It may be client, staff, organization or community focused. In all of these areas, the primary reason for consultation is to increase the knowledge and skills base of the consultee in being of maximum services to the client system. In providing consultation, the consultant must be skilled in recognizing and addressing resistance, transference phenomenon, and particularly in providing consultation to organizations and staff, he/she must be able to distinguish between personal and work-related issues. The emphasis is always directed toward addressing those concerns which are proving to be of a problematic nature or those areas which can be improved so that maximum, effective services are provided to the client system. In Sackheim's view, the consultant in addition to providing therapeutic and educational knowledge also serves as a catalyst for the sharing of ideas, feelings and fostering insights into the situations faced by clients, staff, organizations or communities.

Kadushin (1976) identifies several types of consultation:

(1) Client-centered in which the focus is on a particular client in which the social worker desires to extend his/her knowledge in order to facilitate movement, remove obstacles and achieve stated goals,

(2) Consultee-centered in which the social worker seeks to develop an understanding of his/her interactions with client systems in areas that are proving to be problematic. For example, the social worker may

not be sensitive to the presence of transference or countertransference phenomenon.

(3) In program centered consultation, the focus is on a program. The program may need to be developed and implemented, or an existing program may not be functioning in an intended manner. The objective is to determine what changes are required.

(4) Administrative centered consultation in which administrators seek knowledge on how to address specific areas within the organization which may be proving problematic or stand in need of reevaluation.

(5) Advocacy consultation may be conflictual in nature as it seeks a redistribution of power. While conflict may be present, the purpose of the consultation is the resolution of some problem which requires the assistance of an expert.

Sackheim divides her classification of consultation into those of client and staff. Client-centered consultation seeks to extend the knowledge and skill base for practice with a specific client. Staff-centered consultation centers on helping staff to develop an understanding of their reactions to certain clients or to address areas of concern in the workplace perceived as being stressful. Burnout and how to help workers to deal with it may serve as an area in which consultation is indicated. Peer consultation is also employed by social workers. Usually, it is informal in nature and consists of social workers seeking feedback from peers on how to address specific areas in practice with clients or in the work environment. Professional consultation is formal in nature and is sanctioned by the organization as fees are usually involved.

CONSULTATION PROCESS

Consultation may be provided to individuals or groups. It has a beginning, middle and ending phase. As in all of social work practice, the phases are not mutually exclusive and overlap. The social worker who initiates the consultation process will have recognized the existence of a problem with which he/she desires professional assistance. Ideally, clients should be informed of the need for consultation, and their permission should be secured. In some situations, the consultant may want the client to participate and the client is interviewed before the consultant presents his/her recommendation. The consultant must always clearly understand his/her role. The role is advisory in nature. Contractual obligations should be worked out before the actual process of consultation is initiated. Caplan (1970) states the cornerstone of the consultative process is the coordinate interdependence which exists between the consultant and the consultee. The consultant possesses no coercive power over the consultee and the consultee retains professional authority in determining how he/she will use the consultation outcome. While the consultant does not have coercive powers, the social worker should be on guard against the consultant attempting to persuade him/her to implement recommendations that he/she questions.

The following discussion relates primarily to mental health consultation though it has relevance to any social work setting. The social worker identifies the problem which will serve as the focus of consultation, identifies in his/her mind the reasons for seeking consultation and formulates clear questions that he/she would like for the consultant to answer. The questions are goal-oriented since they represent the information which the social worker would like to secure as a result of consultation. This information is written up in the form of a report or a request. It will contain essentially the following information: (1) referral source and reason(s) for referral, (2) the nature of the problem presented, (3) the attitudes of the client system toward the agency and/or the social worker, (4) salient social history information, including contacts with other agencies and previous consultations, if any, (4) the present status of the case and some of its dynamics, (5) if possible the social worker should include his/her psychosocial assessment or acknowledge his/her difficulties in this area, (6) a picture of the client's strengths, weaknesses and obstacles to full participation of the client in the helping process and (7) the questions which will serve as the focus of the consultation.

A discussion of this report will characterize the beginning phase. It may be sent to the consultant prior to the consultation, or the consultant may read it before the actual process of consultation is started. Following his/her reading of the report, the consultant may have also formulated some questions. These questions provide the essential focus of the beginning phase. Following discussion and analysis of the data presented, the process moves to the middle stage in which the consultant, and possibly other participants in the consultative process, focus on the necessary actions to address the problematic situation. As the beginning phase of consultation focuses on problem identification and contributing factors, the middle phase focuses on the identification of an intervention strategy. The middle phase may extend over several sessions. The consultant may request additional information, or new information may emerge.

The ending phase occurs when the social worker and the consultant have reached agreement on the strategies to be implemented. A follow-up may be indicated to determine the effectiveness of the recommendations following their implementation with the client system.

ELEMENTS OF CONSULTATION

Consultation is an interactional process with a problem-solving focus. The following are features of the consultation process in social work practice:

(1) Consultation consists of voluntary relationships. It is an advisory process which takes place between a consultee (the social worker) and a consultant (an expert) who can provide the required assistance for addressing a particular problem.
(2) Consultation is goal-oriented and characterized by objectivity.
(3) It is time limited in nature and can be provided to individuals or groups.
(4) Consultation is segment-focused, is characterized by contractual obligations and follows the process of beginning, middle and ending phases.

PROBLEMS IN CONSULTATION

Since consultation is an interactional process, the consultant and the consultee may introduce dynamics into the process which can interfere with its effectiveness. In some ways, a parallel process may be introduced which is similar to the problem faced by the consultee with the client system. These behaviors, conscious or unconscious, make it difficult to deal with the problem in an objective manner. A "hidden agenda" on the part of either the consultant or consultee can also have negative results. Within the consultation process itself, distorted perceptions, racist feelings, transference and countertransference may also present themselves. Caplan identifies five reasons for a lack of objectivity in consultation: (1) direct personal involvement in which the consultee has developed a personal relationship with the client and has minimized the professional relationship, (2) simple identification in which the consultee has overidentified with the client system and endowed the participants with either negative or positive attributes, (3) transference in which the consultee reacts to the client system or the consultant as if he/she represented someone from

the past and behaves in an irrational manner, (4) characterological disturbances in which the consultee exhibit psychiatric problems which lead to
distortions in perceptions and behaviors and (5) theme interference
which is similar to transference. Theme interference is temporary in
nature and occurs when the consultee is confronted with a situation
which proves to be upsetting and confusing. It is usually a reaction to a
past event with which the consultee is familiar but has not resolved.
Theme interferences may take on a repetitive nature and needs to be
identified and resolved if the consultee is to be effective in providing
help to the client system.

PREVENTIVE CONSULTATION

In social work, consultation has been essentially remedial in nature. It
is employed following the recognition of a problem with which the
consultee is encountering problems in addressing. The social worker
can also engage in preventive consultation of a proactive nature. He/
she can offer services to people (potential consultees) even when problems have not presented themselves, but circumstances suggest they
may at a later time. When the social worker recognizes existing circumstances which are the precusor of problems, he/she can initiate the
process of consultation with professionals or participants who are involved
in that particular situation. The focus of early consultation is to initiate a change process directed at the prevention of problems through
the early involvement of professionals and others in a proactive change
process. For example, in the school setting, early consultation can
focus on problems faced by immigrants in their adjustment to a new
society, cross-cultural variations in behavior, and the need for sex
education programs. Secondary consultation would focus on populations who are at risk and may focus on teenage pregnancies, drug
prevention and interethnic group conflict. Tertiary consultation would
continue to focus on rehabilitation and remedial efforts with client
systems who have been affected by problems and stand in need of remedial assistance. While the reader will note that these categories are
similar to primary, secondary and tertiary prevention, the author includes
them as consultative efforts as they focus on collaborative relationships
in which the social worker consults with others and engages them in
change efforts as a recognition of those conditions which are viewed as
potentially problem-inducing.

KNOWLEDGE AND SKILLS

As an expert in a particular discipline, the consultant must possess considerable knowledge and skills about the problem area that he/she is addressing. The consultant needs to possess substantive knowledge and analytical and interactional skills. Certainly the consultant must be skilled in individual, group, organization, program and community assessment. He/she must know how to formulate relationships and to maintain them, to purposefully engage people in purposive action and to address and resolve issues of conflict and authority. The consultant must also understand his/her role and the perimeters of his/her power and authority. In the knowledge area, the consultant should possess knowledge of group dynamics, community dynamics and psychosocial dynamics, psychopathology, communication theory, racism, culture, personality theories, organizational theories and social class. It is also important that the consultant possess knowledge of systems theory, the ecological perspective, resistance and transference and countertransference.

SUPERVISION

As an indirect method of social work practice, supervision is worker, organizational and community centered. The primary task of the supervisor as a middle manager is to supervise the work performance of workers assigned to him/her in their daily performance so that the goals of the organization are achieved in an efficient and effective manner. Organizations are goal driven and they must succeed in the achievement of their goals if they are to survive, or they may take on new goals as previous goals are achieved. Kadushin (1976) defines the supervisor as "an agency administrative staff member to whom authority is delegated to direct, coordinate, enhance and evaluate on the job performance of the supervisees for whose work he is held accountable" (p. 21).

FUNCTIONS OF THE SUPERVISOR

Generally, the literature identifies three primary functions for the supervisor: administrative, educational and supportive (Kadushin, 1976). Hester (1954) identifies supervisory functions as those of administering, teaching, consulting and evaluating. The supportive function focuses on the supervisor providing ego-support and encouragement to the worker as he/she encounters organizational and interpersonal stresses which impact adversely on his/her performance. Hester stresses teaching as being the primary function of the supervisor, and states that all of the other functions have teaching aspects.

Schmidt (1973) states that while the expediting and educating roles of the supervisor are of basic importance, the most exciting and creating task is that of enabling. As an enabler, the supervisor enables the worker "to function in a competent and original manner." Even though they are relating to group supervision, Dimock and Trecker (1949) view supervision as a "co-operative leadership." This leadership focuses on activities which are designed to improve the quality of experience and the growth or learning of participants in an agency program (p. 4). Hester emphasizes the role of the supervisor as a consultant. By consultation, she is referring to the supervisor building on the knowledge base which the worker possesses through a discussion and analysis of his/her materials. She states,

> He stimulates him to think about and make full use of the data available in the record, to interpret these in the light of his knowledge of theory and to arrive at a diagnostic formulation of the case. If in this process, it is seen that there are lacks in objective materials concerning the client and his situation, the worker is helped to identify what he needs to know and how he can obtain it from the client and collateral sources. The supervisor encourages him to think through the treatment plan appropriate to the case and the methods of putting this into action (p. 19).

In carrying out this function, the supervisor seeks to develop a research and problem-solving attitude in the worker as the worker researches a problem area in an attempt to gain greater understanding of how to address it. In performing a research function, the social worker also may develop a greater sense of self-awareness as he/she gains knowledge of his/her particular mode of interacting with the client. Similar to casework practice, the effectiveness of the intervention is dependent on the nature of the relationship which is established between the social worker and the client, the same applies to the relationship developed between the supervisor and the supervisee. This relationship has many of the elements which are located in the helping relationship with client systems. Hester states, "The relationship between the supervisor and the worker is the medium through which learning takes place and through which the supervisory purposes are to be reached. It should, therefore, support ego strengths, help the worker to keep emotional balance and so facilitate learning" (p. 17).

Berkowitz (1952) identifies three processes in administrative supervision: implementation, integration and evaluation. Implementation refers to the process of creating the conditions and the resources which are required to get the job done effectively and efficiently. He states, "It ranges from the development of procedure to the innovation of policy. It also includes the detection of policies and procedures that have become anachronistic and the initiative or persistence necessary to bring about their alteration or extinction as rapidly as possible" (p. 26).

Integration refers to the supervisor helping the social worker to integrate his work with the total program of the agency, and evaluation refers to evaluating the performance of the social worker. In general Berkowitz views administrative supervision as "a directing and enabling force, continually endeavoring to create conditions that will improve the quality of the agency's services and increase the importance of its contribution to the community and to its field" (p. 25). Watson (1973) identifies administration and teaching as the primary functions of supervision. Administrative functions include (1) communication linkage, (2) accountability for performance, (3) evaluation, (4) assignment of cases and distribution of work, (5) emotional support of the worker, and (6) utilization by the agency of each worker's experience (Watson). While the first five functions are self-explanatory, the sixth function is similar to that of the consultative function identified by Hester. The supervisor attempts to build on the knowledge and experience which the social worker possesses in carrying out the educational and administrative functions. Evaluation is an extremely important aspect of administrative supervision. The supervisor is called on to evaluate the performance of the social worker. Evaluation determines both the rewards and the punishment systems of the organization. To a large degree, it determines if the worker is to be removed or continued on probation, if a raise is to be given or not, and if the worker is to continue as an employee of the organization. Evaluation relating to job performance is a shared process of an on-going nature and no surprises should exist within it.

Watson also identifies the educational functions of the supervisor. These include (1) social work philosophy and history, (2) social work knowledge, technique and skills, (3) self-awareness, (4) knowledge of available resources within the community, and (5) establishing priorities and developing skills in time management. An educational assessment is an important feature of educational supervision. This assessment identifies the worker's learning patterns, his/her strengths and weaknesses. As a result of the assessment, the supervisor can assist the worker to gain the knowledge and skills which will enable him/her to overcome performance deficits. Student supervision would be heavily educated-oriented as the supervisor is called on to evaluate the capacity of the student for professional development.

In providing supervisees with ego-support, the supervisor attempts to help workers to deal constructively with personal problems, community pressures and organizational frustrations which impact negatively on their performance. The ego is viewed as being over-taxed to the point that the worker's performance is suffering. In carrying out the supportive function, the supervisor guards against becoming the supervisee's therapist. As Hester states, "The supervisor does not "treat" the worker but does give help in handling feeling reactions if they are interfering with performance. The supervisor's focus is always on the worker as a doer of the agency's job, and, therefore, he deals with feelings only when they adversely affect that work" (p. 19).

Middleman and Rhodes (1985) conceptualize supervision as encompassing nine functions: (1) humanizing, (2) managing tension, (3) catalyzing, (4) teaching, (5) career socialization, (6) evaluating, (7) administering, (8) changing and (9) advocacy. In addition they identify three general roles to characterize the changing orientation of supervision over time: (1) the coach who teaches, (2) the counselor who assists the worker in the personality area so that he/she can more effectively engage in the process of giving and receiving help, and (3) the conferee who helps the organization and the supervisee to carry out designated functions. The conferee can assume a variety of roles which include those of helper, enabler, advocate, counselor and broker. Swanson and Brown (1981) focus on the function of the supervisor as a problem-solver in organizational life. They state,

> . . . a primary function of supervisors becomes that of problem solvers in that they mediate worker-management conflicts or advocate for client's welfare. In our view, supervision should be seen as a distinct social work method, quite different from that of social service administration. Supervisors are more enforcers than developers of organizational policies and frequently must negotiate problems among workers, client groups and the agency administration. The change concept of the supervisor's role has been overlooked in the literature (p. 60).

In their view, the supervisor also acts as an advocate for change within the organization as indicated. They feel that advocacy falls within the administrative function of the supervisor and is clearly within the perimeters of the supervisory role.

A PROBLEM-SOLVING APPROACH IN SUPERVISION

The social work supervisor applies a theoretical orientation to supervision in performing his/her designated functions. Munson (1985) states that good supervision should contain the following features: structure, regularity, consistency, case-oriented and evaluation. The case may consist of an individual, the small group, a family, an organization, the community, or interagency and intra-agency conflicts. Munson identifies several theoretical orientations that can underpin the supervisory process: personality, situational, organizational and interactional (p. 5).

Inasmuch as supervision centers around several functions which are directed at enhancing goal achievement and the professional development of the supervisee, the supervisor must address any obstacle which interferes with the ability of the agency to achieve its purpose, the professional development of the social worker, and he/she must identify effective ways of removing these obstacles. A problem-solving approach seems ideally suited for addressing internal and external conditions which interfere with goal achievement and the worker's development. This approach is consistent with the view that a primary objective of the supervisor is to assist workers in problem solving. This approach emphasizes the role of the supervisor as a problem solver whose primary responsibility is to the agency in addressing problems which prevent goal attainment. A number of theoretical perspectives support a problem-solving approach including ego psychology, systems theory, communication theory and an interactional perspective. When the organization performs in an intended manner, and goals are achieved, the survival of the organization is not threatened. The supervisor can direct his/her energies at maximizing organizational effectiveness through carrying out his/her designated functions: administrative, teaching and support. When problems present themselves which interfere with goal attainment and/or quality of services provided, the supervisor activates a problem-solving process by proceeding through the following steps:

- Identification of the problem (in what areas does the situation or problem present itself).
- What are the conditions contributing to it?
- Which of the conditions appear to be having the greatest impact on the situation?
- What type of intervention is indicated?
- Identify the nature of the intervention indicated, develop a plan of action and implement it.
- Monitor and evaluate this plan for its effectiveness.
- Make adjustments in the intervention plan as indicated.

As an example, it may be observed that the agency is servicing a larger number of minority clients than it has in the past. However, workers appear to lack cultural knowledge or sensitivity to these groups, and are imposing dominant group values onto them. The minority clients do not return past two interviews. Research reveals that minority clients do not feel that workers understand them or their culture, present racist attitudes and treat them in an inhumane manner. The supervisor places this problem in the area of educational needs and plans with administration to implement an in-service training or staff development program to address this area. Generally educational objectives center on the following areas: (1) assisting workers to keep abreast of current knowledge and practice skills; (2) helping workers to develop their understanding of client systems such as culture or social class and (3) helping the worker to develop an improved understanding and acceptance of the agency's philosophy, goals, policies, procedures and its place in the community. The in-service training program will address educational objective #2.

KNOWLEDGE BASE OF SUPERVISION

When the social worker achieves the position of a supervisor, the implication exists that he/she has shown leadership abilities in practice with client systems and is now able and ready to transfer this leadership to workers who will be assigned to him/her. The effectiveness of the social worker as a supervisor necessitates that he/she possesses a wide range of knowledge and skills and is able to teach. The knowledge base of the supervisor includes (1) knowledge of the philosophy, objectives and value system of the profession; (2) knowledge of organizational theory and the values, goals and philosophy of his/her employing agency;

(3) knowledge of a variety of theoretical orientations, particularly systems theory, the ecological perspective, the problem-solving approach; (4) knowledge of personality theories; (5) knowledge of social work methods; (5) knowledge of individual, family, group and community dynamics; (6) knowledge of the impact of race and culture on behavior; (7) knowledge of supervision, social and organizational policies, program development and grantmanship and (8) knowledge of research. The skill base includes the capacity to form relationship, to collect data, plan intervention strategies, the constructive use of authority, the capacity to individualize workers. It is extremely important that the supervisor possesses the ability to teach, to administer and to support workers toward the objective of enhancing their professional development so that organizational goals can be achieved in an efficient and effective manner.

CONCLUSION

An analysis of supervision in social work agencies reveals that the supervisor is a part of middle management who is assigned the responsibility of "overseeing" the total performance of the worker as he/she performs work-related tasks which are directed at goal achievement. In performing the supervisory functions, the supervisor acts as an administrator, a teacher and an ego-supporter to the supervisee. The primary objective of supervision is to insure that the goals of the organization are achieved in an effective and efficient manner and that workers are professional and competent. The supervisor also acts as a problem-solver in addressing obstacles which interfere with goal achievement. All members within an organization perform specific functions which are coordinated so that an end product is achieved. Workers and supervisors are guided by policies and procedures, and all organizations have structure for goal attainment. Kouzes and Mico (1979) identify three types of organizational domains in human services organizations: policy, management and service. The policy domain refers to the level of the organization at which governing policies and procedures are formulated; the management domain (supervisory) implements policy decisions, supervises workers to insure that necessary tasks are performed in a creditable manner and engages in problem solving in addressing workers' needs; the service domain consists of workers who provide services to client groups. In order to effectively perform the supervisory function the supervisor must possess extensive knowledge and skills and have demonstrated the capacity to convey this knowledge to workers so that they can develop professionally and provide creditable services to client systems. When obstacles exist to goal achievement, a task of the supervisor is to identify the nature of these obstacles and to report them to administration so that corrective change may be instituted.

Consultation is also an indirect method in social work practice. It is best conceptualized as a problem-solving process in which the client system is the primary beneficiary even though face-to-face contacts with the client may not occur. The social worker may employ consultation in gaining insights into how best to approach a particular situation in which he/she feels the need for outside expertise. The social worker is also a provider of consultation to social systems which request his/her assistance in addressing a specific problem. Consultation may be provided to individuals, small groups, organizations or communities. With the growing complexities of modern society, consultation may become a more dominant method in social work practice as consultees seek to gain knowledge which will enable them to provide more effective services to client systems. Administration and research, other indirect methods in social work practice, are not discussed in this chapter. They have been well covered in the literature and an abundance of materials are available on them.

SELECTED BIBLIOGRAPHY

Berkowitz, S. (1954) The administrative process in casework supervision. In Techniques of student and staff supervision (New York: Family Service Association of America).

Caplan, G. (1970) The theory and practice of mental health consultation. (New York: Basic Books).

Dimock, H. and Trecker, H. (1949) The supervision of group work and recreation (New York: Association Press).

Hester, M. (1954) Educational process in supervision. In Technique of student and staff supervision (New York: Family Service Association of America).

Kadushin, A. (1977) Consultation in social work (New York: Columbia University Press).

Kadushin, A. (1976) Supervision in social work (New York: Columbia University Press).

Kouzes, J. and Mico, P. (1979) Domain theory: An introduction to organizational behavior in human services organizations. JOURNAL OF APPLIED BEHAVIORAL SCIENCE, 15, 449–469.

Middleman, R. and Rhodes, G. (1985) Competent supervision: Making imaginative judgments (Englewoods Cliffs, NJ: Prentice-Hall).

Munson, C. (1983) An introduction to clinical social work supervision. (New York: Haworth Press).

Sackheim, G. (1974) The practice of clinical casework (New York: Behavioral Publications).

Schmidt, D. (1973) Supervision: A sharing process. CHILD WELFARE, LII, 436–446.

Swanson, A. and Brown, J. (1981) Racism, supervision and organizational environment. ADMINISTRATION IN SOCIAL WORK, 5, 59–68.

Watson, K. (1973) Differential supervision. SOCIAL WORK, 18, 80–88.

INDEX